PHONE CALLS FROM THE DEAD

PHONE CALLS FROM THE DEAD

The Results of a Two-Year Investigation into an Incredible Phenomenon

D. SCOTT ROGO & RAYMOND BAYLESS

Postscript by Callum E. Cooper

www.whitecrowbooks.com

Books by D. Scott Rogo

NAD: A Study of Some Unusual 'Other-World' Experiences
A Psychic Study of the 'Music of the Spheres'
Methods and Models for Education in Parapsychology
The Welcoming Silence
An Experience of Phantoms
Parapsychology: A Century of Inquiry
In Search of the Unknown
Exploring Psychic Phenomena
The Haunted Universe
Mind Beyond the Body (editor)
Minds and Motion—the Riddle of Psychokinesis
The Haunted House Handbook
Earth's Ambassador (unpublished) published as *The PK Man* (by Jeffrey Mishlove)
Earth's Secret Inhabitants (with Jerome Clark)
The Tujunga Canyon Contacts (with Ann Druffel)
The Poltergeist Experience
UFO Abductions (editor)
ESP and Your Pet
Miracles
Leaving the Body
Our Psychic Potentials
The Search for Yesterday
Life After Death
Mind Over Matter
On the Track of the Poltergeist
The Infinite Boundary
Psychic Breakthroughs Today
The Return from the Silence
Beyond Reality
Wolf Messing (editor)
New Techniques of Inner Healing

Books by Raymond Bayless

The Enigma of the Poltergeist
Animal Ghosts
The Other Side of Death
Experiences of a Psychical Researcher
Apparitions and Survival of Death
Voices from Beyond
The Case for Life After Death (with Elizabeth McAdams)
Nine Fantasy Tales of Other Worlds (fiction)
Those Below (fiction)

To our friend, Berthold Schwarz, M.D.

Phone calls from the Dead

Copyright © 1979, 1980, 2025 by D. Scott Rogo and Raymond Bayless. All rights reserved.
Postscript copyright © 2025 by Callum E. Cooper.
Published by White Crow Books; an imprint of White Crow Productions Ltd.

The moral right of the authors of this work has been asserted in
accordance with the Copyright, Design and Patents act 1988.

No part of this book may be reproduced, copied or used in any form
or manner whatsoever without written permission, except in the
case of brief quotations in reviews and critical articles.

A CIP catalogue record for this book is available from the British Library.
For information, contact White Crow Books by e-mail: info@whitecrowbooks.com.

Cover Design by Astrid@Astridpaints.com
Interior design by Velin@Perseus-Design.com

Paperback: ISBN: 9781786772725
eBook: ISBN: 9781786772732

Non-Fiction / BODY, MIND & SPIRIT / Parapsychology /
ESP, Clairvoyance, Precognition, Telepathy

www.whitecrowbooks.com

Editor's note: All text in this White Crow Books volume remains the same as the 1979 Prentice-Hall 1st edition of *Phone Calls from the Dead*. Where possible, errors and typos have been corrected, missing references have been updated, and I have included a postscript of where research on the phenomenon is today, finishing off with author biographies.

Contents

Acknowledgments	1
Preface	3
1. Introduction	5
2. In Search of a Strange Phenomenon	9
3. Phone Calls from the Dead: A Survey of Cases	23
4. The Source of the Calls: I. Problems and Possibilities	45
5. The Source of the Calls: II. Communications from the Dead?	59
6. The Mechanics of the Calls	77
7. Further Elements of the Mystery	99
8. Electronic Contact with the Dead: A Wider Perspective	121
Appendix: Some Critiques of the Evidence	153
Postscript: 45 Years Later …	169
Bibliography	187
About the Authors	193
Index	197

Acknowledgments

This book has been extremely difficult to draft since it concerns a subject upon which nothing has previously been written. We are therefore very indebted to several of our colleagues who helped uncover cases, provided us with leads, or directed us to acquaintances who have actually received phone calls from the dead or other types of bizarre telephone calls. In this respect, we would like to thank Dr. Gertrude Schmeidler, professor of psychology at the City College of the City University of New York; Dr. Montague Ullman of Maimonides Medical Center; Dr. Stanley Krippner of the Humanistic Psychology Institute; Dr. Thelma Moss of the UCLA Neuropsychiatric Institute; and Charles Moses, Dr. Jule Eisenbud, and J. Fraser Nicol. Additional thanks are due to Jerome Clark, associate editor of *Fate* magazine; John Bessor, Dr. Walter Uphoff, and Mrs. Rosalind Heywood; Dr. Hans Bender of the University of Freiburg; and to Alan Vaughan. We owe special thanks to Mr. Lucian Landau, who helped us to understand some of the mechanical aspects of our cases, and to Dr. Berthold Schwarz, who provided us with several leads and helped investigate some of our cases. We are also indebted to Vincent Gaddis and Leslie Price, who helped us gather historical information pertinent to the topics discussed in this book, and to Dr. John Palmer of J. F. Kennedy University in Orinda, California, who shared with us his expertise in statistics.

Needless to say, we also thank the many people who freely shared their experiences with us and answered our countless letters and inquiries.

Of course, responsibility for all opinions, omissions, and inadequacies rest solely with the authors.

For use of copyrighted material, the Authors would like to thank the Editors of *Fate* magazine for permissions to quote several cases that originally appeared there. Credit is also due to Patrick Mahony and House of Words Publishers for allowing us to use extracts from *Who's There?* Extracts from Susy Smith's *The Power of the Mind* are reprinted by permission of Chilton Publishing Company; while material quoted from *New Psychic Frontiers* appears by permission of Dr. Walter Uphoff and Mark Jo Uphoff. Short sections of chapters 2 and 6 are based on material that first appeared in *Fate* magazine, and are reprinted by permission. Sections of chapter 5 are loosely based on material that first appeared in *Future Science* (Anchor / Doubleday, 1977) edited by John White and Stanley Krippner. We are also indebted to Taplinger Publishing Company for allowing use of material from Danton Walker's *Spooks Deluxe* and to *Esquire* magazine for use of material which originally appeared in *Coronet* magazine.

Preface

Many of the accounts included in this volume are drawn from cases and incidents that we have personally investigated. Whenever possible, we have tried to use the real names of those involved in these incidents, but in some instances, we have used pseudonyms for our correspondents owing to the very private nature of these experiences. Many of the direct quotes and accounts cited in the text have been extracted from impromptu tape-recorded interviews, phone conversations, and written accounts. On occasion we have edited these transcripts for better clarity and grammatical accuracy, but have in no way materially altered the witnesses' accounts.

Since this book is being issued under two names, we should explain the relative contributions each one of us made to this study. The actual writer of this book is D. Scott Rogo, who was the first to become seriously interested in this unusual phenomenon and who first began collecting cases. Soon, though, Raymond Bayless joined as a collaborator on the project, initiated most of our personal investigations, and carried out much of the grueling legwork of contacting witnesses, taking down their testimony, and transcribing it.

D. Scott Rogo
Raymond Bayless
Los Angeles

1

Introduction

Death has become a subject of ever-increasing importance to the general public. The rise of the human potentials movement, the gradual emergence of parapsychology as science, and our growing desire to find meaning in life have all prompted the American public to take a new and original attitude toward the subject. We are beginning to view death not as the termination of life, but as an adventure and experience unique in itself. At least two books arguing that we possess the *potential* to survive death have made the national best-seller list during 1976-78; the first books on the subject ever to do so. And, in 1978, the publishing market was swamped by not-too-original books on the subject of the death experiences.

Of course, most people who have found themselves taking an interest in the subject of death are concerned primarily with one issue. Will we survive death? It is this question, and the possibility that science itself may eventually answer it affirmatively, which has become so crucial to millions of people across the world. Yet this is a question which parapsychologists have been actively studying for years.

Phone Calls from the Dead is not just another book on life after death. It carries the work of previous investigators one step further by arguing that we not only survive death, but can make contact with the living afterwards. This is, in itself, not a novel claim. But this book *is* novel, since it offers empirical evidence that this contact can be made over the telephone!

We first learned about this phenomenon several years ago, in 1967, when we met a woman named Marge who was eagerly inviting us to some seances being held about town. These dark-room get-togethers had not been very impressive. While all of Marge's pet mediums claimed to enter trance and bring through the dead, certainly none of our deceased relatives had put in an appearance at these often all-too-grim affairs. And we weren't making any bones about our disenchantment. Our friend, though, was a kind of credulous soul who believed everything *any* medium or fortune teller told her, and she was becoming more and more nonplussed over our own boredom with the whole affair. We even told Marge that if her mediums were any indication, we doubted whether communication with the dead was actually possible at all.

Although we meant our little jibe only as good-natured "dig," Marge immediately went on the defensive. "Well, how can you explain this?" she asked us with a hint of righteous indignation in her voice. "A friend of mine once received a phone call from her dead son. He called and simply said, 'Hello, Mother?' and then the line went dead." Marge went on to explain that her friend had recognized the voice of her mystery caller; it was identical to that of her late son who had died as a result of a motorcycle accident two years before.

At the time we really didn't feel we had to supply Marge with an explanation for this incident. We thought that in all likelihood her friend had either been pulling her leg or just plain lying, and we had to restrain ourselves from saying so; instead we tried to reason with Marge and asked her just what proof her friend could offer that this alleged phone call had actually occurred.

Marge sorrowfully admitted that this little story had been told to her on trust. Having taken it as face value, she had never interviewed her friend in depth about the incident or tried to find out if the woman actually ever had a son at all. Marge's friend was apparently home alone when the call came through, so there wasn't even a witness who could verify the story.

And that, so far as we were concerned in 1967, ended the matter. Marge's account was merely an anecdote in the worst sense of the word.

If this story were told to us today, though, our reaction to it will probably be very different: we would take it much more seriously. Our shifting attitude toward cases such as this one has been the gradual product of a whole new approach we began taking a few years ago toward the study of psychic phenomena.

Introduction

Most parapsychologists study such commonplace types of psychic phenomena as ESP, mind over matter, psychic healing, hauntings, and the like. In 1974 both of us began to realize that there were many weird things going on in our vastly complex universe that most conventional parapsychologists—who are trained to study and personally confront the supernatural—prefer to ignore rather than to examine. Some UFOs, for instance, act more like apparitions or psychic materializations than nuts-and-bolts machines. Religious miracles, such as weeping holy statues and angelic visitations, are occurring today just as they presumably did in Biblical times. Even monsters such as Bigfoot and other mystery animals might be more the product of our minds than the exclusive creations of nature.

After coming to this conclusion, we subsequently found ourselves studying and investigating these aspects of the psychic world in just as much depth as we were giving to more conventional ESP and mind-over-matter research.

It was also during this time of discovery that we started to come across many people who claimed that they had received phone calls from the dead. These stories were, in many respects, similar to the one Marge had told us about years before. Quite frankly, we still didn't know what to make of this phenomenon—a phenomenon which struck us as probably the most bizarre mystery of all. Of course, we thought back to Marge and her claim and began reconsidering it. Could the telephone, we wondered, actually be used on occasion as a channel for psychic communication between the living and the dead?

The very idea might strike you as blatantly ridiculous. But after two years of research, we have come to the conclusion that these enigmatic phone calls actually do occur and are, indeed, probably more common than you might imagine. We have come to the invariable conclusion that the people who report these experiences are not perpetrating hoaxes, but have had genuine and sometimes shocking experiences—experiences that most para psychologists have been ignoring for years.

This volume, then, represents the results of a two-year investigation into the phantom phone call mystery. We've written it not only to present this fascinating material to the general public but also to make some sense of this bizarre phenomenon. We feel that we have quite literally stumbled upon a new form of psychic communication and, after several months of research, we feel that we know a little about *when* these calls are prone to occur, *who* will receive them, and *how* they are actually produced.

Although this book deals with an almost unbelievable subject, we hope that it will be read as a serious study of a very unusual phenomenon. Certainly we, as parapsychologists, have found the case reports included in this book just about the strangest we have ever encountered during the course of our work. Yet we have found working on this project one of the most provocative endeavors of our careers. We have spent hundreds of hours together discussing what these cases might be telling us about our psychic potentials, our universe, life, death, and the possibility that we might be able to make electromagnetic contact with the dead. We have never ceased being fascinated by our discoveries and correlations. Hopefully, the readers of this book will feel the same sense of wonder and excitement as we did when talking first hand with the witnesses involved.

2

In Search of a Strange Phenomenon

Being psychical investigators by profession, we often receive phone calls and letters from people who seem eager to tell us all sorts of stories about their psychic experiences. Consequently, over the years our files have become full of letters reporting everything from prophetic dreams to telepathic flashes, or even about a ghost or two the writers may have seen or met. Sometimes we run into people whose experiences are even more bizarre. But if our work has taught us anything, it is to be totally open-minded, though at all times, skeptical. We've learned through long and hard experience never to reject anybody's story about a personal psychic experience or encounter without first giving it a fair hearing. Why? Because some of the craziest stories we've investigated have turned out to be absolutely authentic.

Just such a credulity-stretching story was run in the September 1969 issue of *Fate* magazine, which is one of the country's leading and most long-standing occult/psychic publications. It was reported by one of the magazine's many readers, Mr. Don B. Owens of Toledo, Ohio, who obviously felt compelled to share his personal encounter with his fellow subscribers:

> Until late October 1968, had a very close friend. Lee Epps and I were closer than brothers and it seemed that when he wasn't at our house we were at his.

Lee was a bachelor with a good paying job he had held for years. While he had no money worries, he never had much luck with women. Anyone could see he was a lonely man, one who valued his few friends. He didn't make friends easily, for he was pessimistic and a little inclined to complain. But we liked him and understood him. He was fond of my wife Ethel and she of him. He called her "Sis" and often did little things for her.

Lee Epps and Owens once lived in the same neighborhood. But then Lee moved to another area, and, as the years rolled by, the two gradually drifted apart. After Lee's move, a casual dinner engagement, evening out, or telephone conversation was the only contact they had but then, writes Owens:

> ... at 10:30 p.m. on October 26, 1968, while I was out, a phone call came from Lee: it was urgent. My wife answered and immediately recognized his voice. What little he said or the way he said it greatly upset her. She tried to call him back a few minutes later but got no answer. The message he had given her was this:
> "Sis, tell Don I'm feeling real bad. Never felt this way before. Tell him to get in touch with me the minute he comes in. It's important, Sis."
> The message upset me as much as it had Ethel. I called his number but got no answer. I called again and again. No answer.

The sequel to this urgent call was bound to shock and upset the Owenses even more than the message itself. As Mr Owens concludes his account:

> That very evening, I learned later, Lee lay in a coma in Mercy Hospital less than six blocks from our place. He died at 10:30 p.m., the time he had called our home. My wife talked to him and readily recognized his voice—no doubt about it—Lee made that telephone call.

How can this unusual incident be explained? When we first read Owen's account our first reaction to the case was that Lee Epps must have recovered from his terminal coma long enough to make the mysterious call. But then one day I got into a discussion with my family doctor about the medical aspects of deep coma.

Patients in this state rarely regain consciousness before death. This depends, of course, on the nature of the disease and the age of the patient. However, patients who do manage to regain some alertness before death

In Search of a Strange Phenomenon

rarely engage in any type of normal conversation, usually mumbling only a sentence or two about "being in heaven" or thinking that they are already dead. As for motor functioning, these patients achieve practically no digital dexterity and usually do not move their fingers at all. In fact, they rarely even move their eyes. Under these circumstances, then, had Lee Epps genuinely been in a coma, there is practically no possibility that he could have made the call right before death.

From a medical standpoint, it doesn't seem likely that Lee Epps could have placed the call. But it doesn't appear as though the Owenses were mistaken about the experience either. Could they have actually received a phone call from the *dead* Lee Epps? While perhaps an almost unbelievable idea, that is precisely what appears to have happened.

Now, admittedly, this case is not a very strong one. No corroborative statement from Mrs. Owens verifying her husband's account was printed with the story; nor was *Fate* sent a copy of Lee Epps' death certificate, validating the time of his death. Do we don't have any real *proof* that the events described in the report actually happened.

Nonetheless, I don't think we can merely dismiss this case as just a put-on... and for one very good reason.

Back in 1976, out of pure curiosity, Raymond Bayless and I began collecting, investigating, and tracing "phone calls from the dead" cases. We wanted to see if these types of psychic phone calls were worth studying seriously. And what we did discover came as quite a shock. If the research and case files we have accumulated over the past two years are any indication, Mr. and Mrs. Owens are apparently only two of the hundreds of people who have received just this type of phone call from the dead—or who have received other types of "phantom" phone calls.

When we first began our careers in parapsychology (I entered the field in 1966 and Raymond started his researches back in the 1940's), we tended simply to dismiss cases like Mr. Owens's out of hand; they struck us as just too unbelievable. Although we had heard and read of such experiences, we just couldn't bring ourselves seriously to believe that the dead could contact the living through any medium as mundane as the telephone. This now seems a rather odd position to have taken, since our job as psychical investigators is to study just such "impossible" phenomena as ESP, out-of-body travel, hauntings, poltergeists, and psychic contact with the dead. But when we investigated some of these cases ourselves, talking with dozens of witnesses and analyzing their experiences, we gradually came to realize that these phone call mysteries represent a very important type of psychic phenomenon, one few writers or parapsychologists have ever been willing to study seriously or comment on. We became so engrossed in them that by the middle of 1977 we found ourselves engaged almost exclusively in investigating these phone call cases.

Our research has proved, at least to us, that these types of calls are not only disturbingly real but also surprisingly common.

For example, the July 1974 issue of *Fate* magazine ran another "phone call from the dead" story. (By our count, *Fate* has published some five of these cases between 1950 and 1977.) It had been submitted to the editors as a true anecdote, by a Mrs. Viola Tollen of Indianapolis, Indiana.

Mrs. Tollen had been very friendly with her neighbor's caretaker, Davis Stone, as well as with his young daughter Ruby. This bond of affection came to a tragic end when the little girl died at the age of seven. Sometime later, Stone himself was severely injured when he fell from a ladder on his employer's estate. He was nearly crippled by the accident, which naturally limited his ability to work. If he so much as sat or fell asleep in the wrong position, the strain on his muscles would incapacitate him for weeks. Not willing to admit defeat, though, Stone kept up with his job despite his handicap.

"Not long after his fall, Davis's employers went on vacation and Davis had complete responsibility for the estate," writes Mrs. Tollen. "The job was really too much for one person, and I was continually on watch to see that he did not cripple himself again. One evening just before dark my telephone rang, and I answered it. I heard a voice I recognized but could not place—it was the tiny voice of a child."

Their conversation was brief. "They told me I could not telephone, but I just did, didn't I?" the peculiar voice explained.

Mrs. Tollen was puzzled and could only respond, "I know your voice, but who are you?"

"You know me," the voice answered. "I am Ruby."

Mrs. Tollen was alarmed by the call and immediately realized that something must be wrong with Davis. After giving the caller a quick "good-by" (and receiving a polite "thank you" in return), she darted next door to make sure everything was all right. Her agitation became even more intense when no one answered her knock. So, after finding a rear door which had been left unlocked, Mrs. Tollen searched room after room of her neighbor's house until she found Davis Stone. He had fallen asleep in an awkward position, one that would have crippled him. Luckily, the frightened woman was able to waken him before any damage had been done to his spine or legs.

In Search of a Strange Phenomenon

This incident, like the Owens one, is a typical "phone call from the dead" case. The voice identified itself openly. It also apparently had a specific reason for making contact with Mrs. Tollen, since the call may have saved Stone from a permanent injury. (Although the voice never actually imparted this warning, Mrs. Tollen seemed somehow to intuit the meaning of the call.) There is one curious feature about this case, though, which is especially intriguing. Who were the mysterious "they" who told Ruby she *couldn't* contact the living over the telephone? Other discarnates, perhaps? Or maybe even some other extradimensional beings? These are questions we'll leave for further discussion.

Probably no one would blame you if you tended to dismiss this report as just a piece of imaginative fiction. Certainly it is much more convenient simply to ignore such reports than come to grips with them. But the fact remains that this case, just like the Owens one, differs very little from the dozens of cases we have personally investigated and believe to be genuine.

But if these cases *are* so common, why has so little material been written on the subject? Why have parapsychologists paid so little attention to these mysterious phone calls?

If you've been asking yourself these questions by now you're in good company. This is exactly what we began asking ourselves as we came to realize just how common these calls are. While parapsychologists study everything from telepathy to haunted houses, the embarrassing fact remains that "phone calls from the dead" are not mentioned in most serious books on psychic phenomena. Despite their apparent frequency, in fact, very few of these cases have ever found their way into print at all.* And to date, no parapsychologists other than ourselves have ever attempted systematically to study phone call cases or even given them much thought.

As we proceeded with our work, we soon realized that we had stumbled onto quite a paradox. On one hand, we continually kept coming across all sorts of people who either had had one of these phone calls or knew somebody who had. Yet when we spoke with other

---

* The only book we know of which seriously discusses phone calls from the dead in any depth is S. Ralph Harlow's *A Life after Death*, published in 1961. A Congregationalist minister, Harlow cites two cases in his book. But even his discussions are extremely brief. During our attempts to track down cases, we perused well over 100 books dealing with psychic phenomena. Yet we could find only four or five which even mentioned phone call cases.

parapsychologists about our work, we found that most of our colleagues had never even *heard* of this phenomenon, much less tried to study it! How, we began to wonder, could such an amazing phenomenon have remained so long unknown to science or organized parapsychology?

There are several possible answers to this question, but the most likely one is simply that people who have received these calls are usually very reluctant about reporting them unless specifically encouraged to do so. As a general rule, people are very reticent about reporting experiences or observations for which they might be ridiculed. This is a simple principle of human nature.

As you probably know, psychic experiences are not rare. Just about all of us will have some sort of psychic encounter during our lifetime. However, most people never bother to report their experiences to anyone other than perhaps another family member or a close friend. A person who has had a startling psychic experience will only rarely contact a parapsychologist to tell him or her about it. This is a problem which continually plagues those of us actively involved in studying psychic phenomena. So let's take a look at this issue in greater depth. This will not only help you understand the many problems we faced as we tried tracking down the reports which appear in this volume, but will also cast some interesting light on just why so few parapsychologists have ever bothered studying these phone call cases at all.

A hundred years or so ago many people refused to discuss any type of personal psychic experience, fearing that they might be labeled liars or, even worse, crazy. Fortunately, this situation has drastically changed. Over the last few decades, parapsychology—the scientific study of psychic phenomena—has begun to achieve more and more scientific recognition. Several sophisticated laboratories across the country, such as the Stanford Research Institute in Menlo Park, California, and the Brooklyn-based Maimonides Medical Center, have been actively engaged in studying everything from ESP to mind over matter and out-of-body travel. A few universities in the United States and Great Britain are even granting Ph.D.'s in parapsychology. The upshot of this vast amount of scientific research into the psychic field has been that the study of psychic phenomena has outgrown its reputation as a "taboo" subject and has become a socially and scientifically acceptable area of inquiry and discussion.

Likewise, it is now socially and scientifically acceptable to talk about one's own psychic encounters—but only to a certain degree. No one would bat an eye if, for instance, you talked about a precognitive dream you had about a friend's being injured in an automobile accident. Probably no one would even be too surprised if you claimed to have received a telepathic message—or if you knew someone who had. Those forms of psychic interactions occur to practically all of us at one time or another during our lives.

During the course of our work, though, we have constantly found that many people are still very reluctant to discuss *unusual* types of psychic experiences. No doubt afraid of ridicule or recrimination, many individuals are still wary of talking openly about such extraordinary experiences as out-of-the-body travel, UFO encounters, or poltergeist attacks. These experiences seem to go a bit beyond the limits of "scientifically acceptable" psychic experiences! Even the supernatural, it would appear, has its conventions.

In this same light, Raymond Bayless and I have found that many people are very reluctant to talk about "phone calls from the dead" encounters. During our interviews we sometimes find that our witnesses seem almost irrationally to doubt and question their own experiences. Though perhaps eager to tell us about their encounters, many of them have refused to allow their names to be published. Some of them will even go so far as to admit their experiences openly, yet deny them at the same time!

Just this sort of thing cropped up when Dr. Montague Ullman, one of this country's leading psychoanalysts as well as a parapsychologist of note and formerly a chief administrator of Maimonides Medical Center, told us of a fellow psychoanalyst and colleague of his, Dr. Lester Gelb of Riverdale, New York, who had once received an extraordinary mystery phone call. Raymond Bayless lost no time getting in touch with Dr. Gelb, who responded by giving us one of our most detailed cases.

Dr. Gelb's mother died in January 1970 at the age of 90. She had never suffered any overt ill health during her lifetime, although in her later years she became blind and hard of hearing. This handicap, understandably, was a painful blow for a woman who had led a healthy and active life, and in consequence, she committed a rather passive form of suicide: she simply stopped eating until her health gave out completely. During these last months of her life, Mrs. Gelb lived with her daughter, and Dr. Gelb phoned her frequently. During this period they shared dozens of phone conversations. Dr. Gelb told us that as soon as his mother recognized his voice over the phone, she would always say, "Lester?"

A few months after his mother's death, Dr. Gelb and his wife and two children were just about to leave their New York home for a casual

Sunday outing. As they were getting ready to step out the door, the phone rang.

"I remember feeling annoyed," the New York psychoanalyst told us. "I picked up the wall phone in our kitchen. After I said 'Hello,' the 'telephone voice' only said one word. 'Lester?' it asked inquisitively. I was shocked and perplexed to hear the exact voice of my mother."

Stunned, Dr. Gelb repeatedly asked the caller to identify herself. But the voice, always speaking in the same tone of voice, only kept echoing the doctor's name. Finally, after what Dr. Gelb described to us as a "clacking sound" came over the line, the phone went dead. He continued to talk, hoping to get a bit more conversation out of the mystery caller, but there was no response.

"After hanging up," Dr. Gelb went on to say, "I joined my waiting family. My wife asked me who had called, and I answered only that it was someone who asked for me and had then hung up. I felt too disoriented and perplexed to provide further details until a week later."

Curiously, this voice—unlike that of Don Owens's friend—did not *specifically* identify itself or announce its death. This seems to be a pattern to which many of the cases we have collected conform, even though the receiver of the call may have no doubt as to the caller's identity. Dr. Gelb, for instance, had no doubt whatsoever about his recognition of the voice of his caller at the time of the incident.

Yet even more interesting than the call itself was Dr. Gelb's psychological reaction. What did Dr. Gelb think about his other-worldly experience? Trying to resolve this question obviously presented quite a dilemma to the psychoanalyst.

"Was this the voice of my mother, or only a very similar voice?" Dr. Gelb wrote to us. "I do have an excellent 'ear.' I had musical training from early childhood. I pride myself on being able to recognize almost anyone's voice after a first hearing. I recognize local radio stations instantly by the sound of the various announcers' voices, etc. My mother had a very distinctive way of calling my name. Her voice had a quality, a crackle, a timbre and manner that I had lived with all my life. The voice I heard on the telephone that early spring morning was the same voice!"

But his certainty regarding the nature of the voice did not include belief as to its source. "To the question of what I believe about the matter of 'the dead' communicating with a living person, my answer is that I am a skeptic," Dr. Gelb explained to us. "Although it sounded as though my mother called me, this personal experience of itself does not lead me to believe that communication from the dead is possible. I do not have a clear explanation for what I experienced, and I remain intrigued. My best guess is, simply, that some living person with a similar voice and plaintive manner of speaking called me."

This case illustrates the constant self-doubting and questioning of people who have had these experiences. It also helps explain why so few of them report their encounters at all. Like UFOs and hauntings, these phenomena seem much easier to rationalize away than to explain.

Nonetheless, it is hard for us to accept Dr. Gelb's own explanation for his experience. Even the good doctor himself makes a strong case for the probability that the voice was actually that of his mother: its distinct timbre was the same as the elderly woman's; it seemed unable to carry out a normal conversation; it called his name just as his mother had always done. This was obviously no normal phone call. It's hardly likely that the call came from one of his patients, who certainly would not have addressed the therapist by his first name.

There are other reasons why people do not like to talk about their weird phone calls. Many of them, we have found, will not discuss these cases unless they are first assured that *other* people have had similar experiences. Still another reason many witnesses have for keeping these incidents secret is a very personal one: in talking with some witnesses, one senses that these people somehow view their experiences as something very personal, private, and not open for discussion—almost sacred, as one might say. A woman who receives a phone call from a deceased son on Mother's Day (as in one case we traced) or who receives a call from a deceased relative during a time of personal crisis may feel compelled to keep quiet about it. Even Mrs. Tollen, quoted above, described her encounter as "a treasure in my memory." Obviously, this is not the type of experience one goes blabbing about indiscriminately!

So, all in all, it really isn't too surprising that not very much material has been available on this subject until now. Since very few cases have ever been reported or published, most parapsychologists simply have never had their attention drawn to this phenomenon.

Not all "phone calls from the dead," however, are as brief or uninformative as the one Dr. Gelb received. Sometimes these mysterious Callers will give their contact—the person who answers the call or to whom the call is addressed—information that only the dead person could possibly possess. The Don Owens case, cited above, is a typical case in point. The voice called Owens's wife "Sis," a pet nickname which only Lee Epps ever used. Other cases which we have collected are even more impressive and evidential. In some instances, the phone voice will use an expression which the deceased person often used while alive.

One outstanding case of this nature was told to us in confidence by a well-known Hollywood television and motion picture actress who specifically asked us to keep her name private. (The incident was a family secret, and the actress didn't want to cause any upset by having her name associated with its publication.) However, Miss Patricia Adams—as we will call her here—had no reservations about telling us about the bizarre call which she had taken as a child. In this unusual case, the phone call was placed collect and through a long-distance operator, yet no record of the call could be traced; nor was it ever charged to the family who received it. (Since our investigation of this case, interestingly enough, several other "long-distance" phone calls from the dead have come to our attention. We now have a handful of such cases on file.) This voice also used an expression which the dead had often used in life—and used it word for word.

Here is Miss Adams's story, which has been edited from our interviews with her:

> When I was about eight years old, I was living in Texas. My mother had a very dear friend whose daughter had gone away to college. The daughter came back home around the first of the year, each year. The third year, while on her way back home, she was killed in an automobile accident.
>
> A couple of years later we were over at the home of this friend of my mother's for Thanksgiving, which was one of the holidays for which the daughter used to come home. The telephone rang. I was at the age when, if the grownups were away in the living room, and the kids were always running around, I would answer the phone. I picked it up and heard the long-distance operator say, "I have a collect call." She mentioned the name of my mother's friend and she mentioned the name of the daughter. [In other words, the call was addressed to the friend, and the operator told Miss Adams that the call was from the deceased daughter.] This threw me a little bit even as a child, and I said, "Just a minute." I went and got my mother's friend. She came to the phone. I stood watching her, because I had heard the name and thought that maybe somebody was playing a joke on me or her or something. She listened on the phone, turned absolutely white, and fainted.

Later on I heard what happened. There was a great hushing up about it, but I learned that she had heard her daughter—who had been dead two or three years—speak to her. She said the same thing she always did before she came home: "Mommie, it's me," she said. "I need twenty dollars to get home."

The mother always sent her twenty dollars for good luck. She said she recognized the voice. They called the phone company, but they had no record of any phone call.

Miss Adams told Raymond, who conducted the interview, that there was a long-standing joke between her mother's friend and her family. Whenever any of the children were about to come home for a visit, they would always call first and ask for twenty dollars. Her mother's friend often joked good-naturedly about this inevitable request when her daughter was still alive.

The fact that this mystery voice used a significant phrase—that is, one which the woman would immediately recognize and associate with her deceased daughter—is probably the most interesting aspect of this case. But why should the voice make such an odd and (under the circumstances) obviously meaningless request? As Raymond suggested to me after interviewing Miss Adams, it seems as though this mystery voice was deliberately trying to prove its identity as forcefully as possible.

Notice how most of these calls are exceedingly brief. It would seem that the psychic force needed to establish this type of contact is short-lived, as if these phantom callers may not have much time to get their messages across. Now, *if* this call had actually come from the woman's dead daughter (which we consider one possible explanation for this case), the caller may have wanted to say something which would immediately establish who she was. The phrase "I need twenty dollars to get home" may have been used as a code or signal—a phrase she knew had special meaning for her mother.

Actually, many people do this sort of thing quite naturally when calling up close friends or relations, especially ones they haven't seen for a long time. I can remember, while on a business trip, phoning an old college friend of mine whom I hadn't seen for some ten years. When I heard his voice on the line, the first thing I said, quite jokingly, was, "You still owe me fifteen dollars." I knew my friend would immediately recognize me, since my remark alluded to an old college joke between us. At the time, it seemed more forceful to identify myself by using this phrase than by merely offering my name. Perhaps these voice-entities engage in a similar type of shenanigans.

The Patricia Adams case contains several characteristics that can be found in other such incidents. For one thing, the voice called on a special and emotionally meaningful day—on Thanksgiving—a day on which the caller usually returned home. In several other cases we have collected, which will be discussed in Chapter 5, the callers also seemed to choose for making contact a specific day that had some meaning in their terrestrial lives or in the lives of the persons they contacted.

The fact that the collect call was never billed to the number Miss Adams answered is yet another mysterious aspect of this case. Since the operator placed the call, it should have been registered by the phone company. Or was the operator's voice, too, a phantom voice, "staged" by the phantom caller to make the call seem more normal? In many other cases we have collected, these voice-entities try to give the impression that they are still alive. Now whether this is a conscious act or merely inadvertent is a moot point. (We'll have more to say about this phenomenon in Chapter 4.) But we cannot dismiss the idea that these voices engage in a deliberate charade. The operator's voice may have just been a lark. On the other hand, could the intelligence which produced the call have first contacted a living operator who then actually placed it? If this were the case, perhaps the call was not registered because no geographical location could be ascertained as the origin of the call. It's too bad that at the time no one thought to ask the operator just where the call was coming from.

As I suggested above, at first we thought that these types of phone calls and other forms of telephonic shenanigans were very rare occurrences. In March of 1977, when we first decided to undertake a *major* study of this phenomenon, we were aware of only about four or five "phone calls from the dead" cases on record. I subsequently wrote up and published them as an article under the title "Phone Calls from the Dead?" in the October 1977 issue of *Fate* magazine. Only after the appearance of this article, however, did Raymond Bayless begin coming across additional previously published accounts. Slowly but surely, we started hearing about still other cases which had been included in autobiographies and in other non-parapsychological books. Some of these cases date back many years.

Finally, many of our friends and acquaintances started informing us about people *they* knew who had received similar mystery calls. We also began contacting many of our colleagues in the field of parapsychology and asked them if they had heard of this phenomenon or had cases in their research files. The upshot of our informal survey among this country's leading parapsychologists was at once helpful, enlightening, amusing, and frustrating. A few of them stoutly maintained that no such phenomenon even existed! Yet others became interested in our work and admitted that they too either had known someone who had received such a call or had a case or two in their files which they had never published. So it seems to us that even our rather large file probably represents only a fraction of the cases potentially available. Hundreds of such calls are probably received every year across the country.

When we began our research into this bizarre mystery, we were breaking new ground in the true sense of the phrase. We had no preconceptions as to what we would find or what our data would reveal. At first, we were primarily interested in collecting only "phone calls from the dead" cases. Our original goal was to see if we could determine whether these calls actually emanated from the dead, as they purport to, or if other types of psychic explanations could account for them. For instance, could the receiver of the call actually have used his own psychic abilities to create the phenomenon? (This is a possibility which will be discussed in another chapter.) But as our work continued, we discovered that just about all of our cases have fallen into one of three basic and very different categories:

1. *Apparent phone calls from the dead*: As in the cases in this chapter, the witness receives a call—usually brief—from a person who either has just recently died or who has been dead for some time. Occasionally the person receiving the call does not know at that time that the caller is dead and believes he/she is talking to a living person.

2. *Intention cases*: The witness usually receives an urgent message by phone from a friend or relative, or even from an unknown individual who explains that he is placing the call for the former. Later, the witness learns that the friend *never made the call, although he or she thought intently about doing so*. The phone voice will often mimic that of a living person perfectly. However, a few witnesses have described these voices as "mechanical" or "drunk sounding," although this is rare.

3. *Answer cases*: Rarely, the witness himself places the call and carries out a conversation with a person whom he later discovers either (a) was dead at the time the call was placed or (b) could not possibly have been home to receive it.

It soon became clear to us that we had stumbled across a greater series of mysteries than we had originally suspected.

By far, the vast majority of the cases we have collected fall into the first category. "Phone calls from the dead" seem to be the most common form of telephonic hi-jinks, or at least the most commonly *reported* type of phantom phone call, even though these cases actually represent only part of a wider phenomenon. Over the past hundred years there have been reports about voices of the dead speaking over record player amplifiers, appearing on magnetic tape, communicating over telegraph keys, or coming through a host of other types of electronic equipment. To understand these mysterious "phone calls from the dead," we must delve into these related enigmas as well.

3

Phone Calls from the Dead: A Survey of Cases

The incidents reported by Mrs. Tollen, Marge, Don Owens, and others are at the same time both scientific reports and parlor anecdotes. As scientific reports, they have been placed on record for our scrutiny and evaluation. But as anecdotes, they have often been reported in a casual and undocumented campfire-story sort of way. It is for this reason that the reports of such cool-headed witnesses as Dr. Gelb, Patricia Adams, and others are so important. Dr. Gelb's call was overheard by his family, so he at least has witnesses who can testify to his receipt of his mother's mysterious call. Miss Adams can be placed in the same category, since she was not the only one who witnessed the call from her friend's deceased daughter.

Despite the purely anecdotal nature of so many of these phone call cases, there are nonetheless on record many well-authenticated cases of this phenomenon. Some of them have been published as brief reports in books and popular magazines dealing with psychic phenomena, and as pointed out earlier, we've tracked down several ourselves. As we came across more and more of these "phone calls from the dead" cases, it gradually dawned on us that there existed a substantial variety of these calls. That is, there seemed to be different and specific types of "phone calls from the dead." Let's look at the four cases we've already recounted. The voices of Lee Epps's and Miss Adams's contacts were able to impart important, though brief and concise, messages. It seems almost as though these communications were well prepared and planned out in advance of the actual call. Yet the mystery voices which spoke to Dr. Gelb and Mrs. Tollen were a bit confused. They seemed stunned, or at least surprised that they had been able to make contact with the living at all. This would seem to be the same sort of call that Marge's friend received.

Despite the fact that these cases represent a wide variety of phenomena, Raymond and I soon realized that all of our reports fit neatly into either of two basic categories. In some of our accounts, only a brief—and often interrupted—interaction took place before either the line went dead or the conversation was otherwise terminated. We started calling these "simple calls" or Type 1 cases. In others, the phone voice carried out a lengthy conversation with the person who answered the call. We immediately began to call these "prolonged calls" or Type 2 cases. So before trying to analyze just what these calls mean or how they are produced, let's examine a number of previously published reports with cases drawn from our own files.

One account of a rather extended phone conversation with the dead was written up by the well-known writer Susy Smith in her book *The Power of the Mind*. The witnesses to this typical Type 2 call were two acquaintances of the author, Bonnie and C. E. MacConnell of Tucson, Arizona, who even supplied Miss Smith with a notarized statement about the incident. Here is the story as they related it to Miss Smith:

The MacConnells had been very friendly with a philanthropic but harshly realistic author named Enid Johlson (pseudonym). Now in her old age and having given much of her money away to the needy, Enid found that she didn't have enough left to care for herself or to cover her skyrocketing medical bills. The MacConnells had hoped that Enid would write another book in order to stabilize her finances, but the book was never written. As befalls so many of the elderly, Enid was hustled from one hospital or nursing home to another. Eventually the MacConnells lost touch with her completely. This depressed the couple because they had always spent Christmas with her, each year bringing her a bottle of blackberry wine as a present.

After losing touch with Enid, several months went by before the MacConnells heard from her again. Then one Sunday evening in May of 1971 they received a surprise phone call. Mr. MacConnell answered the phone and, after speaking with the caller, brought the phone to his wife.

"Do you know who this is?" the voice queried.

Of course, Mrs. MacConnell immediately recognized Enid's voice. It was a healthy, clear voice—one wouldn't have suspected that the elderly author had been so sickly—and the two women spoke for quite some time.

Enid began by explaining how she had been transferred to the Handmaker Jewish Nursing Home for the Aged in Tucson. According to Mrs. MacConnell, these opening remarks preluded what was to become a thirty-minute conversation.

As she explains in her deposition which she later turned over to Miss Smith:

> Enid said it was too bad we hadn't been able to see each other, and I explained all the problems I'd had. It had been more than a year since I'd visited her and I realized that the following Tuesday would be her birthday. I said, "Enid, I owe you a bottle of blackberry brandy ... I'll bring you a bottle Tuesday for your birthday."
>
> She said, "I don't need it now." I said I'd bring it anyway. I mentioned that she sounded as if everything was great with her. She said, "It is. I've never had such good care." She also said, "Wasn't it too bad we didn't get that book finished?" I said, "You will," for she sounded absolutely wonderful. After the call, my husband, who had been participating in our conversation from the bedroom phone, said, "That sounded like the Enid of 20 years ago."
>
> Among other things, I said to Enid, "Do you have a phone by your bed again?" And she replied, "No." Then I said, "Do you mean you can get up and go to the phone?" And she said, "Oh, I get around fine." I commented that she sounded so happy and she said, "I've never been happier."
>
> We must have talked for half an hour, just reminiscing and referring to personal matters.

On Friday night of that same week, Mrs. MacConnell started thinking about Enid, so she phoned the Handmaker Nursing Home and asked the receptionist to connect her with her friend's room. But the operator was a bit taken aback by the request.

"Why, Mrs. Johlson died last Sunday morning," she sadly reported.

From what the MacConnells could gather, Enid Johlson had apparently died at 10:30 on the previous Sunday, several hours before they had received her phone call. Just to make sure of her facts, Mrs. MacConnell verified that that particular Sunday was the *only* Sunday during which Enid had been at the Home, so there could be no error about the date of the call. As Mrs. MacConnell told Miss Smith:

So two of us talked to her for 30 minutes after 5:00 in the evening of the date she died at 10:30 in the morning, reminiscing over old times and verifying her identity repeatedly. She probably deliberately called at a time when we were both home so that we would be able to confirm each other's data. We were so impressed that we wrote up the entire episode and had it notarized.

This case stands in striking contrast to most of the ones we cited in Chapter 2. In those instances, the phone calls were rather hurried and exceedingly brief. This case is particularly impressive since *two* witnesses recognized and spoke to the voice of the dead woman. (Since the MacConnells had the account notarized, it had obviously made quite an impact on them.) Now if the MacConnells' rather lengthy conversation with the deceased Mrs. Johlson were unique, the only case of its kind ever recorded, I'm sure most of us would simply dismiss it. The MacConnell case, however, is *not* unique! A number of other cases are on record in which people have reported long—and apparently perfectly normal—talks with the dead. For instance, a similar case was reported in 1975 by Dr. Berthold Schwarz, a New Jersey psychiatrist.

Although a psychiatrist by profession, Dr. Schwarz has had a long association with conventional parapsychology and is author of several books and reports on ESP (his latest being *Parent-Child Telepathy*). Dr. Schwarz is somewhat unconventional though, in that over the years he has investigated everything from UFOs to phantom phone calls. In 1975 he published an account of one phantom phone call case which he had personally investigated. His short report on the case appeared in his essay "Telepathic Humoresque," which is included in Dr. Stanley R. Dean's anthology, *Psychiatry and Mysticism*.

The recipient of the call was a New Jersey woman named Marie D'Alessio. Although the phone call had been made years prior to the investigation (Dr. Schwarz doesn't mention the year), the details were still vivid in her mind when he interviewed her about the incident.

The entire episode began one night with a dream in which Mrs. D'Alessio saw a childhood friend named Lana sinking into a pool of blood. Obviously, the dream was symbolic, and Mrs. D'Alessio immediately suspected that something horrible had happened to her friend. When she recounted the dream to her husband, he reminded her that Lana was only a phone call away. The distraught woman put a

Phone Calls from the Dead: A Survey of Cases

call through immediately, and her husband thereby became the chief witness to this bizarre series of events.

Lana answered immediately. She admitted to Mrs. D'Alessio that she had indeed been sick and had even been hospitalized. She said she had been temporarily released but added that she was due back in the hospital the very next day. Mrs. D'Alessio listened patiently and sympathetically to this very normal conversation, suggesting that she would like to visit her friend in the hospital. Lana asked her not to, however, but promised she would call back later. (Interestingly enough, Mrs. MacConnell similarly suggested to Enid that they get together on her elderly friend's birthday, but the phantom caller put a damper on the idea.)

Several days later, when Lana had not called back, Mrs. D'Alessio decided to call her again. But try as she might, no one ever answered her several calls. Finally, she called Lana's neighbor, who, rather surprised at the call, informed Mrs. D'Alessio that Lana had died. She added that the deceased woman's husband, who was currently away on a business trip, could give her more information. Mrs. D'Alessio was understandably surprised, but apparently hung up without finding out exactly *when* Lana had passed on. Later, Lana's husband told the D'Alessios that they must have been mistaken about the call to his wife. He said she had died a full six months before Mrs. D'Alessio first called her!

This is more a case of a "phone call to the dead"—a rarer phenomenon than a "phone call *from* the dead'—but we have collected a few similar reports during our investigations.

When we first read this account, we tried to track down Mrs. D'Alessio ourselves. Unfortunately, we were never able to get in touch with her, so there is little more we can add to Dr. Schwarz's summary of the case. However, when I first met Dr. Schwarz in the summer of 1977, I asked him about this account. He assured me that he considered Mrs. D'Alessio a perfectly honest witness and added that he had no doubt but that the incident had occurred just as she had reported it to him. According to Dr. Schwarz, Joseph Dunninger—who before his death was one of the country's foremost magicians as well as author of two books "exposing" fake mediums and mind readers—had also investigated the case and considered it genuine.

Interestingly enough, Dr. Schwarz ran into another one of these phone call cases two years later. While investigating a UFO case in Ohio, the psychiatrist asked the principal witnesses, Mrs. Geri Wilhelm and her family, if any of them had ever had any other type of anomalous experience. Mrs. Wilhelm's mother, Mrs. Sherrin, immediately chimed in with a story about one of these odd "prolonged" or Type 2 telephone conversations with the dead. About 18 months before, Aunt Lorraine, her favorite relative, had been killed in an automobile accident. The call from her came about six months later. As she told Dr. Schwarz:

"We were like sisters. We talked about different things we had done in the past, places we had been together, just sort of reminiscing. I was home alone. This went on for about half an hour. When I hung up, I thought, 'It was Lorraine! But she's dead. She was killed instantly in an automobile accident six or seven months ago!' I even get chills now, talking about it. In fact I was so upset I dialed her number, but nobody answered."

This case is doubly interesting since Mrs. Sherrin noted how *long* the conversation lasted. Most people who have received these calls do not mention just how long they spoke to their callers. However, it is rather obvious that even if the mystery voices try to communicate lengthy messages, the duration of most phantom phone calls is rather short. Mrs. Sherrin's half-hour conversation is the most extended phone call in our files. But this case is extremely intriguing on another count as well.

Every phone call case we run across presents its own unique puzzles. This report, brief though it is, is no different. As far as I am concerned, the most curious aspect of this case is not so much the call itself, but—as with the Gelb report cited in the last chapter—the witness's reaction to it. Although she *knew* her aunt was dead, Mrs. Sherrin seemed to have suffered a selective amnesia as soon as the call came through. Never once during the course of the conversation did she remember her aunt's tragic death. She carried out the phone conversation under the perfect conviction that her aunt was still alive, yet she regained her memory immediately after the call was over. Now, the more Raymond and I thought about this case, the more we began to realize that there were two very different explanations for Mrs. Sherrin's amnesia. One is a psychological explanation, while the other is a psychic one. Each possibility may be telling us something very important about the nature of these calls, as well as the type of reaction people are prone to have in the face of them.

People react to stress and trauma in a variety of ways. Some people seem able to handle emotional upsets rather easily. Although they might suffer some momentary anxiety, emotional upsets do not seem to interfere with their capabilities for continuing with their lives and work. We often refer to such people as "stoic" or "unaffectable." Other people, though, have violent reactions to anxiety-provoking situations. For example, a person who was beaten as a child or who witnessed a murder might repress his experience. In other words, he might forget his experience by pushing it out of his conscious memory and into the dark realms of the subconscious. This type of restricted amnesia can be incredibly selective. An accident victim, for instance, might remember being involved in a collision but not recall what happened to him immediately before or after the ordeal.

This is really nothing more than a simple shock reaction to a life-threatening situation, but sometimes these forms of temporary amnesia can become even more bizarre. Several years ago, for instance, a friend of mine was home from college, out working in his yard, when he received the awful news that his girlfriend had been killed in an automobile accident. After hearing the news, my friend literally blanked out. He found himself walking along a deserted street some 24 hours later; he even had to be reminded about his fiancée's death. To this day he does not know what happened to him after receiving the news. This type of amnesia is not rare. Many people seem able simply to "block out" stressful life experiences by conveniently forgetting them. "Forgetting," though, is rather a weak description of what really happens. Actually, the mind forcefully coerces the painful memories out of consciousness.

It is therefore possible that Mrs. Sherrin's amnesia was purely psychological in nature. Let's not forget just how traumatic these phone calls can be. If you recall, Patricia Adams's friend fainted at the sound of her deceased daughter's voice, and Dr. Gelb—who is a trained psychiatrist—described himself as "disoriented" after his experience. So Mrs. Sherrin's amnesia may have been a defense her mind used to help her deal with her experience. When she answered the phone, the sound of her aunt's voice may have been so frightening that she instantly and selectively blocked out all memory of the woman's death. This amnesia may have kept Mrs. Sherrin from suffering a devastating emotional shock as a result of the call. Yet, at the same time, it allowed her to maintain enough presence of mind to carry out a very natural and extended phone conversation with the voice-entity. The fact that she remembered her aunt's death right after the call doesn't strike us as odd either. When the phone conversation came to an end, the potentially trauma-producing episode was also terminated. At that time, it may have become psychologically safe for her to remember her aunt's accident and death.*

While Mrs. Sherrin's amnesia was probably psychological in nature, it is also possible that it may have had a *psychic* or paranormal cause. Could it be that somehow the intelligence that structured the phantom call also telepathically *forced* Mrs. Sherrin to forget that her aunt was dead, so that she would not become distressed during the call? Although bizarre, this theory is feasible. This is a suggestion to which I'll return later. For now, we'll just mention it as a possibility.

All in all, Mrs. Sherrin's report is one of our most interesting cases. It proved to us that we should study the personalities and individual psychologies of the people who have received these psychic phone calls as well as the calls themselves.

I should add at this point that when Raymond and I first started coming across these cases of "prolonged calls from the dead," we were a bit puzzled by and biased against them. While we had already come to the conclusion that phone calls from the dead genuinely occurred, we were much more impressed by the brief sort of interactions such as Dr. Gelb and others had reported. They struck us as just the type of contact between the living and the dead that might occur over any mechanical medium such as a telephone—i.e., a momentary and fragmented conversation. These reports of extended phone calls which are much rarer than Type 1 cases, struck even us as contrived and

---

* This explanation might strike you as farfetched, but in 1977 I came upon just such a case of selective amnesia while I was investigating a haunting in Los Angeles. The chief witness, a young man who had been taking care of a house while the owner was out of town on business, had heard various raps, moans, and groans in the house throughout the preceding several days. One evening, the noises became more prominent, and the witness even saw an apparition in the house. He became so frightened by the phantom's appearance that he ran from the house, hopped into his car, and drove over to his own home. As he drove, though, what he described as an "eerie serenity" came over him—and he totally forgot about his psychic experiences that evening. In this instance, the cause of the amnesia was no doubt psychological in nature, since the victim was trying to block out the memory of a terrifying psychic experience. While remembering everything that had happened *before* and *after* seeing the apparition, the memory of actually seeing the ghost became completely blocked from his conscious memory, apparently within three or four minutes after the experience, even though his memory returned spontaneously several hours later.

unbelievable. But as we kept running into more and more of these lengthy phantom calls, we once again realized that our prejudices were unfounded.

Only after we had collected about a half dozen of these Type 2 cases, however, did we realize that they had one conspicuous element in common. Predictably enough, this is an element which also links together the MacConnell, D'Alessio, and Sherrin cases. Notice that in each of these cases, *the recipient of the call thought he or she was talking to a living person.* They did not know at the time that their callers were quite dead. When we made this discovery, Raymond and I went back over our files and collected all the "prolonged" phone call cases we could find. (We arbitrarily decided that any case in which the phantom voice spoke over 30 intelligent words constituted a "prolonged" type of case). In all cases but one, the witnesses did not know that they were speaking to the dead at the time of the call.

Could it be, we thought, that prolonged conversations between the living and the dead *can occur* only when the witness is totally unaware that he or she is receiving a psychic phone call? Could this have something to do with Mrs. Sherrin's strange amnesia? This certainly seems to be the case. But why? This is a question to which we'll return in the next chapter.

Despite the challenge posed by these Type 2 cases, the vast majority of phantom calls is rather brief. In our collection of cases, short or Type 1 calls outnumber prolonged calls at the rate of four to one. However, they are certainly no less fascinating.

As we pointed out in the last chapter, one of the few investigators of the past who ever took any interest in these phone cases was the late Rev. S. Ralph Harlow. Besides being a rather active psychic investigator, he was also professor of religion at Smith College in Northampton, Massachusetts. Harlow included two phone call cases in his book, *A Life After Death*. (Originally published in 1961, this book was in one sense a landmark in parapsychology. It was one of the first books ever written by a Christian minister to actively support the contributions parapsychology could make to the study of life after death.) Although Harlow never commented on or offered any explanation for these two cases, he was obviously impressed by them.

Dr. Harlow never divulged the names of the two women involved in the first of his cases, but he refers to his main correspondent, whom he calls Mrs. Smith, as "a woman of marked intelligence and common sense." Since this woman also worked at Smith College, we can presume that Harlow knew her personally, and possibly quite well. One simply doesn't discuss phantom phone callers with strangers!

Mrs. Smith always spent her summers in a small New England town, Dr. Harlow explains. There she met and became friends with the elderly son of the famous Civil War admiral David Farragut. One summer day the elderly man died, and no doubt Mrs. Smith thought that the death would be the end of their relationship.

The next day, though, a relative of Mrs. Smith who was staying at her home answered a rather odd long-distance phone call from San Francisco. The caller was a man who identified himself as a retired Naval officer.

"Is Farragut there?" he asked.

"Who? No," answered Mrs. Smith's relative. Perplexed, she was about to tell the caller about Farragut's death.

"Well, where is he?" he interrupted almost brusquely. "He called me yesterday, and we'd only started talking when the line went dead. I haven't heard from him in years. At first I thought he was here in San Francisco, but he hadn't said before the line went dead."

The caller went on to say that he was sure it actually had been Farragut on the line. The caller had even addressed him by a nickname Farragut had called him years ago. The Naval officer had apparently spent all day trying to locate and phone him back. (Unfortunately, Harlow doesn't explain how the man came to call the Smith residence.)

As Mrs. Smith's relative talked with the officer, she realized that Farragut's bizarre call had apparently been placed to the officer three hours *after* the man's death.

Harlow's second case is very similar. It, too, was a short and abrupt call that was terminated suddenly and mysteriously. As he comments in his book:

> A similar case, in which I personally know the persons involved, happened recently. In this instance a young woman answered the telephone to hear her husband's voice clearly say only one word, "Good-by." And then the phone went dead. A short time later she was informed that her husband had died of a heart attack shortly after reaching his office. When she compared the time of his death with the time of the telephone message from the husband, she found that she had received the call about thirty minutes after her husband had died.

Phone Calls from the Dead: A Survey of Cases

This latter case is very similar to a case we ourselves collected. In this instance, too, the voice was only able to garble one or two words. We stumbled on this case quite by accident when Raymond, on a hunch, decided to phone Dr. Thelma Moss of the UCLA Neuropsychiatric Institute. Dr. Moss often appears on local television and radio programs and also teaches adult education courses at the university. Raymond thought that she might have a phone call case or two in her files, perhaps sent to her by a student or viewer. As usual, Raymond's hunch was right. She immediately replied that one of her students had indeed reported a "phone call from the dead" to her a couple of years before, and she promised to look it up for us. A week later Dr. Moss supplied Raymond with all the fascinating details.

The woman who received the call, a long-time resident of Los Angeles, was very devoted to her son, who was an amateur mountain climber. In 1975 he visited India to scale some of the notoriously treacherous Himalayan peaks. Only a few weeks after he began his climb, he was reported missing and was never seen again. Local Indian officials concluded that he must have fallen while making his climb and presumed him dead shortly after his disappearance. Even the *Los Angeles Times* ran a story about the supposed accident.

Naturally, when Dr. Moss's student received the first cable from India advising her about her son's disappearance, she was panic-stricken. "One night," Dr. Moss told us, "she had tried to put in a telephone call to the police in the place in which he had been staying. It was a large Indian city—New Delhi, I think. Communications are very difficult to get through by telephone. I know, I've been there and I've tried."

The overseas operator was anything but helpful and kept telling the distraught woman that they would call her back as soon as they placed the call successfully. Then, as Dr. Moss told us:

"It was quite late at night, around midnight I think, when her phone rang, and she thought, 'Oh, thank God.' She picked up the phone and heard her son's voice say, 'Hello, Mother.' Thinking that he was all right, she said, 'Hello, how are you?' The voice again said, 'Hello, Mother.' She tried to establish contact, but there was a click and the receiver went dead. She was sure that it was her son's voice."

This case, in turn, reminds us of an incident a woman from Australia once told us about. In this case, too, the voice could only eke out a couple of words before losing contact completely:

Phone Calls from the Dead

Last year a friend of mine named Elsie died. She was the only Elsie I knew apart from an old lady aged 82, who hasn't got a phone and has never rung me anyway. A few weeks after the death my phone rang, so I answered "Hello." But all I heard was a faint, "Elsie, Elsie," repeated a few times and getting fainter and fainter till it finally faded out. I kept on saying, "Put your money in," but that was all I heard. It was not till some time later that I suddenly realized that it could have been Elsie. I was not surprised as I believe in this kind of thing, having [had] one or two experiences of a similar kind.

This incident is somewhat similar to the Gelb case. In both instances, the phone voice seemed impervious to anything said by the person answering the call, just as though a faulty connection had been established. In fact, these types of abortive communications are often reported by people who have received phantom phone calls. We're continually impressed by the similarities that many of our cases seem to share. For instance, we've noticed that calls from people who have died only recently—say, within 7 days of the call—tend to be abortive, confused, and exceedingly brief. On the other hand, more prolonged calls are most often received from people who have been dead for several months. (The D'Alessio incident is a good case in point. The woman she spoke to over the phone had been dead for some months before phone contact was made.) While this is not a hard and fast principle, to date we have come across only one instance where a lengthy phone conversation took place immediately or shortly after the caller's death—the MacConnell case cited earlier. If not brief, these contacts seem confused—as though the deceased party really didn't know what he or she was doing. As Raymond has suggested to me, it sometimes seems as though at first these phantom voices don't even realize that they have made successful contact with the living.

A good example of just this sort of call was reported to us in August 1977 by Dr. John Medved, a prominent Los Angeles physician. Dr. Medved had been so perplexed by his experience that he called UCLA to report the incident to Dr. Moss. Later, he called the Beverly Hills-based Society for Psychic Research (S.P.R.) and reported his experience to their secretary. It was apparent to the S.P.R. staff that Dr. Medved was desperately trying to find some explanation for his experience. So they, in turn, suggested that he call Raymond, who routinely investigates hauntings and other reports of psychic phenomena for the S.P.R. Dr. Medved had been searching three years

Phone Calls from the Dead: A Survey of Cases

for someone who could help explain his experience or at least discuss it with him intelligently.

After hearing the doctor's story, Raymond realized we had a gold mine on our hands, not so much because of the content of the call, but because we were able to talk with Dr. Medved in such great depth. We were therefore able to dig out several interesting aspects of the case which we would probably not have been able to uncover through correspondence. And we really became excited when we found out that there was a witness to Dr. Medved's experience.

Dr. Medved's mother died on July 13, 1974. It had been her long-standing wish to be buried in her family's old hometown in Idaho, so, shortly after her death, her remains were duly transported there by plane. Dr. Medved made the long trip to the funeral by automobile. He remained in Idaho only a day or two before driving back to his practice in Los Angeles. His phantom phone call, which was to puzzle him for months to come, came through the day after his return:

> Being very tired from the long trip, I had gone to bed early the night before. I got up with the sun about 6:00 o'clock in the morning and went out and got the paper. I put on the coffee, had a cup, watered some plants, and went into the bathroom to clean up when the phone rang.
>
> It was exactly 6:30, and I thought that it was no time for my exchange to be bothering me. In the bathroom, behind the sliding door, I have a "banana phone," but I rarely ever use it. I went down the hall and stopped at the desk just inside the front door entrance. There is a phone there, but I went on to the kitchen. There is a counter there with a phone, pad and pencil. I wanted the pad since I assumed that it was the exchange calling.
>
> When I said hello, the voice on the phone said, "Johnny." It was a little odd sounding, and I thought it was one of my sisters. It sounded a little dismayed, as if she was calling to report a problem. I said, "What's the matter?" and the voice said again, "Johnny."

At this point in his story, Dr. Medved imitated the way the voice called out his name. "John-n-n-n-y-y-y-," it said, drawing it out eerily at the end.

> I again said, "What's the matter? Who is this?" I don't know whether the voice said "Johnny" again, but then I began to get rather excited. The next thing the voice said was, "Is that you, Johnny dear?" By this time I didn't know if someone was pulling a joke on me or what, and

my voice really got high. "What's the matter?" I said. "Who is this?" I kept repeating this, and the voice said, "Your mother."

Dr. Medved explained that the voice exactly matched his late mother's. At the end of these two words, the voice trailed off into a whisper.

Dr. Medved kept talking, but it was no use. The phone line remained open (in other words, it didn't go dead), but after fading out, the phantom voice just ceased talking. Neither did Dr. Medved hear a "click" over the line as though some one had hung up on him. Finally, when the doctor realized that the call was over, he himself reluctantly hung up.

Although Dr. Medved was the only one who spoke to the phantom voice, this case is not merely an unsubstantiated anecdote. Medved explained to us that a friend of his, whom we'll simply call Mr. B. to protect his privacy, was visiting him when the call came in. Although Mr. B. hadn't actually witnessed or overheard the call, Medved had excitedly told him about his weird experience within half an hour of the occurrence. Since Mr. B. was still living in Los Angeles at the time we investigated this case, Raymond felt that it would be wise to track him down and interview him. If the witness's story matched Dr. Medved's, we reasoned, this would give added support to the case's evidentiality.

Luckily, it didn't take Raymond long to locate Mr. B., who remembered the episode quite well.

"He told me about it right after it happened—within 15 minutes," he told Raymond. "He was visibly shaken, and said, 'I don't know what is going on, but I just talked to my mother.' "

Mr. B. recounted exactly what Medved had told him about the call back in 1974. This version of the story was identical to the one Dr. Medved told us three years later. To us this indicated not only that Dr. Medved was telling us the truth about his experience, but that his memory of the incident was accurate in all details.

Even though most "phone calls from the dead" are exceedingly brief, they are not *always* abortive, and this is true of "simple" as well as "prolonged" cases. The callers are sometimes able to get through a message—occasionally short, urgent calls for help, such as the one Don Owens and his wife received (see Chapter 2). In other cases, these callers will communicate some short allusion to their terrestrial lives. Patricia Adams's report is an excellent case in point: In this instance the voice of her friend's deceased daughter made the same request over the phone that she invariably made when calling her mother during

Phone Calls from the Dead: A Survey of Cases

her life. This feature occurs in several of the cases we've collected; for the sake of space, though, we'll cite only one or two examples here.

On July 18, 1978, we received a letter from Dr. Berthold Schwarz informing us that he had just run into a "phone call from the dead" case while investigating a haunting in Montclair, New Jersey. While talking with the family who lived in the haunted house, Schwarz learned that Mr. Karl Uphoff, a young man who was currently boarding with them, had received a mystery phone call about a year before. Knowing of our interest in these cases, Bert tracked down all the witnesses to the incident he could find and immediately sent us the result of his investigation. This case is doubly impressive since two people spoke to the phantom voice while two others witnessed the call. However, this account is unusual in one major respect: Most people receive phantom phone calls while in their own homes; this call, though, was not made to Karl's home, but to that of a friend he was visiting at the time.

Here, then, is a summary of the case as Dr. Schwarz pieced it together for us:

Karl was only 18 years old when his 80-year-old maternal grandmother died. He had been her favorite grandchild, and there had been a close bond of affection between them. During the last years of her life the elderly woman had grown quite deaf and would often call up Karl when she needed his assistance. Karl was a typical teenager with plenty of errands to run and friends to visit, so if his grandmother had to get in touch with him urgently, she would often call at his friends' homes while trying to track him down. No matter who answered the phone, she would invariably ask, "Is Karl there? Tell him to come home now."

Only two days after his grandmother's death, Karl decided to pay a call to the home of Mr. and Mrs. Sam D'Alessio.* Peter, the D'Alessio's son, was a good friend of Karl's, and both the elder D'Alessios were home when he dropped by. The visit was just a social one and had nothing to do with his grandmother's recent death. In fact, the D'Alessios didn't even know that Karl's grandmother had died. As Karl and Peter were talking together in a downstairs room, the phone rang unexpectedly.

So that the boys wouldn't be disturbed, Mrs. D'Alessio went upstairs and answered the phone. "It was Karl's grandmother asking to speak to Karl," Mrs. D'Alessio told Schwarz later. "She said, 'This is Karl's

---

* (No relation to Mrs. Marie D'Alessio, whose case was also investigated by Dr. Schwarz.)

grandmother.' And when I hollered down to Karl, my son said he turned all colors."

According to what Mrs. D'Alessio told Schwarz, the voice delivered the same message she often delivered when alive: She requested that Karl come home. At first, when Karl told her that his grandmother had recently died, Mrs. D'Alessio thought the call was a prank. Nonetheless, Karl himself got on the line, but by this time, though the phone line remained open, the voice had stopped speaking.

Fortuitously, Dr. Schwarz brought this case to our attention just a few weeks before I was scheduled to fly to the East Coast, and right then and there I decided to interview Karl personally if at all possible. Bert provided me with Karl's phone number, and I called Karl a few days after arriving in New York.

Karl turned out to be a friendly and open young man, just a couple of years younger than myself, and quite willing to discuss his unusual experience. Since I was planning to make a trip to Montclair to meet with Bert anyway, I invited Karl to drop by when I arrived in town so that we could all discuss the incident together. Karl was ready and willing, so on May 1 all of us—Karl, Bert, and myself—got together at Bert's splendid, huge, turn-of-the-century home. But Karl had at least one surprise up his sleeve for us: He brought Peter D'Alessio along with him. Since Peter had witnessed the call, he was able to help fill in several details about the case. Peter was now Karl's roommate and served as an independent witness to everything Karl told us.

Karl, a young jazz musician in his mid-20s, had a fairly good recollection of the incident and verified the version of the story Mrs. D'Alessio had given Bert several weeks before. In fact, his version of the incident was even more impressive than hers had been.

"When I was a little kid," Karl explained, "my grandmother was about 80 percent deaf. We had a phone with an amplifier on it so that she could amplify whatever was coming through, but it still didn't help very much. Up until the time I was 16 or 17, I would leave her a list of numbers and tell her where I was going. If she needed me for an emergency or something, she would call any place I went. She'd merely dial the number—she wouldn't know if it rang or if anyone answered—and she would keep repeating over and over, maybe four to six times. 'This is Karl's grandmother, and would you please send him home, I need him,' or something to that effect. It was a regular occurrence for me; it happened all the time. The last phone call like that I might have gotten at anyone's house was when I was, maybe, 16.

"This incident was in 1969, and I guess I was 18 at the time. It had been two years since she had done anything like that because my sister, who was in the area and around a lot more, took care of everything. But by the way, none of my friends knew about this."

Karl told me that he never brought up the subject of his grandmother's habit to his friends and had not even known the D'Alessios very long at the time of her passing. As was pointed out earlier, he didn't even tell them about his grandmother's death when he visited them two days after her demise. Although Peter knew of her passing, he had not mentioned the matter to his parents either. Karl and Peter were forming a rock combo and the purpose of Karl's visit was to work out some of the details. They were talking together in the D'Alessio basement when the upstairs phone rang.

Peter concurred. "We were talking or playing or something," he added, "and I heard my mother, not arguing—I don't recall any words—but I know my mother's tone of voice, and she was getting a bit miffed." They didn't pay much attention until Mrs. D'Alessio yelled down to Karl. As he explained to us:

"Mrs. D'Alessio said to me, 'There's an old woman on the phone. She says she's your grandmother and she says she needs you. She just keeps saying it over and over again.'"

"She hollered it down the stairs," Peter interjected. 'Downstairs, we heard her on the upstairs phone, and in all my life I've never seen anybody turn as white as Karl turned. He was like marble white, and he did my cellar stairs in three bounds."

From there, Karl took up the story again: "When I grabbed the phone," he said in a voice full of disappointment, 'no one was on the line."

In reconstructing the events of the day, both Peter and Karl were in general agreement about what had happened. For instance, Karl told me that after the incident, Mrs. D'Alessio said that the voice had repeated its message over and over, "a few times." She had tried to communicate with the woman on the line, she said, but the voice merely ignored her attempts. Mrs. D'Alessio had even tried to tell the voice that she would get Karl, but the voice seemed oblivious to her.

At this point, the witnesses became a little confused about certain details pertinent to the call. Mrs. D'Alessio had told Bert that the voice identified itself as Karl's grandmother. Karl also remembers that Mrs. D'Alessio identified the caller when she hollered down to him. Peter's recollection, however, was that his mother yelled down to Karl only that "an old woman" was on the phone for him. In discussing the incident, however, all three witnesses agreed that at one time or another Mrs. D'Alessio recalled that (1) the voice called for Karl by name, (2) it said that she needed him, (3) it said that he should come home, and (4) this message was repeated several times. So under the circumstances, whether or not the voice actually identified itself as Karl's grandmother is of no great importance. The message, which is the most evidential aspect of the case, was identical to the one the deceased woman had made to Karl for many years while alive.

But this was not the end of the attempted communication. Later that night Karl answered several phone calls back at his own home. Each time, there was no one on the other end of the line. Peter had gone home with Karl that evening and also witnessed these calls. While the calls could, of course, have been due to some sort of mechanical malfunction, Karl could not remember this ever happening to his home phone before. It therefore seems likely that these abortive calls may have been further attempts at communication. At least, that was Karl's gut reaction to the calls. If so, this would be a semi-unique aspect of this case, since we have run into only one other case in which the witness received a series of mysterious "silent" phone calls. This report will be cited in Chapter 6, when we discuss the mechanical aspects of these cases.*

---

*While investigating this case, Schwarz ran into some wild coincidences that are interesting enough to be mentioned here. In December 1977 I wrote to Dr. Schwarz and asked him if he had come across any new "phone calls from the dead" cases since investigating the Marie D'Alessio case, cited earlier. Bert wrote back to me on January 4, explaining that he had just run into the Karl Uphoff case. In fact, my letter had been right on his desk when he himself learned of the case. He had decided to answer my letter right after phoning the witnesses to the Montclair haunting he was investigating and it was during this phone call that he learned of Karl Uphoff's experience.

This in itself was a striking coincidence, but it was only the beginning of a long series of synchronicities. (Synchronicity is a term coined by the great psychoanalyst C. G. Jung and refers to "meaningful coincidences," i.e., events which seem totally coincidental but which indicate some sort of cosmic planning on the part of the universe.) Before running into this case, Bert had personally looked into only three other "phone calls from the dead" incidents. The first, reported to him by Marie D'Alessio in the early 1970's, was discussed earlier in this chapter. The second was reported to him by Dr. Walter Uphoff and concerned a call presumably made by his deceased secretary. (This case will be summarized shortly.) Now, Karl Uphoff turned out to be Walter Uphoff's second cousin, although the two had never met nor even knew

Phone Calls from the Dead: A Survey of Cases

Sometimes these Type 1 "message" cases can be incredibly touching. (By nature, psychic investigators are supposed to be cold, critical, and dispassionate, but some of these accounts pack an emotional wallop that would melt even the iciest heart.) One woman, who had read a magazine article that we had written on the subject, wrote to tell us about a personal experience she had about four months after her husband's demise. Only 45 years old at the time, he succumbed to a heart attack while out on a camping trip with his two teenaged sons. He died that same day, before his wife could even reach him. She wrote:

> Just before he left on his trip he crouched down in front of the refrigerator to pick up [our daughter] Lynn. He turned to me and said something he often repeated with a smile. "Darling, have I told you lately how I love you?" That was the last thing he ever said to me. One Sunday afternoon in March 1957 I was alone in the house. The phone rang and when I answered it, a voice—it was so faint I could not tell if [it was] a man's or a woman's—started reciting Elizabeth Barrett Browning's poem, *How Do I Love Thee, Let Me Count the Ways.* The voice became fainter and fainter till there was no more sound."

Although the woman did not actually recognize the voice, she intuitively knew that her late husband had been responsible for the call. "No one else has ever come up with any other explanation,"

---

about each other's experiences. Notice the phenomenal interplay of names: Schwarz investigates two phone call cases, concerning a Walter Uphoff and a Marie D'Alessio, and then runs into a third case in which the two primary witnesses are named Karl Uphoff and Mrs. Sam D'Alessio. Coincidence? Or something more?

One runs into these types of coincidences all the time while investigating the paranormal. By studying such synchronicities, we might eventually discover some cosmic clues about the intelligence which seems to be masterminding these phenomena. A classic example occurred during a UFO flap which spread over the Eastern part of the United States in 1957. On November 6, twelve-year-old Everett Clark saw a UFO in Knoxville, Tennessee. The object had landed on the ground and the boy saw four occupants, two men and two women, standing by the craft. Although he didn't communicate with the beings, he heard them speaking in a strange language. On that same evening, a Mr. John Trasco of Everittstown, New Jersey, saw a UFO hovering over his barn. He, too, saw an occupant near the vehicle who approached him and asked if he could take his dog away.

she told us. We tend to agree—at least, we don't think this was any normal phone call.

So far, we've summarized two different types of phone call cases, arbitrarily labeled as "simple" or Type 1 cases (such as the ones Karl Uphoff, Owens, and Medved received) and "prolonged" or Type 2 cases (such as those reported by Marie D'Alessio, the MacConnells, and Mrs. Sherrin.) There is another type of case, however, which strikes us as even more perplexing. These are instances in which a third party—usually someone who never knew the deceased person making the call—is deliberately contacted by the phantom voice. Usually the voice simply delivers some sort of urgent message or communication, and the person who has received the call often remains totally unaware that he or she is actually speaking to a phantom!

We only have two or three cases of this very rare type of call in our files. The following incident was reported to us by an acquaintance, Dr. Walter Uphoff, who is a former economics professor now living in Wisconsin. He cites the case in his book, *New Psychic Frontiers*, but Dr. Uphoff also supplied us with some further details pertinent to the case.

Back in 1965 Uphoff was teaching at the University of Colorado, where his secretary was a conscientious and dedicated woman named Mrs. Iris Brace. During her tenure with Uphoff, however, she suffered a gall bladder attack and her doctor advised her to have the organ removed by surgery whenever convenient. As Uphoff reminisces in his book:

> We were working at that time on a book about the long strike at Kohler, Wisconsin. When Memorial Day weekend drew near, we decided to spend the last days of May and the first week of June in Wisconsin on further investigations. "Since you will be away," Mrs. Brace told me, "I think I will go to the hospital for surgery."
>
> I told her that would be quite all right as far as the work was concerned, "But when I get back," I asked, "would you be sure to remind me to call the insurance firm of Trailbush and Hedgecock to ask one or both of them to speak on personal life insurance programs at the Steelworkers' Institute?" She promised she would. We ordered a plant to be sent to her at the hospital and left for Wisconsin. The following Friday, our son phoned to tell us that Mrs. Brace had died unexpectedly from an embolism. We returned to Colorado that weekend. The memorial service was set for Monday afternoon.
>
> I spent Monday forenoon at my office, working on final plans for the Steelworkers' Institute. I remembered to call the insurance firm and

placed the call about 10 a.m. Glenn Hedgecock answered the phone and I had just begun to explain why I was calling when he said, "Just a minute! My other phone is ringing!" I waited a few minutes until he resumed. "Your secretary just called to remind me that you wanted me to participate in your Institute program..."

Dumbfounded, I said "I'm sorry, but she died last week!" It was his turn to be surprised. "All I can say is that's for you to figure out. When I told her that you were on the other phone, the voice said, 'In that case I'll consider the message delivered.'" That was all he heard and there had been no clicking of the telephone receiver.

My first reaction was not very logical. I checked with the secretary of the Economics Department to see if she had called. Then I asked a student who worked part-time in my office, and called Mrs. Brace's sister-in-law, all of them denying that they had made such a call. Finally it dawned on me that someone going to the hospital expects to recover and would not likely ask others to take over so trivial an assignment as this; and, if Mrs. Brace had asked someone to call, they surely would have said, "I am calling on behalf of, (or for) Professor Uphoff's secretary" not "This is Professor Uphoff's secretary."*

Like so many of the cases we have collected, this one, despite its bizarre nature, has certain features in common with other cases in our files. For instance, note that the recipient of this call did *not* hear the phone being hung up at the end of the call. Neither did Dr. Medved when he received a phone call from his deceased mother. However, this case is somewhat different in that this phantom voice was motivated to deliver a precise and somewhat urgent message. (In fact, as I suggested earlier, we've come to call these types of calls "message" cases.)

Most phantom callers do not seem motivated to do anything more than make simple contact with the living. Mrs. Sherrin's aunt, Farragut, Dr. Medved's mother, Karl Uphoff's grandmother, even Mrs. D'Alessio's friend—none of these "voices" seemed to have any special purpose for placing their calls; they just seemed to want to share a consoling word or two with their former friends and relatives. Although Enid Johlson and Mrs. D'Alessio's friend engaged in lengthy conversation with the living, they did not seem to have any pressing need for making contact.

---

* We were able to contact Mr. Hedgecock ourselves. He fully corroborated Uphoff's version of the incident, adding, "The voice did not sound peculiar. I do not remember hearing the phone being hung up."

If we may be permitted a rather banal colloquialism, these cases seem more like "social calls" than emergency ones.

We do not mean to deprecate the importance of these less complex cases, however. Obviously, they are telling us something very important about the nature of "phone calls from the dead." Perhaps it is only natural for the dead to wish to contact us—and in any way possible. But another type of motivation seems to have prompted Iris Brace's call—the need to deliver a specific and *impersonal* message to complete work left unfinished at the time of death. These "message" cases are much rarer than the simple calls that Karl Uphoff and Dr. Medved received, but they are infinitely more important—that is because, more than any other type of case, they supply us with several clues about the nature, purpose, and very source of these calls. So, at this point, perhaps we should start trying to figure out where these calls come from and just who, in fact, are making them. Are the dead really trying to contact us? Or is some other force at play?

4

The Source of the Calls:
I. Problems and Possibilities

Raymond and I had two goals in mind when we first started collecting these phone cases. Of course we wanted to amass as many firsthand accounts as possible. The examples recounted in chapters 2 and 3 are typical of what our endeavors turned up, and we have several more still under investigation. But we have never really been content with merely collecting these reports and charting their characteristics. Our second and much more difficult goal was to answer two questions these cases prompted us to ask: (1) What is the nature of the intelligence that lies *behind* these calls? and (2) How are they mechanically produced over the telephone system? Neither of these questions is easy to answer, so for now we will concentrate just on the first.

At the beginning of our research, Raymond and I felt that three different explanations could account for these phantom phone calls. Our reasoning went generally along the following lines:

1. To begin with, we, of course, felt that these alleged phone manipulations might indeed be masterminded by the dead during attempts to contact us. This explanation might be called the *spiritistic* or *survival* theory.

2. However, we could not dismiss the possibility that some other type of paraphysical or extradimensional being—perhaps invisible

denizens that co-inhabit the Earth with us or exist in some parallel universe—might be playing a huge cosmic joke on us. Such beings might be endowed with the ability to manipulate our phone system and mimic the voices of the dead. Several experts on the paranormal (such as writers John Keel and Brad Steiger, as well as the famous naturalist Ivan Sanderson) have seriously postulated the existence of such beings. Steiger and Keel especially believe that these intelligences might deliberately set out to trick or bewilder us in any way possible. Many American Indian legends talk about a similar race of beings. Although admittedly an extravagant theory, it should nonetheless be taken seriously. We'll explain why later. For short, we've come to call this explanation the *EDB* (extradimensional being) theory.

3. Finally, we also thought that the witnesses themselves might be unwittingly manufacturing these calls through their own innate mind-over-matter (*or psychokinetic*) abilities. In other words, we wondered whether or not we might be playing some sort of psychic joke on ourselves! This might be called the *PK-from-the-living* theory.

Now just how does one go about trying to determine which of these explanations best fits the facts? To be blatantly honest, at first we weren't sure. There are pros and cons to each explanation, and a good case could be made for any one of them. Of course, it would certainly have been easy for us merely to assume from the start that these calls come from the dead, but nothing is that simple in parapsychology. So, as we tried to determine just what guiding force is lurking behind these calls, we found ourselves taking a much closer look at the reports we had assembled.

We started by mapping out the characteristics of our cases. We graphed out how long they lasted, how many words were spoken by the phantom voices, what time of day they occurred, *ad infinitum* and *ad nauseum*! After we graphed, diagramed, "statisticalized," and scrutinized our data, we were hoping that some clues might become apparent to us. Things didn't quite work out as neatly as we had hoped, but we did uncover several clues that led us to believe that these calls actually do come from the dead.

Now you still might be asking yourselves why didn't we merely assume this to begin with? Isn't it self-evident? The answer to this question is clearly negative. This might surprise you a bit, so let me explain.

Parapsychologists are roughly divided into two camps. Some, whom we call "survivalists," are researchers who believe that some forms

The Source of the Calls: I. Problems and Possibilities

of psychic experiences (such as apparitions, hauntings, and psychic communications received through mediums) are due to the activities of the dead. In other words, the survivalists believe that some element of the human personality survives, persists after death, and can subsequently make psychic contact with the living. Out of convenience these entities are usually called "Theta-agents." On the other hand, many other parapsychologists classify themselves as "anti-survivalists." Not only do they *not* believe that the dead can communicate with the living, but most do not believe in any type of a life after death at all. They argue that we, the living, often use our own innate psychic abilities to *trick* ourselves into believing that the dead are trying to contact us or are otherwise influencing our lives. (There are also, of course, many parapsychologists who are totally agnostic on the survival issue and who prefer not to think about it at all!)

Consequently, there are two ways any case of an alleged "contact with the dead" can be explained, that is, along either survivalistic or anti-survivalistic lines. For example, take a look at the following case, originally reported around the turn of the century:

> I had a very dear brother (my eldest brother), Oliver, lieutenant in the 7th Royal Fusiliers. He was about nineteen years old, and had at that time been some months before in Sebastopol. I corresponded frequently with him, and once when he wrote in low spirits, not being well, I said in answer that he was to cheer up, but that if anything did happen to him, he must let me know by appearing to me in my room. This letter (I learned subsequently) he received as he was starting to receive the Sacrament from a clergyman who has since related the fact to me. Having done this, he went to the entrenchments and never returned, as in a few hours afterwards the storming of the Redan commenced. He, on the falling of the captain of his company, took his place, and led his men bravely on. He had just led them within the walls, though already wounded in several places, when a bullet struck him on the right temple and he fell amongst heaps of others, where he was found in a sort of kneeling posture (being propped up by other dead bodies) thirty-six hours afterwards. His death took place, or rather he fell, though he may not have died immediately, on the 8th September, 1855.
>
> That night I awoke suddenly, and saw facing the window of my room, by my bedside, surrounded by a light sort of phosphorescent mist, as it were, my brother kneeling. I tried to speak but could not. I

decided that it must be fancy, and the moonlight playing on a towel, or something out of place. But, on looking up, there he was again, looking lovingly, imploringly, and sadly at me. I turned, and still saw poor Oliver. I shut my eyes, walked through it, and reached the door of the room. As I turned the handle, before leaving the room, I looked once more back. The apparition turned round his head slowly and again looked anxiously and lovingly at me, and I saw then for the first time a wound on the right temple with a red stream from it. His face was of a waxy pale tint, but transparent-looking, and so was the reddish mark. But it is almost impossible to describe his appearance. I only know I shall never forget it. I left the room and went into a friend's room, and lay on the sofa the rest of the night. I told him why. I told others in the house, but when I told my father, he ordered me not to repeat such nonsense, and especially not to let my mother know.

Though it is not clearly stated in the account, the witness had absolutely no idea that his brother had been killed the very day he saw the soldier's apparition. He only learned of the death ten days later.

Now there are two very plausible explanations for this psychic experience. The survivalist might unhesitatingly argue that some element of the dead soldier's personality survived death, "traveled" to England, and manifested before his brother in the form of the apparition. This explanation is logical, plausible, and consistent with all the facts of the case. The anti-survivalist, however, would argue that the witness had actually received only a telepathic message from or about his brother which informed him of the death. What he really saw was not his dead brother's "Theta-agent," but a telepathically triggered *vision* and nothing more. Of course, one could argue for hours over which theory is the more cogent, but there is simply no way to *prove* which one is, in fact, correct.

In this same light, take the following case which appears in Dr. Louisa Rhine's book, *Hidden Channels of the Mind*:

A spring evening about twenty-eight years ago in our home in Massachusetts, my dad, mother and I were reading aloud when suddenly, at twenty minutes after seven, the clock struck once—a clock which struck only the hours and had been doing so for years. This striking was so unusual we all noticed it and about five minutes later a telephone call told us my mother's favorite sister had died suddenly of a heart attack—at seven-twenty. The clock never struck out of turn again.

The Source of the Calls: I. Problems and Possibilities

Once again, the survival-oriented parapsychologist would probably have no difficulty explaining this odd "death coincidence," and would argue that at the moment of death some component of the deceased woman's mind traveled to her sister's house and caused the disturbance. The anti-survivalist, on the other hand, could argue just as convincingly that the witness probably unconsciously received a telepathic impression about her sister's death. Her unconscious mind may then have projected some sort of psychokinetic force that made the clock chime. The witness's mind may have used this mechanism to bring the information to conscious attention instead of, for instance, producing an apparition.*

Note that in both these instances—the soldier's apparition and the mysterious clock chiming—it appears that the witnesses themselves created psychic phenomena which only *looked* as if they were produced by the dead; but they may well have been, and most likely were, constructed by their own minds. One must never underestimate how cleverly our own minds can deceive us.

Raymond and I ran smack into this same problem when we started studying "phone calls from the dead" accounts. Let me illustrate this point by talking a little bit about the nature of psychokinesis; suggesting a possible mechanism by which these calls might be produced; and then showing how they can be explained in two very different ways.

Despite the years that went into its development, the telephone is not an overly complicated device. When you speak into it, you are, in fact, talking into a diaphragm which vibrates and converts your voice into electrical impulses. These impulses are then transmitted over the telephone wires and are reconstructed by the speaker in the phone of the person you're calling. What he or she hears is not your actual voice, but a series of electrical impulses that are mimicking you. Now, you might ask, what does all this have to do with psychokinesis?

---

* In fact, a great deal of evidence indicates that ESP usually works through the unconscious mind in just this way. Most psychic messages reach us in dreams, visions, "hunches," or "intuitive feelings," all vehicles by which the unconscious mind transfers information into the conscious mind. If a friend of yours were injured in an accident, you might dream about it, have a vision of it, or undergo an odd mental impression at the very moment of the accident. It seems that our unconscious minds are probably bombarded by ESP impressions constantly, although few of them are strong enough to break into consciousness. It is also possible that we use ESP like radar to unconsciously scan about psychically, and that we might use PK unconsciously on rare occasions as well.

All of us are apparently endowed with two types of psychic ability. The first, of course, is ESP. While not very many of us have any control over our ESP abilities or can use them consciously, there seems little doubt that all of us have an ESP *potential* locked within us. There is even some rather impressive evidence that ESP can be developed through training. (See Dr. Charles Tart's book, *Learning to Use Extrasensory Perception*. Chicago: University of Chicago Press, 1977.) That we all probably possess some modicum of psychokinetic (or PK) ability as well was aptly proved by Dr. J. B. Rhine years ago when he began his famous research at Duke University back in the 1930's. By 1934, Rhine was able to report in his book *Extrasensory Perception* that one out of every five people seem to have some ESP talent. He had reached his conclusion after testing students, colleagues, visitors to the lab, and everyone else he could lay his hands on.

In 1934, Rhine suddenly became interested in seeing how many of his subjects had PK abilities as well. His initial interest was aroused when a young gambler visited the Duke Psychology Department one day and claimed that he could psychokinetically influence the fall of the dice. Rhine tested the man by carrying out a simple series of tests; he merely rolled some dice and asked the gambler to make them land on certain sides more often than chance could account for. The experiment was apparently successful, and soon Rhine and his colleagues began testing everyone in sight, hoping to discover just how widespread PK abilities are among the general public. The upshot no doubt surprised even Rhine. The Duke team, as well as other parapsychologists working in independent laboratories, discovered that many ordinary kinds of people—like you and me—do have a rather weak ability to influence the fall of dice, spinning coins, the growth and yield rate of plants, and so on. PK seems to be an ability almost as widespread as ESP. Eventually, some parapsychologists even discovered that PK *can disrupt delicate electrical systems.*

Dr. Hans Bender is a noted German parapsychologist who, until his recent retirement, headed a division of parapsychology at the University of Freiburg. In 1967, he was called in to investigate some haunted law offices in Rosenheim, Germany. The poltergeist was causing quite a commotion and had singled out the office's electrical equipment for the greatest amount of mischief. The phones' call buttons would activate wildly, phone calls that had never been placed were billed to the office phones over and over again, and other mechanical malfunctions plagued them as well. Later, light bulbs started exploding, furniture began moving around by itself, pictures on the walls would swing back and forth, and the overhead light would sway to and fro in an eerie dance. Even a 2,000-pound storage cabinet once slid across the floor.

Of course, the managers of the building immediately called in electrical experts from the local community and the power company. They checked the building over thoroughly and could find no normal reason for the disturbances. But once Bender arrived on the scene, it didn't take him long to isolate the cause of the disturbances. It quickly became apparent that these odd PK and electrical phenomena occurred only when a teenaged employee, Annemarie Schnabel, was present in the offices. Nothing would happen when she was gone, but as soon as she came in for work, phones started malfunctioning and objects would start moving about inexplicably.

Sometimes the PK disturbances would center right on Annemarie. According to Bender, the lights often swung about in the office corridor as soon as the girl walked by them. Light bulbs would also explode in her presence, and the broken fragments would invariably fly toward her. Finally Annemarie was terminated from her job, but similar PK phenomena broke out in her new place of employment—and even in a bowling alley she visited one day.

But just how and why was Annemarie related to these PK outbreaks? Bender was able to come up with a good explanation for these enigmas. By talking with the girl, Bender—a trained clinician—could see that she was extremely disturbed. On both a conscious and unconscious level, she was trying to cope with deep hostility toward herself and her job. Her romantic life wasn't going too smoothly either, and Annemarie apparently had no normal outlet for expressing her anger, hostility, and frustration, which could do nothing but well up within her.

In view of his clinical findings, Bender came to the conclusion that there certainly wasn't a spook loose in Rosenheim. The office wasn't really haunted. Rather, Annemarie's own troubled mind was responsible for the PK attacks; Annemarie was probably causing the disturbances psychically—but unconsciously. Disrupting her employer's office may have been her way of expressing the hostility seething within her. Some psychic violence was erupting within her unconscious mind, and her boss was the unfortunate victim.

The Rosenheim case certainly indicates that our PK abilities might have a particular penchant for disrupting electrical systems—telephones included! It is therefore also plausible that PK force might also *be able to set up and manipulate electrical impulses sent over telephone wires.*

Thus these "phone calls from the dead" cases might actually be a very bizarre form of PK function—either carrying out the dead agent's wishes to contact us *or being the projections of our own minds.*

If, for instance, a friend of yours thinks of you right before or even after his death, it is quite possible that he might release some sort of PK force. This PK force, liberated by the agent's death, might then be able to "travel" to your home and cause a clock to chime unexpectedly, stop a clock, or push a plate off a shelf in your kitchen. But why couldn't this force also affect your telephone system and wires, perhaps by initiating a series of electrical impulses that would imitate a human voice? Such a process would result in a "phone call from the dead." On the other hand, it might also be possible that *you* produced this force as the result of an unconsciously received telepathic message. Having learned of the death unconsciously, your own mind might then project a PK force capable of manipulating your phone system and putting the call through.

There is one problem with this latter theory, of course. Why do some witnesses receive phone calls from people who have been dead for several months, even years? What possible purpose could these belated calls serve? In answer, I can only say that all of us yearn for immortality; recent opinion polls have shown that a vast majority of the American public believe in some sort of life after death. I doubt whether anyone who has ever lost a close friend, relative, or even a pet has not fervently hoped that, somehow, they have survived death. So "phone calls from the dead" could be a psychic and symbolic way by which we attempt to prove immortality to ourselves.

Now, I am not saying this theory is really the explanation for these phantom phone calls, but it is a way of looking at them, which we cannot logically dismiss. In other words, one can accept the existence of these phone calls *without actually believing that they are produced by the dead.* On the other hand, it may be that there are different types of these curious phone calls. Perhaps some of them do come from the dead while others are the product of our own minds.

Only after we had come to this conclusion did our colleague Dr. Berthold Schwarz develop a similar theory. In a letter to us dated January 19, 1978, Schwarz admitted that "whether these calls come from the dead or are created by PK [from the living] is obviously impossible to prove." However, he went on to theorize that a person who has a strong need to believe in life after death might be "so psyched up by the actual situation and combination of other complex psychic factors

The Source of the Calls: I. Problems and Possibilities

that an independent energy could be split off from the witness's mind that might have some type of ghostlike existence—that hypothetically continues as long as it is fed by the needs of the various participants and other understood psycho-physiological influences."

Schwarz is actually describing what might be called a "thoughtform"—a psychic entity created by our own minds and endowed with formidable PK powers. Once created, this being might take on a life of its own, as he suggests. This "mind-ghost" might be very sensitive to the thoughts and motivations that gave it birth in the first place. Could these hypothetical beings be the cause of these mysterious calls? Could we in fact be talking to some dissociated part of our own minds, lobotomized and existing independently in time and space? While this theory is pretty strange, it is certainly no stranger than many things you invariably run into while exploring the psychic world.

Dr. Schwarz does not dismiss the possibility that some of these calls do come from the dead, though. As he also pointed out in a letter to us, " ... some of the communications are so spectacular that the most fetching hypothesis is some type of actual spirit communication. Maybe we are the unreal world, and the other is the true reality." He went on to suggest that perhaps we are being *deliberately* led by these phone contacts to accept things such as life after death, which normally we might find unacceptable.

Now you can see why these phone calls represent such a puzzle. There is simply no way to prove unequivocally that they come from the dead. Too many alternative explanations are just as feasible. Even so, long before we began serious work on this project, Raymond and I felt that our cases themselves might supply us with obvious clues about their ultimate nature. And we were not disappointed when we began studying our cases and started coming across several indications that they had a spiritistic source. However, before explaining just how we came to this conclusion, I would like to backtrack a bit and discuss our initial reactions to these phone calls and how our present attitude gradually evolved.

My own first feelings about these cases were somewhat different from Raymond's. From the beginning he felt that these calls were probably exactly what they purported to be, i.e., attempts on the part of the dead to contact us. I was less sure, and at first it was hard for me to believe that our departed friends and relatives have nothing better to do in the next world than to cavort around, calling up the living over some astral pay phone. I was much more prone to believe that these calls were produced by some form of PK-from-the-living. I also felt that some of these calls were probably being produced by some sort of extra-dimensional beings, out having a little fun at our expense by manipulating our telephone system and mimicking the voices of the dead.

This might strike you as a preposterous idea, but some of the first cases we collected indicated that these phantom callers were engaging in an elaborate—and very cruel—charade. I was immediately puzzled, for instance, by the MacConnell case when I first read it in Susy Smith's *The Power of the Mind*, in 1975. Although the MacConnells recognized the voice of their friend Enid Johlson, never once did the voice let on that it was speaking from beyond the grave. It struck me as highly unusual that the phone-entity actively pretended to be still alive. If Enid Johlson really were the one making the call, why hadn't she told the MacConnells about her death? The voice-entity even went out of its way to carry off the pretense. When, for instance, Mrs. MacConnell suggested that they all get together for a reunion, the voice made rather weak excuses for avoiding the meeting, yet never explained the *real* reason why such a meeting would have been manifestly impossible.

As I began collecting more phone call cases, I noticed other examples of this same type of trickery. In the Marie D'Alessio case, recounted in Chapter 3, Mrs. D'Alessio carried out a long conversation with a woman who had actually been dead for several months. Of course, the witness merely assumed she was talking to a flesh-and blood human being, and never once did the voice-entity try to dispel the illusion. It even ridiculously claimed that it had to go to the hospital the very next day, and when Mrs. D'Alessio offered to come to visit her, the voice immediately told her not to! It seems that this phantom was out to deliberately dupe Mrs. D'Alessio.

A similar "charade" case was reported to us by one of our colleagues. Some years ago, he received a letter from a young woman whose father-in-law had received a call from his dead daughter. The voices were identical, and the call was not very mysterious at all. The first words the caller said were, "Hi Dad. It's me. When are you going to pick me up?" This was a request his daughter had often made while alive. The witness could not believe that he was actually speaking to the dead, so he assured the caller that she must have misdialed the number. "Come on, Dad, don't kid," was the voice's reply. The caller then gave her name, as well as those of her mother and father. They all matched. But never once did the caller make any allusion to her own death; she continued to ask that she be picked up just as though she were alive. (The witness, by the way, never did come to believe that he had received a psychic phone call. He chalked it all up to coincidence!)

After studying similar cases, I rejected the notion that these calls, and others like them, came from the dead. Why would a Theta-agent want to pull such a stupid and pointless charade on its surviving friends and relatives? I thought. Instead, these cases indicated to me that at least some of the calls are being produced by some sort of "trickster." I continued to accept this theory for quite some time—until one day it dawned on me that my line of reasoning was all wrong.

In February 1978, just as the first phase of our research was coming to an end, I began mapping out the characteristics of all the accounts we had collected so far. I was particularly interested in determining the length of time the conversations usually lasted. It was then that I made the discovery that I spoke about in the preceding chapter: *If* the witness knows he is talking to someone who has died, the call tends to be extremely short; but if the witness thinks he is talking to a living person, the conversation can, on occasion, last much longer. This pattern has consistently cropped up in our data. At first, neither Raymond nor I could figure out an explanation for it. But a few days after our initial discovery, one theory came to mind that fits the facts beautifully.

It had gradually become clear to us that these phone contacts can occur only when many delicate conditions—psychic and otherwise—are met. Most likely, the person receiving the call must be in just the right frame of mind before contact can be made at all. (This probably goes for the intelligence making the call as well; otherwise, these phone calls would be occurring all the time.) You might have noticed by now that most of the witnesses whose accounts we've quoted were in a very passive, unoccupied frame of mind when their calls came in. They were usually engaged in pleasant conversation, household chores, or just sitting home alone. At the moment psychic contact was made, all seemed to have been in a rather "receptive" frame of mind. Now, while many of our witnesses have described their initial reactions to these calls as "shock" or "disorientation" (and one even fainted), these reactions were reported only by people who *knew* they were talking to the dead. Certainly one might expect a person to become extremely upset once he realizes that a ghost is on the line, and one can hardly blame him. We feel, though, that this state of emotional shock probably destroys the psychic conditions that have made the phone contact possible in the first place. These calls are, therefore, bound to be short or interrupted.

This theory can also explain why someone who does not know he or she is talking to a phantom voice can engage in a lengthier conversation. These witnesses probably stay in their "receptive" frame of mind during the course of the conversation and do nothing to disrupt the contact. The phone call from the girl who wanted her still-living father to "pick me up" may have gone on so long because the witness *refused* to believe he was talking to the dead and never became emotional or upset during the call.

This theory, by the way, is more consistent with the spiritistic theory than with the PK-from-the-living idea. Were a person using his own PK to produce a "phone call from the dead," it is unlikely that he would allow himself to fall into a frame of mind that would automatically abort the call. But more important, our theory can also explain why the voices of Enid Johlson and Mrs. D'Alessio's friend engaged in their little deception. They may have intuitively known that their contact with the living would be instantly aborted should they let on about their deaths. So in order to keep the conversation going as long as possible, they merely pretended to still be alive. Perhaps this is the reason Mrs. Sherrin "forgot" that her aunt was dead during her 30-minute phone conversation with the woman. While it was possibly a shock reaction, it also seems feasible that somehow the deceased caller *psychically* caused the woman to lose her memory momentarily.

It didn't take me long to give up my extradimensional being theory, once I realized the psychic importance of the MacConnell and D'Alessio cases. There was probably nothing sinister about them at all. In consequence, I gradually joined Raymond in believing that these calls were deliberately produced by the dead.

Our analyses of our cases didn't end with that, though. Our belief in the spiritistic nature of these calls was reinforced even further when we decided to take another detailed look at our cases.

Most forms of "death coincidence" phenomena occur close to the actual time the presumed agent has died. Most cases of mysterious clock-stoppings or chimings such as the one Mrs. Rhine reported occur within 24 hours of death, and then become *less* frequent as time goes by. This fact has a significant bearing on "phone calls from the dead" cases, so we'll discuss it in some detail. For close to 100 years it has been known that this same pattern holds true for apparitions.

Back in 1889 a group of psychical investigators in Great Britain under the direction of Professor Henry Sidgwick, a noted philosopher of his day, carried out a poll among the British public. The investigators were primarily interested in discovering just what percentage of the population had psychic or other "hallucinatory" experiences to report. Sidgwick and his co-workers reaped a rich harvest: no fewer than 17,000 people responded to the poll. While the vast majority denied ever having had any hallucinatory experiences, 2,272 affirmative replies were received. Three hundred, surprisingly enough, claimed to have seen apparitions.

Of course, Sidgwick and his group had no way of telling how many of their witnesses had merely suffered pathological hallucinations, had brain dysfunctions, or had actually seen objectively real apparitions. However, they soon began to focus their keen attention on 80 very special reports that had resulted from their poll. These came from people who claimed that they had seen apparitions resembling friends or relatives who had just died. Many times the witnesses didn't even know of the deaths until *after* seeing the phantom. Upon re-analyzing their data, Sidgwick and his colleagues determined that most apparitions are seen within one day of the death of the agent (the person whom the apparition resembled). These were subsequently called "crisis" cases. Fewer were seen during the subsequent weeks, and only very few were reported a year or so after death. It was this discovery that led the early investigators to believe that apparitions were nothing more than "telepathic hallucinations" produced by the unconscious minds of the witnesses.

Later researchers were able to corroborate Sidgwick's findings. Around the turn of the century, Camille Flammarion, a well-known French astronomer, began collecting reports of apparitions and hauntings. As he reported in his massive three-volume study, *Death and Its Mystery*, his data matched Sidgwick's in all details.

When we began collecting "phone calls from the dead" cases, we fully expected to make a similar discovery—that most of our cases would represent calls produced within a day or so of the caller's death, and that these calls would then become less frequently reported as weeks and months went by. Therefore, right at the onset of our research we immediately placed each case we collected into one of five categories:

1. "Crisis" calls, received within 24 hours of the caller's death.
2. Postmortem calls, received within 7 days after death.
3. Calls within 30 days.
4. Calls within from 2 to 6 months.
5. Calls after 6 months.

After we had collected our first 30 cases or so, though, we discovered that our reports did not conform to the expected pattern. To be sure, about 27 percent of our total collection fit into the "crisis" category. But phantom calls made a few days or even many months after death were equally common. A full 22 percent of our cases came from witnesses who had received calls from persons dead six months or longer.

Our data turned up one additional and curious fact, though. Most "phone calls from the dead" seem to be received either *within* one week or *after* one month or more from the time of death. We have practically no cases on file from agents who had been dead 8 to 30 days.

Raymond and I both felt that these data, once again, indicated that "phone calls from the dead" are actually produced by Theta-agents. If these calls are being produced by the witness's own minds, one might expect the majority of them to be "crisis" cases. In other words, one would expect a greater number of these calls to occur during those times when the witnesses have the greatest psychological need to communicate with the dead—soon after one has lost a spouse or sibling and before the shock of the loss has subsided. If a person has the PK power to produce one of these phone calls, why would he or she do so only some six months *after* a friend's or relative's death? Or after two years? On the other hand, the dead might be motivated to contact us at just about any time—especially immediately after death, or perhaps only after they have recovered from the shock. This can explain why most phone calls from the dead are received within 24 hours of death or else after a couple of months or so.

By this time, it looked to us as though we were finally making progress. Our statistics were beginning to make some sense to us. But after graphing out the above set of data, we realized that our work was only beginning. And the more we studied our cases, the more clues we uncovered about their nature. Our cases came from witnesses who had received calls from persons dead six months or longer.

5

The Source of the Calls:
II. Communications from the Dead?

Our first major clue about the nature of these phone calls came when we uncovered yet another pattern in our data. Our phantom callers seem to have an absolute penchant for phoning on days that had held special meaning for them during their earthly lives. These "anniversary" cases, as we started dubbing them, constitute about 10 percent of all the accounts we've collected. Birthdays, anniversaries, Mother's Day, and even public holidays are all times on which these calls are especially prone to occur.

A typical anecdote of just this kind was reported in the January 1960 issue of *Fate* magazine by Mrs. Ruth Pritchard of Denver, Colorado. Her son had died on October 12, 1957. Mrs. Pritchard was understandably depressed by his death, and on the morning of February 1, 1958—her first birthday since losing her son—her misery was especially acute. "As I sat there choking back the tears, I longed to see him and thought that I would give all I have just to hear him call me 'Mom' today," she admitted.

Mrs. Pritchard's depression must have lightened a bit when her husband came down for breakfast. They were enjoying their meal when the phone rang. "I lifted the receiver and said 'Hello?'" she reported to *Fate*. "A young man's voice said, 'Mom?' I stood there shaking—unable to say a word. In the silence I heard the receiver at the other end of the line click. I walked back to the table crying..."

Mrs. Pritchard wasn't positive that the voice was really her son's. But she adds, "The memory of the experience has lived with me these many months. And the question sticks in my mind: was the voice on the phone the answer to my heartfelt prayer?" The following "anniversary" case was reported in the September 1953 issue of *Fate* by Mrs. Mary Cahill of New York, who tells about receiving a phone call on Mother's Day from her daughter Peggy. The girl had died six months before, at the age of 12. Like the call Patricia Adams told us about, this one too, was seemingly placed by a long-distance operator.

> As I relaxed in my easy chair one evening in May 1943, listening to my favorite radio program, the phone rang insistently. The operator told me it was a long-distance call and put it through. In a confusion of sound I heard what seemed to be several persons talking all at once. Then I nearly fainted as I heard the breathless voice of my little girl, Peggy, 12.
>
> "Hello, Mom! How are you? Can you hear me? Hello, Mom!"
>
> The whirring as of many winds and the mumbling of voices continued. I begged the operator to clear the lines or at least to relay the other messages.
>
> The beloved voice I remembered so well went on talking, "Mom, can't you hear me?"
>
> I talked to Peggy but it was like talking through a storm. Then silence fell. "Operator," I said, "this call must be intended for someone else." I gave her my name and phone number.
>
> She repeated this and then to my surprise she said, "You positively are the one they want."
>
> Again Peggy's voice called to me through a rushing as of great winds. The winds rose to a roar and then died into sudden silence. Frantically I called Peggy's name—but there was no answer.
>
> I asked the operator to trace the call, but she replied with finality, "We have no record of incoming calls."
>
> My eye filled with tears of joy. I realized that Peggy had called me not only on Mother's Day, but from beyond the grave—for she had died six months before.

It has been very difficult for us to shed any new light on phone call cases we have found published in books and magazines. Usually we have been unable to trace writers; and many more have been unwilling

The Source of the Calls: II. Communications from the Dead?

to answer our letters. This certainly hasn't made our work any easier. This is especially true of Mrs. Cahill's case, which was published over twenty years ago. When we first came across it, we doubted whether we could ever trace the writer after so many years. This was doubly annoying because we were a bit suspicious of this account at first. This overly literary and melodramatic style in which it was written suggested to us that it was not really an account of a genuine occurrence.

We were, however, able to throw a little added light on this case in January 1978. By that time, Raymond and I had already published an article and a letter in *Fate* magazine about the phantom phone call mystery. After our second publication had appeared, we received a note from Jerome Clark, *Fate*'s young and energetic associate editor. Among other news, he informed us that he had just received a letter from a Mr. John Bessor of Butler, Pennsylvania. Bessor, who had seen our publications, [and] told Jerry in his note that he, too, had long been collecting phone call cases. Jerry naturally knew we would be interested and sent Bessor's name and address directly to us. We contacted Mr. Bessor immediately, since we hoped he would be willing to let us examine his files. Bessor answered us within a few days, but apologetically admitted that he had turned over all his cases to another parapsychologist and had only a few he could send to us.* Although disappointed, we were interested to find that several years ago Bessor had independently received a letter from Mrs. Cahill telling of her rather emotional experience. This version of her story was virtually identical to the published report, which indicated to us that her account was not dramatized or fictionalized for publication.

We think these "anniversary" cases are telling us quite a bit about the phantom phone call mystery. First, they reveal an especially strong motivation on the part of the callers to communicate with the living. They also indicate that whoever is putting these "anniversary" calls through is very aware of our emotional needs and thoughts. Neither do they seem to be happenchance affairs, but, rather, carefully planned communications—almost as if a special effort were being made to get the contact established on just these days. Of course, it could once again be argued that these calls are actually produced by the witnesses'

---

* Interestingly enough, we had contacted this same parapsychologist ourselves at the beginning of our work and had asked him if he had any "phone calls from the dead" cases in his files. He replied that he "thought he had one case" but declined to dig it up for us and generally took very little interest in our project.

own minds. Birthdays and anniversaries are times when our thoughts instinctively turn to those we miss, and perhaps this mental state triggers the unconscious mind to project some sort of PK force that produces the calls via the telephone system in answer to our personal needs.

While plausible, this explanation strikes us as just too facile. If we ourselves can produce the calls, why don't they occur more often? People who had these experiences invariably report that they were once-in-a-lifetime occurrences. If "phone calls from the dead" can be produced through PK-from-the-*living*, there is no reason why a person who has produced one of these calls shouldn't go on to produce many more of them. But that just doesn't seem to happen. We have received reports from only two people who ever received more than one phone call from the dead during their lives. (In one instance, the witness had her first experience as a young child and her second during adulthood.) One might also ask why we don't ever produce phone calls from *living* relations and friends from whom we have become separated by time and distance?*

Instead, it appears as though the intelligences that produce these calls lose their motivation to talk with the living once contact has been successfully achieved. These callers appear to have their own plans and motivations and seem totally independent from our own minds.

Earlier, we pointed out that it is highly likely that these communications can occur only when the recipient is in a certain delicate frame of mind. This fact, too, might help us to understand "anniversary" calls. No doubt Mrs. Pritchard and Mrs. Cahill were thinking intently about their children when the calls came through. Mrs. Pritchard admits this quite candidly in her report. And who wouldn't think of a lost son or daughter on a birthday or Mother's Day? But this may have been a very special type of concentration—that is, not so much an agitated, hand-writing episode of grief and depression but an almost passive form of mourning. Grief and anger go hand in hand. But as genuine mourning takes over, this type of angry injunction and self-recrimination about the death of a close relative usually fades away. I tend to doubt that Mrs. Pritchard and Mrs. Cahill were undergoing these fierce dual emotions

---

* There *are* cases on record in which phantom callers have mimicked the voices of living persons. These cases, which will be examined in Chapter 7, seem extremely rare and of an altogether different nature from "phone calls from the dead." For instance, they are invariably made to people who had no particular desire to talk to the presumed agent.

The Source of the Calls: II. Communications from the Dead?

when they received their calls. Anniversaries may well help us to think about the dead in a very special way. And when we concentrate on them, we invoke them or memories about them. Could it be that this special state of mind also *summons* the dead and makes communication all the more possible? If telephone contact between the living and the dead can occur only when both the witness and Theta-agent have a mutually strong need and will to communicate, then anniversaries and other significant days might especially prompt just such emotions.

In some respects, our data also fall neatly in line with what some clinical psychologists are finding out about death, mourning, and possible postmortem communication. Ever since the 1960s more and more psychologists and psychiatrists have become interested in the psychology of the death experience, and many of them are now turning their attention to helping people cope with death and prepare for it, counseling their families, and analyzing the therapeutic value of mourning. Thanatology, the study of death and dying, is fast becoming an integral part of conventional psychology. *Human Behavior*, one of this country's leading psychology magazines, even devotes a monthly department to the subject, and there are now at least two professional journals devoted to research on death. Although few thanatologists seem genuinely interested in whether we actually survive death, a few researchers have accumulated data that bear significantly on the survival issue. And these studies also shed some interesting light on "phone calls from the dead."

In 1971, for instance, Dr. W. Dewi Rees, a British physician, published a paper in the *British Medical Journal* entitled, "The Hallucinations of Widowhood." Rees polled some 293 widows and widowers and discovered that 47 percent thought they had been in mental contact with their deceased spouses at one time or another. According to Rees's respondents, these contacts have sometimes occurred years after death. While some were presumably telepathic contacts, many of Rees's subjects believed that they actually had been visited by objective "physical" presences of the dead. These findings were also confirmed in 1971 by Dr. Robert Kastenbaum, then a staff member for the Wayne State University's Psychological Studies of Dying, Death and Lethal Behavior. (He now teaches at the University of Massachusetts and is editor of *Omega: The Journal of Death and Dying*.) Speaking before the 1971 annual convention of the American Psychological Association, Kastenbaum reported that 63 percent of the people he polled reported back to him "an experience which seemed, at the time, as though it involved communication with another mind, since deceased and invisible."

Widows and widowers do seem especially prone to these experiences, but few of them find their postmortem contacts frightening; instead, they usually describe a feeling of great comfort from these visitations.

It is of course impossible to determine whether these witnesses really made contact with the dead or were merely deluding themselves. Wish fulfilment and psychological need can do strange things to the mind. But in light of our own research, as well as the research that parapsychology has massed on the survival issue, it is highly likely that these witnesses were having genuine objective experiences.

The research of Rees and of Kastenbaum does not literally "support" our findings and views, but their data are strikingly consistent with ours. They, too, have found that postmortem contact seems to take place even years after the agent's death. Their data also suggest that the motivation on the part of the dead to contact the living is a long-term and continual process, but that this motivation is lost once contact with the living is made. For example, relatively few of their respondents reported multiple experiences. This finding is also in keeping with our phone call data. Their findings also help explain why "phone calls from the dead" are often received on emotionally loaded days. These special days, and the intense but resigned, angerless mourning they invariably bring, may help set up just the right conditions for the long-awaited psychic contact to take place.

But now, let's get back to Mrs. Cahill.

When we first ran across the Cahill case, Raymond and I were puzzled by Mrs. Cahill's report that "I heard what seemed to be several persons talking all at once." This account is very different from the majority of cases in our files, since most witnesses usually hear only one voice over the phone. So we at first chalked up Mrs. Cahill's account as an anomaly and left it at that. We really didn't expect to run into other accounts describing this exact phenomenon, but, as you might have guessed, that's precisely what happened. These cases gave us our second major clue—the fact that many voices came through—about the source of the calls.

In February 1977 Mrs. Evelyn Paxton of Chevy Chase, Maryland, sent John Bessor an account of one of these "multivoiced" calls. He turned over the report to us, and we contacted Mrs. Paxton for an independent account of the incident. As she reported:

> My daughter Eileen... died in Montgomery County Hospital, Sandy Spring, Maryland, around 9:30 am on November 12, 1969, from

The Source of the Calls: II. Communications from the Dead?

cancer of the lungs. She died on the anniversary of her first wedding, November 12, 1942, in Washington, D.C. Her funeral was set for Wednesday or Thursday the same week.

I was at her sister's home just outside of Damascus. Around 6:00 am the telephone rang and I answered it. It was a faint voice which I recognized as Eileen and it asked for Ann [her sister] and I could hear faint sounds in the background—people sustaining someone. By the time Ann reached the phone the voice faded but the line stayed open until we hung up. This was the morning of the funeral. It must have been Thursday.

An even more spectacular case of this type was published in 1955 by Alfred Hitchcock, that master of suspense, whose films have thrilled moviegoers for over 30 years. Writing in the September issue of the now-defunct *Coronet* magazine, he presented the little vignette as part of an article entitled, "My Five Greatest Mysteries." An editorial preceding the article stated:

"Alfred Hitchcock, Hollywood's master mystery-maker, has filmed the most incredible of crime stories. Yet, these real-life thrillers frustrate him. A movie, he explains, must be believable. But these true tales are too improbable. They would never be believed." (Perhaps so, though fictionalized phone calls from the dead have served as the subject for at least one *Twilight Zone* scenario*• and they play a key role in

---

* The plot of this episode concerns a young boy who is able to speak to his dead grandmother over a toy telephone. Eventually the mother hears the voice as well. I first saw this episode in July 1978 and was surprised to note that the name of the perplexed family is, synchronistically, Bayles. The star of the episode was Phillip Abbott (best known for his supporting role on *The F.B.I.*) who, by another coincidence, is an acquaintance of mine whom I met through our mutual interest in parapsychology. By yet another coincidence, Mr. Abbott's son is named *David*. Thus, his son's name matches that of the pioneering magician and psychical researcher, David Abbott, who pioneered the study of paraphysical voice effects at the turn of the century. Mr. Abbott did not know this at the time of his son's birth. (See Chapter 7) Himself an actor, David has a supporting role on the daytime serial, *For Richer, For Poorer*.

While I am not claiming that these coincidences have any relevant meaning to the nature of this book, I have brought them up for the sake of anyone interested in the phenomenon of synchronicity. The name coincidences are similar to the ones Berthold Schwarz ran into during the Uphoff-D'Alessio investigation.

Phone Calls from the Dead

Anthony Burgess's novel *Beard's Roman Women!*) Here, in any event, is Hitchcock's case in full:

> Arne Gandy's mother had been hoping for a call from him, so she was not alarmed when the telephone rang at 3:00 am that night in January 1934. In San Francisco, across the continent, it was midnight
>
> She got out of bed and hurried to the phone. When she picked up the receiver she was surprised to hear a strange man's voice.
>
> "The kid is here, and for God's sake forgive him and give him another chance," he was saying. "What I said about him in my letter is all true, he is a fine kid."
>
> Next morning, Mrs. Gandy gave police this account of what followed:
>
> "I asked who was speaking. He replied with a hollow laugh. I told him he must have the wrong number, that I had no letter. I asked what number he was calling and he repeated our number, which is unlisted.
>
> "There were several voices. All seemed to come from another part of the room. I couldn't understand what he was saying.
>
> "'Oh,' I said, 'let me talk to my boy.'
>
> "There was a lot of laughter. The strange voice said, 'Your son is in hospital in San Francisco. He's in bad shape. But never mind. He's on his way home now.'
>
> "'I am helpless,' another voice said. 'Here I lie propped up on pillows. I can't move.' Then a sigh, a groan, and the voice faded like music, and the other voices came over the phone. Then everything stopped.
>
> "I jiggled the receiver and got the operator. She told me that the call came from San Francisco. My husband immediately contacted the police."
>
> Next morning, Arne Gandy's body was found in San Francisco Bay. He must have drowned at least two days before, the coroner estimated. Yet Mrs. Gandy insisted she heard his voice on the phone.
>
> The story caused a sensation.
>
> Arne had been the 20-year-old son of an advertising artist. He had signed on at New York as mess boy for a world cruise on a Dollar liner. But when the ship docked in San Francisco, he hurried ashore, without stopping to get his clothes and private papers from his locker, and never returned.
>
> That day he wrote a cheerful letter to his parents, giving no hint that he had quit. Then he dropped from sight. Six days later, his corpse was fished from the bay.

The Source of the Calls: II. Communications from the Dead?

Police investigation led nowhere. There were no clues as to why he rushed off the ship, where he went, how he spent the few days before his death. The phone call remains unexplained.

Hitchcock ends this account with a succinct editorial. "To me," he writes, "the Arne Gandy case is one of the five most baffling real-life mysteries of our generation. If I made it into a movie, no one would believe it."

No doubt Hitchcock's judgement was correct; but that doesn't alter the fact that the unsolved mystery of Arne Gandy is similar to other "phone calls from the dead" reports. It's certainly a bit stranger than most of our other cases, but as we pointed out before, every account we've come across seems to contain at least one unique characteristic. This case is particularly intriguing because it was made to an unlisted number.

The Gandy report, like the Paxton and Cahill accounts cited earlier, can serve as especially convincing evidence for survival for several reasons. It is hard to believe that Mrs. Gandy actually used PK to place the call to herself. This suggestion just can't explain any of the facts in the case. Why should she have psychically produced so *many* voices—and mocking ones at that—instead of merely the voice of her dead son? (This, or course, holds true for Mrs. Cahill and Mrs. Paxton as well.) During the entire duration of the call, Mrs. Gandy was apparently *never* able to talk with her son, whose attempts at communication seem to have been blocked by the cackles and messages from the other phantom voices. Yet these voices were well aware that something dreadful had happened to the boy and tried to communicate this information to the puzzled woman. On the other hand, though, some of their communications were totally misleading. They deliberately told Mrs. Gandy that her son would be all right when he was already dead, and one voice even mentioned a letter which was obviously never written or received. Why would Mrs. Gandy have produced such a jumbled phone call if her own mind were responsible for it—a phone call which served absolutely no conceivable purpose?

However, this case *can* be explained if we accept the possibility that the call was instigated by the dead boy. When these phone calls the dead are produced, some channel may open between our world and some other dimension of the universe. Why should we assume, then, that *only* the intelligence responsible for the call has access to this channel? Once such a "window" is open, it seems plausible that other Theta-agents or extradimensional beings might want to barge in. As one psychical researcher of the past suggested, the dead may be as eager to contact us, as we are to communicate with them. All sorts of unseen intelligences might be eagerly waiting for some opportunity to make their presences known.

If you've ever read Lovecraft's masterpiece *The Dunwich Horror*, you'll understand what we're getting at. The story concerns, in part, a race of beings existing in a fourth-dimensional world who are just waiting for an opportunity to enter our own. All they need is a channel. Any window between our world and the next would be enough for all of them to infiltrate into our securely (?) material universe. Lovecraft's story is, of course, pure brilliant fiction—and admittedly tainted with more than one sinister overtone. But the basic theme of the story has some bearing on phantom phone call cases. Any channel which opens between our world and any other dimension might instantly become a released floodgate.

If this speculation is correct, then the "multivoiced" calls received by Mrs. Cahill, Mrs. Pritchard, and Mrs. Gandy become perfectly understandable. One might almost *expect* them. These cases, therefore, constitute our second major clue about the nature of these calls.

Most of the cases we've collected have been rather simple in content. Phantom voices don't usually say very much, offering no startling revelations either about the universe or about their present state of existence. They seem guided more by raw motivation than by actual intelligence. Nor, except for "anniversary" cases, do most of these calls seem very well planned; often they appear to be almost accidental contacts. In many instances it seems as though the phantom voices are as shocked as the people who receive them! Nonetheless, every so often it appears that the phantom voice is deliberately seeking to communicate vital information to the living. Two cases of this nature have already been presented. In Chapter 2 we discussed one case in which the voice of a young child called to warn her father's neighbor that he was in trouble. Likewise, Walter Upoff's secretary returned from death to complete a task assigned to her before her unexpected demise. Of all our cases, these are perhaps the strongest evidence for survival we've collected. Since they are the hardest to explain away as the psychokinetic product of our own minds, they represent our third major clue (or point of evidence) as to the spiritistic nature of these calls. For example, just consider the following case which we investigated in 1977 in which a phantom voice desperately tried to warn the witness about events which tragically came to pass several months later.

The Source of the Calls: II. Communications from the Dead?

The witness to the call, Mrs. Elsie Pendleton of Palos Verde, California, is a former actress. She had been particularly close to her mother, Mimi. Since Mrs. Pendleton then lived in Portuguese Bend, California, and her mother lived in Hollywood, the two often communicated by phone, sometimes talking together three to four times a week. Shortly before her death, Mimi was incapacitated by a stroke, so she moved into her daughter's apartment building. During these agonizing months, Mrs. Pendleton called her mother each morning to make sure she had passed the night comfortably.

Unfortunately, Mimi wasn't the only family member Mrs. Pendleton was concerned about during these trying weeks. At the same time that her mother lay incapacitated, the actress was growing more and more worried about her teenaged grandson, Scott. A rather rambunctious 17-year-old, he was a hell-raiser of sorts and was quickly becoming a serious discipline problem to his parents. Mimi's eventual death was the proverbial last straw. She had been a stern influence on the boy and was one of the few people who seemed able to manage and reason with him. The boy took his great-grandmother's death hard and, almost in anger, became even more reckless in his habits. Neither Mrs. Pendleton's daughter Connie nor the boy's stepfather could handle him at all.

One evening in February of 1975, about six months after Mimi's death, Scott got so out of hand that Connie and her husband decided that perhaps they should send him to live with his natural father in Hawaii. Mrs. Pendleton tended to agree. "Well, it's too bad that Mimi isn't here to take care of this," she told her daughter in resignation.

Then that evening:

"I was alone at the time; my husband was at sea," she told us, "and I always had a telephone by my bed because he called me from all over the world. The minute I hear the phone, I am wide awake. If it's a long-distance call, I can't hem and haw and not remember who I am. So when the phone by my bed rang, I was instantly awake."

The forthcoming experience was so vivid that Mrs. Pendleton had no problem remembering her brief conversation with the voice on the line—which she instantly recognized as her late mother's.

"Elsie, I can't find Connie," it blurted out.

At first Mrs. Pendleton didn't realize that her mother was actually dead; she could only reply, "Mimi, what are you calling me for at this time of night?"

"I can't find Connie. I've been trying to get in touch with Connie for two or three days and I can't get in touch with her. I can't in touch with Connie," the voice continued.

"What's the matter?" replied Mrs. Pendleton.

"It's Scott. I've got to talk to Connie. Tell Scott, *No*. Write it down so you won't forget when you see Connie. I said to tell him, to tell Scott, *No!*"

After that, the line went dead.

The call didn't make a real impact on Mrs. Pendleton until the next day when she awoke and realized what had happened. Her shock was compounded when she saw the words, "Tell Scott, *No!*" written hastily on a message pad by her phone. And the writing was in the exact handwriting of her deceased mother! The words were crimped and slanted forward, whereas Mrs. Pendleton, a "lefty," writes with a characteristic backhand slant. Mrs. Pendleton also told us that she did not doubt that the voice on the line was her mother. "There was no other voice in the world like hers. She had a Boston accent," she remarked at the end of our interview.

The voice's concern eventually turned out to be well founded. Scott's recklessness became worse and worse, and finally, as a result of one of his escapades, he was killed in a senseless automobile accident.

Now, was Mimi's call the psychokinetic result of Mrs. Pendleton's own anxiety and concern? A problem which she wished her mother were still alive to handle? Or was the call made by the deceased but surviving intelligence of the elderly woman? Either explanation fits the facts, but the survival theory seems more logical, since Mrs. Pendleton simply had no real psychological reason to stage the call. Yet the voice seemed to sense imminent danger and tried to communicate this fact to both Connie and her daughter. And if Mrs. Pendleton's own mind had produced the call, why did she place it to *herself* when the call was obviously meant for Connie? Why didn't Mrs. Pendleton produce the call in her daughter's home? These questions just can't be easily explained by the PK-from-the-living theory. But the facts are consistent with the idea that the call was placed by Mimi's Theta-agent, which, finding itself unable to contact Connie, decided to deliver the message by proxy.

This case also provides a clue to the greatest mystery these cases pose. Just why do some Theta-agents attempt to communicate by phone, of all things, instead of by some sort of telepathic contact with the living or by appearing as apparitions? At least according to Rees's and Kastenbaum's statistics, these latter types of postmortem contacts

The Source of the Calls: II. Communications from the Dead?

are certainly more common than "phone calls from the dead." (In fact, over the years, hundreds of accounts of apparitional visitations by the dead have been placed on record.)

Frankly, this problem has puzzled us ever since we began collecting these accounts. It wasn't until we stumbled across Mrs. Pendleton that one possible answer struck us. In her report she mentions that the telephone was her *chief* method of communicating with her mother during the last months of the invalid's life. On looking back over our cases, it dawned on us that Dr. Gelb had made the same remark to us about the call he received. The daughter of Patricia Adam's friend had also communicated with her mother chiefly by phone during the last two years of her life. Could this all be merely coincidental, or could it be that when trying to reach us, the dead use the one method they are most *accustomed* to employing? Mimi's anguished phone call may have been the product more of habit than design.

This speculation my seem contrived and farfetched, but I feel that I have some personal evidence supporting this explanation—a sequence of events every bit as bizarre as a phone call from the dead.

In the summer of 1977 I had to fly to New York on business. During my trip I was staying with relatives and, about a week after my arrival, I started having chronic out-of-body experiences. (This is an odd experience during which the witness feels that his mind has physically detached itself from the body. Often the person undergoing the experience will find himself draped in some sort of apparitional form. There is both anecdotal and experimental evidence that the mind can "travel" and can accurately observe transactions taking place in cities miles away during this experience.) Each night after I fell asleep I would suddenly find myself out-of-body and visiting my Los Angeles home. Eventually these experiences became more realistic than a dream could possibly be. And, for some reason, I *always* found myself projected to my suburban three-bedroom home, and during one of these visits I even saw the brother of a friend of mine at the house, sleeping in the spare bedroom. This surprised me, since he had no reason to be there, yet later I was able to verify that the young man had indeed spent that night in my house, just as I had seen him. During one of my last such experiences, I once again found myself at home and standing in the hallway. The first thought that came to mind was to try to contact Raymond, so I immediately attempted to phone him. I approached my hallway phone and tried to dial it. When I suddenly realized that there was no way I could place a phone call while out-of-body, I aborted the attempt, returned to my physical body in New York, and "woke up" soon afterwards.

Phone Calls from the Dead

This incident is fascinating for a number of reasons. It is especially pertinent that while out-of-body, I tried to *phone* Raymond instead of simply visiting him. Since I had apparently "traveled" instantly from New York to Los Angeles, it shouldn't have been hard for me to traverse the additional 15 miles or so that separate my home from Raymond's. But instead I tried to call him, and the reason is simple. I've known Raymond for ten years, yet we visit each other only about once or twice a month. Instead, we usually talk by phone and call each other one or twice practically every day. While psychically visiting my home, I tried to phone Raymond from force of habit. I didn't even think twice about the matter, and only abandoned my attempt when my reasoning powers became stronger than my instincts.

Phone calls from the dead may be the result of a similar type of habit or intention. By merely thinking about contacting the living by phone, the dead may, on rare occasions, actually succeed. These contacts could also be accidental. Maybe this is why so many voice-entities seem so surprised when they have successfully made phone contact.

This, of course, is only pure speculation—pertinent speculation, however. But let's get back to Mrs. Elsie Pendleton, who turned out to be one of our all-time star witnesses in more ways than one.

After telling us about her own phone call from the dead, she related how she had once witnessed an identical type of call many years earlier when she was rooming with the noted actress Ida Lupino in Los Angeles during World War II. The fact that his call was independently witnessed is extremely important because this voice of the dead offered information *that no living person could have known*. A call came from Miss Lupino's father, who had died six months before. Unfortunately, Mrs. Pendleton knew only the essentials of the case, not the specific details, but though incomplete, her testimony is based on what Ida Lupino told her personally. The following extracts are taken from a personal interview that Mrs. Pendleton gave Raymond on November 20, 1977:

> This was during the war years. Her father, Stanley Lupino, the actor had died. Somewhere along the line their [London] home had been bombed or partially destroyed... Because of the circumstances under which he had died—the time, etc.—there apparently was no will... Stanley called her and told her exactly where to find some very important papers in regard to the estate.
>
> Whether it was a will *per se* I do not know, but they were very important papers, something very important to the family and quite

necessary. He told her on the phone exactly where it was. They had many times looked for these papers, perhaps even close to where they were, and had never found them. He told her exactly where and, as I understand it, the area that they had searched was more or less rubble at the time.

We were also interest in what Mrs. Pendleton has personally overheard:

> Ida and I shared adjoining rooms, and I recall hearing her talking to somebody on the telephone. I remember her screaming for me. I ran into the room, and she said, "My God, my God, it was Stanley on the phone, it was Stanley." She always called her father by his first name.*

Unfortunately we were never able to get in touch with Miss Lupino directly; therefore we have no further information to this intriguing case. It is interesting to note, though, that Miss Lupino once answered a phone call from the dead when she was a child. This account will be discussed in Chapter 6.

If Mrs. Pendleton's version of the story is accurate—and there seems little reason to doubt it—it would be very hard to dismiss the incident as being due to anyone but Miss Lupino's deceased father. The only other possibility would be that Miss Lupino's unconscious mind somehow located the documents clairvoyantly, then used PK to place the call and manipulated and oscillated her telephone wires to produce the voice of the elderly man. Again, it's impossible to prove or disprove such a theory. But it certainly doesn't strike us as a particularly parsimonious explanation for Miss Lupino's strange phone message!

By this time, it should be pretty clear just why these cases have prompted us to adopt the survival theory. I hope, though, that we have also made it clear that we didn't naively jump to this conclusion. We adopted it fully only when we realized how cogent it was and how well it seemed to explain all the clues we uncovered. But before concluding this chapter, we will cite one last case that supports this

---

* Several months after we received this account, we came across some autobiographical material written by Miss Lupino. She specifically mentions that she called her father by his first name, and we subsequently learned that these "papers" consisted chiefly of the deed to the Lupino home which Stanley had placed in the cellar for safekeeping.

view. In this instance, it seems as though the surviving intelligence of a recently deceased man was trying to contact his still-living wife through *two* different psychic channels, one of them the telephone.

The following case was originally investigated by Patrick Mahony, a writer and investigator of the psychic scene who includes a complete summary of the incident in his book *Who's There?* Mahony first learned of the case when two sisters approached him during a lecture he gave in San Diego in 1959. The younger woman, whom he calls Mary in his report, recounted to him a sequence of events that led up to a phone call from the dead:

> My husband was one of those insignificant-looking men who somehow capture one's attention and hold it. We met on the ferry going to Coronado. I never felt I would fall in love with him, but I did. We had sixteen years of utmost bliss until, six months ago, he fell victim to terminal cancer.
>
> He was a small, neat man, with a pleasant pale face and soft blue eyes in which there was a wondering look. Soon after we married I found there were many terrors hidden in his heart and they all came from one dreadful thought. Supposing one day he should be unable to work and support me and our child; what would become of us? Sometimes he would awaken at night almost weeping because of some dream he had just experienced in which he seemed to be dying. He would awaken in a frightened sweat. The thought of sickness terrified him as much as the thought of old age...
>
> Then, when disease struck him down, an extraordinary change came over him. He came out of surgery with a smile. His poor face, waxen and wrinkled, smiled bravely and somehow his alarms and anxieties had gone, and in their place was a deep calm. There had developed in him one distressing symptom when death was near. His voice became thin and reedy and the doctors said that this was an extension of the generalized cancer in his body. The strain of hearing him trying to speak was ghastly. I was not present when he finally expired, but the attending nurse told me that he said goodbye as if thankfully—with that voice which is difficult to describe except to say it was dead—the voice of a dying man.

Right after the funeral the two sisters went to a nearby café along with another couple who had attended the services. Their attempts

The Source of the Calls: II. Communications from the Dead?

to cheer up Mary were soon interrupted when Bill suddenly put in an apparitional appearance. As Mahony reports:

> And then, just as the party was to begin eating, the man opposite gripped the table with both hands, shaking the dishes as he did so. "Don't look now," he said with faltering voice. "Bill is standing beside us."
>
> Naturally the widow and her sister did look and both gave muffled screams. There, lifesize and pathetically ravaged by the malignancy which had killed him, was the tragic figure of the dead husband. He was wearing a white hospital wrap, and as he tried to speak he raised one of his arms in a semi-apologetic gesture. All four persons in the café booth could see the ghostly apparition, also hear the wheezing and creaking voice as it tried to utter sounds, which were absorbed by the chatter elsewhere. There he stood somewhat casually, but with that tortured smile which he had displayed so bravely before life left him forever.
>
> "And then suddenly he wasn't there," sobbed the widow, "not there anyway for outward eyes to see."

Mary was so upset by the experience that she had to be taken home immediately; she was given a sleeping pill and told to get some rest. The ordeal was hardly over, though. Again, to quote from Mahony's account:

> Just as her sister [Mary] was half undressed, the telephone bell rang. She went to the instrument, took off the receiver and held it to her ear. Then, after what she heard, she dropped it as if it had been red-hot—sending it sprawling on the floor with the mouth of it screeching undistinguishable sounds. Somehow, she steeled herself and went to awaken her sister.
>
> "Mary!" she cried, agonized. "It's Bill. He can't be dead after all. He's on that telephone, and he must have thought it was you instead of me. I know it's him. He spoke in that death-rattle voice.
>
> ...He said distinctly 'Mary, I've something to tell you...'
>
> Shivering with fear, Mary went to the instrument and held the earpiece shakily to her head. But the voice had gone as mysteriously as it had come.

Mahony doesn't mention the names of the four people involved in the case, but when we decided to carry out a follow-up on the report, he supplied us with their full names and addresses. All four are still living in San Diego.

What is so appealing about this case is how both the apparition and the phone call were in keeping with the deceased man's personality. Horrified by the thought of death, he was keenly anxious about his family's welfare should anything happen to him. This anxiety was apparently translated after death into a fierce desire to contact his wife. Both the apparition and the phone voice were clearly trying to communicate a message to Mary, even though they never succeeded. These two phenomena apparently were two psychic channels, which the dead man tried to use during his attempts at communication. Failing at one, he resorted to the other.

Of course, you could always argue that Mary unconsciously placed the call herself by PK. But if so, who created the apparition—an apparition so physical and lifelike that it was collectively seen by four people?

6

The Mechanics of the Calls

"Okay," a skeptic once challenged us, "so the dead can phone up the living. Just how do they do it?" We wish we could give a precise answer to this disturbing question. To date, unfortunately, no phantom caller has ever explained to his bewildered listener just how he produced his call, so all we can do is guess.

Nonetheless, Raymond and I have been able to develop some rough idea about what physical mechanisms operate behind these calls and lead to their production. When we first began collecting phone call cases, we really didn't believe we would uncover any clues about *how* they were produced. But once again, we had underestimated just how much information would be contained in the various accounts we received. We've already pointed out the many clues we uncovered about the source, nature, and intelligence behind these calls. Much to our surprise, we were also able to uncover several surprising clues that might help explain how these calls are physically produced.

The first mechanical puzzle these calls pose is a rather basic one. Are they genuine *incoming* calls—i.e., calls produced from some distant location which are then routed to the witnesses' homes through a central phone exchange—or are they psychically produced directly over the individual telephones on which they are received? This may not strike you as a particularly important question, but it is critical as far as we are concerned. If these calls are incoming signals, then the phantom telephone voices would have to be an electromagnetic phenomenon. In other words, our witnesses really heard only a pattern of electrical oscillations that imitated human speech. We've come to call this the *electromagnetic theory*. If, however, these voices are somehow being produced over or within the *specific instruments on which they are received*, their nature might be very different. They might be some sort of human speech or "independent voice" (that is, a disembodied voice created out of thin air) speaking directly over the amplifier in the receiver. This might be called the *paraphysical theory*.

Are the dead contacting us by manipulating electrical currents, or are they literally "speaking" directly to us during the course of these mysterious calls? We think we have some tentative answers to these questions, and it could well be that the dead can contact us *either* way.

That's not meant to be a cop-out, either. We came to this conclusion only when we realized that the intelligence responsible for these calls is capable of making contact with the living both ways. Some phone calls probably are electromagnetic phenomena, while others seem to be purely paraphysical voice-effects. We'll take a look at each of these mechanisms in turn.

There seems little doubt that at least *some* phantom phone calls are produced from a distant location and are then routed to the witnesses' homes quite normally through a local central telephone exchange. We reach this conclusion on the basis of three clues we uncovered in our data:

1. In some instances, *all* the extension phones in the witness's home rang when the phantom call was placed. We have one case on file in which the witness especially noted this phenomenon. Dr. Medved, whose case was recounted in Chapter 3, first heard his hallway phone ring but deferred picking it up until he could get to another household extension where he had placed a message pad. Both phones were apparently ringing at the time. This case has a crucial bearing on the phantom phone call mystery for the following reason:

When someone calls your number, a charge of alternating current is sent to your phone through a central phone exchange. This charge then activates your phone and causes it to ring. The only "orthodox" way to make your phone ring from *within* your home would be by somehow manipulating the DC current available in the phone itself. However, this DC current is specifically blocked from the bells by capacitors. While it does not seem hard to believe that a PK force could oscillate the two small bells inside the telephone, it is a moot point whether PK could vibrate it at exactly the right frequency. When activated, your phone rings at a specific oscillation, vibrating at between 50 and 60 cycles per second. If it were to vibrate at any other speed, the ring would probably strike your ears as peculiar sounding.

In any case, it is *not* possible to ring two or more phones in a home by manipulating the phone system from anywhere *within* the house. So Medved's call could have been produced only in one of two ways:

(a) either the call was placed through an exchange that routed the calls and caused the phones to ring, or

(b) the witness or some Theta-agent somehow released a PK force that simultaneously and directly affected *all* the household phones. Since it appears as though many of these phone calls are in fact produced by the dead (as we argued in the last chapter), the first explanation seems more plausible and parsimonious. The voice with whom Dr. Medved spoke was therefore probably not the actual voice of the dead. It was most likely an electrical effect produced over the telephone system from some distant location.

2. We were a bit amazed when we realized that some phone calls from the dead are placed through long-distance operators. Although we can't dismiss the possibility that the phantom callers only "staged" the voices of these operators, we don't have any direct evidence to this effect. Yet the handful of these unusual cases that we have certainly represent one of the more enigmatic aspects of the phantom phone call mystery and also indicate that some "phone calls from the dead" are naturally produced incoming signals.

3. When somebody hangs up on you, you invariably hear a "click." The sound is made when your connection is terminated. A few of our witnesses have specifically mentioned that they heard this "click" at the end of their conversations. Usually the sound of the dial tone was reinstated—and quite naturally so—afterwards. If a phantom call were paraphysically produced *directly* over your phone, you probably wouldn't hear this noise when the call was terminated; most likely the line would just stay open. Even though many of our witnesses have reported this effect, too, we still cannot dismiss the self-evident fact that some of these calls terminate mechanically just as normal incoming calls do.

These three clues lead us to believe that some phone calls from the dead are—mechanically speaking—electromagnetically produced.

We should note in passing, though, that this theory is not a new one by any means. Back in 1931 H. Ernest Hunt, a British psychic investigator of sorts, reported a curious phone call from the dead in the pages of

Light, a newspaper that reported all the latest news and gossip on the psychic and spiritualistic scene during those years. (Its format was very similar to *Psychic News*, which is still published weekly in London.) Two of Hunt's acquaintances were talking over the telephone, he reported, when they were interrupted by a third voice. This voice claimed to be that of a person who had recently died, but its attempts to communicate were interrupted by frequent and unpleasant noises over the line. (Hunt doesn't give any further details.) Later that night, the two witnesses renewed their conversation, and *again* the mystery voice butted in.

Hunt realized that this "voice" may have been nothing of the kind, but only some sort of paranormal electrical effect. As he commented on the case: "Perhaps the actual circuit as between the two subscribers produced a wavelength upon which something could be superimposed which was subsequently heard as sound." So even before World War II, at least one psychical investigator was toying with the idea that the dead could contact us by manipulating electromagnetic forces.

Other phantom phone callers may rely on a different set of mechanics, however. As we studied our cases, it gradually dawned on us that most of these calls are probably produced directly over the specific instruments on which they are received. Many of our witnesses may not have been listening to electrical effects, *but no human voices produced directly within the phone itself!*

This process may seem more bizarre than it really is, but it might become clearer once you understand a little about how the receiver of a typical telephone is constructed. The earpiece of the phone is actually connected to the mouthpiece microphone. Subsequently, you will hear over the earpiece any voice produced in the microphone. It would even be amplified on the way. So a phantom caller could contact you by making your phone ring, getting rid of the dial tone which you normally hear on picking up the receiver, and then creating a tiny voice inside the mouthpiece. A Theta-agent could produce the ring of the telephone by direct PK action. Getting rid of the dial tone would be easy, too—the entity would merely use PK to disrupt some inner workings in the phone.

You might think we are contradicting ourselves at this point, since earlier we suggested that any sort of direct PK manipulation of the bells within a telephone would probably result in a peculiar-sounding ring—unless they could be vibrated at exactly the 50 to 60 cycles required. Yet to all appearances most of the calls we've investigated were presaged by quite normal-sounding rings, just as though they were activated by a normal AC charge from a phone exchange. However, this fact might be more apparent than real, as we soon found out.

Our eyes were opened to all these possibilities and paradoxes by Lucian Landau, a British industrial consultant and inventor who is also a gifted psychic. Mr. Landau became interested in our research at the onset of the investigation and became our more or less official technical advisor on the project. Well versed in both mechanics and electronics, he was responsible for alerting us to many potential clues about their nature which we might stumble across while analyzing our cases.

Shortly after offering his help, Landau suggested that these phantom calls were probably not PK-mediated electromagnetic effects, but are most likely produced directly by the dead, who are somehow able psychically to manipulate our telephone system. On the theory that (a) the calls are probably not produced through a normal exchange and (b) both the "ring" and "voice" represent some sort of paraphysical manipulation of the phone the witness is answering, he therefore predicted that these calls would sometimes be announced by abnormal-sounding rings.

When Mr. Landau made this forecast we were somewhat skeptical, since none of our witnesses so far had made any mention of such an effect. But as we received more and more cases, a few cropped up in which the witnesses specifically noted that their calls *were* presaged by odd-sounding rings. These cases indicated to us—as they did to Landau—that at least *some* phantom phone calls are produced directly over the witnesses' phones.

Our most spectacular case of this nature was reported to us from Germany in 1978. During the course of our worldwide search for cases we had contacted our colleague, Dr. Hans Bender at the University of Freiburg. As he is Germany's leading parapsychologist, we thought he might know of some untranslated cases. Bender informed us that a young man living in a small German town had just written him; he was searching for someone who could help explain his frightening experience. Luckily, the witness had written out his account within a few days of the incident, when it was still fresh in his mind. Dr. Bender kindly translated the account and sent it to us for our files. The following excerpt quotes the key portions of this lengthy report:

> On January 30, 1978—a Monday—I got a telephone call in the evening. It [the person] did not ring normally but in a deadened sound, so at first I did not know if it was a call or not. I picked up the receiver, asking, "Hello, hello?"

> All of a sudden I heard, distinctly and unmistakenly real, my father's voice... My father died on September 24, 1974, at the age of 56 years.
> I heard his voice quite clearly: "I am here, Daddy... here, Daddy." At the third time, he said it more intensely: "Here, Daddy," asking immediately afterwards: "how is Mommy, how is Mommy?" And all of a sudden, the whole thing was over and gone.

The young man's wife was also at home when the call came in and witnessed the entire conversation. Her husband became so agitated that at first she thought he had received some sort of bad news. The witness was so shocked by the call that he couldn't speak for several minutes afterwards.

Our second example is a rather old one and was reported in the Summer 1974 issue of *Tomorrow* magazine by Julian Franklyn, a well-known British author who died just a few years ago. The incident had occurred when he was living in one of the suburbs of London. This phone case is a bit unusual in that the phantom caller apparently made several abortive attempts before finally getting through. However, in this case, the peculiar phone ringing occurred two days *before* the caller's death, while he lay dying in a nearby hospital. As Franklyn writes:

> On Sunday, February 7th, [1954], my telephone, which is situated on the staircase, so as to be equidistant from all rooms, began to ring. It is true that I did not jump to it as though it were a fire-alarm, but I did not particularly dawdle; however, before I could answer, it stopped ringing, and when I did pick it up, it gave back only the dialing tone. I returned to my desk, sat down, and off went the phone again. I was quicker this time, but not quick enough. I replaced it, but before I had gone out of reach the thing began again. *This time it gave only a half-hearted tinkle*, and though I grabbed it in record time, I only got the dialing tone once more. [Italics ours.]

At first Franklyn merely thought the phone was acting up, but he didn't bother to report the problem to the phone company. Later that day, a woman Franklyn knew, whose husband, Tom, was dying in a local hospital, phoned to complain that she had been trying to reach him during the day. Franklyn logically concluded that his phone's incessant ringing had been caused by the woman's attempts to reach him. Two days later, though, the phone started ringing again; another series of "malfunctions" was in the works:

The Mechanics of the Calls

I scrape my hand against the dinner bowl, rinse it in a basin of water, peel Paddy [the kitten] off my neck, and make a beeline for the stairs, but the phone stops. Well, I can't help that. Back in the kitchen I finish mixing for Laddie [the dog], cut Paddy's meat, and have barely finished that, when the phone begins again. I fly to it and snatch it up quickly. It remains "alive," but nothing else. Conventionally I give my number (someone in a slot-machine callbox may be waiting for that) and I hold on a second—then I hear the irritating, slightly nasal, high-pitched, singsong of Tom. It is a little muffled, a little irritable, and contains a slight note of urgency, as though it were coming over long-distance rather than local, and he is a bit peeved at the delay, but it's him all right.

"Oh! Hullo Tom!" I cry boisterously, and I want to burst into a peal of merry laughter, because I perceive that he is now sufficiently recovered to sit up and not simply "take notice" but conduct his own affairs by phone. That is pretty good for a man who only nine days ago had "brought up" too much blood for the surgeons to risk his removal to hospital.

"Are you there? Are you there?" he is demanding, and I am overjoyed to hear the voice I cannot normally tolerate for two minutes.

Franklyn terminated the call when the voice of a man interrupted, explaining that he wanted to talk to Tom. The voice promised to reconnect them after he as through, but the return call was never placed. Franklyn contacted his local phone company to complain about his phone's capricious behavior. Service representatives checked out the complaint, but could find no problem in the lines going to the author's home. Only several hours later did the writer learn that Tom had died about 9:30 that morning, several hours before his call was received.

Could the odd tinkling sound which Franklyn heard coming from his phone have been caused by the dying man via long-distance PK? In a future chapter we'll explore this issue in depth.

By now you have probably noted that phantom phone calls are terminated in any of three ways. As we pointed out a few pages ago, several witnesses heard a "click" over the line followed by the subsequent reinstatement of the dial tone. Many other witnesses noted that their lines either stayed open or suddenly went dead. A surprising number have noted these same effects. This fact, too, tends to indicate that these are not incoming calls carried over telephone lines, but some sort of paraphysical manipulation of the witnesses' phone instruments. The witnesses usually terminated the calls *themselves* by hanging up when the lines remained open and they realized that their mystery callers were not about to engaged in any further conversation.

While the paraphysical theory might still strike you as unlikely, we know of two individuals who received calls which could not have come through ordinary channels. Ida Lupino reported a case of this nature years ago; the other came to light during our personal investigations.

Ida Lupino, who was later to receive her own phone call from the dead, answered one of these strange calls when she was a child. This incident may well have prepared her, or served as the prototype, for her own experience years later. She told the well-known writer Danton Walker about it, and he placed the account in his book, *Spooks Deluxe*:

> My father belonged to a club in London similar to the Lambs Club in New York. He had the title of Treasurer of Secrets, which carried with it Masonic responsibilities. The story involved a fellow member, and one of his closest friends, to whom I shall have to give the fictitious name of Andrew Meyer, for a variety of reasons.
>
> Uncle Andy, as I called him, was a frequent visitor at our home and I was very fond of him; in fact, all of us were.
>
> At the time, we were living with my grandmother at her home in the outskirts of London, while my parents—whom I always called by their first names, Stanley and Connie—were playing an engagement in one of the London variety houses.

That night was a restless one for the young girl. Alone with her grandmother that evening, she tried to sleep but was awakened by a nightmare about Meyer. (In a recent comment on this case, Miss Lupino claimed that she was disturbed by an *apparition* of the man and not by a nightmare.) She was so upset by the dream that she decided to recount it to her grandmother, who was still up and working in the kitchen. Ida was in the midst of describing her dream when the phone rang. Since her grandmother had her hands full at the moment, Ida answered it.

> I went to the phone, took the receiver off the hook, and heard a voice on the line, but it was so faint that I could scarcely understand the words. Finally, the voice became stronger and I could understand the message, repeated monotonously several times:
> "I must talk to Stanley. It is terribly important."

The Mechanics of the Calls

I answered: "Oh, it's you, Uncle Andy! Daddy isn't home yet." But the voice kept repeating the same words and this time quite distinctly: "Stanley—I must talk to Stanley—it's terribly important."

I asked him to hold the line until I could get Granny. She went to the phone and I heard her say, "Why, Andy—are you ill?" Then the phone was cut off, and there was no further talk.

This incident occurred in 1929, some years before the British telephone system went to an automatic direct dialing system, which was put into effect only after World War II. Callers still had to contact an exchange operator, who then put the calls through. Ida's grandmother was perturbed by the interruption and contacted her local exchange to complain.

"She was even more exasperated," Miss Lupino ended her account, by saying "when the operator said *she didn't believe there had been a call on the line during the past hour.*" [Italics ours.]

Ida's parents returned home later that night and her grandmother told Stanley about the phone message, adding that Andy sounded ill. Miss Lupino's father was flabbergasted; he had not yet told anyone that Andrew Meyer had hanged himself three days before.

Our second case is even more spectacular. Since the incident was told to us in confidence, we can't reveal the names of the people involved, but the following summary is an accurate resumé of this most revealing case.

The principal witness was vacationing alone in San Francisco and staying at local hotel, where she was awakened one morning at 5:30 am when her phone started ringing. Her aunt was on the line, but could speak only a few words before being cut off. The witness immediately clicked for the switchboard operator and complained about the interruption. The operator was a bit surprised by the complaint since *she had not put any calls through for five hours!* Three hours later, the bewildered woman received a long-distance call from her husband, who informed her that her aunt had died at 5:30 that morning.

Any normal phone call to the hotel would have gone through the central switchboard. There was simply no way a normally placed call could have bypassed the hotel's exchange. But this one did, and we have the operator's assurance to that effect. It must therefore have been some sort of psychic effect on the instrument itself, that is, some sort of psychic action which first rang the bell, disconnected the dial tone, and then produced a voice in the mouth or earpiece. There is simply no other way this call could conceivably have been made.

The discovery of the paraphysical mechanics by which many of these calls are produced came as quite a surprise. Originally, we had thought that these communications from the dead were probably some sort of electromagnetic effect. However, as should now be obvious, this explanation cannot account for *all* the cases we investigated. As our case analyses drew to a close, we began to realize that *most* "phone calls from the dead" are probably paraphysical mechanisms—that is, the production of a voice inside the phone mouthpiece microphone-cum-amplifier—are surprisingly consistent with some discoveries we had made a few years earlier while investigating quite different genre of "electronic communication with the dead."

In 1956, long before I knew him, Raymond inaugurated a lengthy series of experiments to see if the "voices" of the dead could be caught and impressed on electromagnetic tape. He was assisted in this project by a remarkable psychic named Attila von Szalay, a commercial photographer. They carried out their joint research during 1956-65 and later, when I joined them, between 1968-75. Since this research has a crucial bearing on phantom phone call cases, we will devote some discussion first to the topic of paranormal tape-recorded voice phenomena, and then to a recap of the Bayless-von Szalay investigations by reviewing the experimental methods they used and the results they achieved. Some surprising results of Raymond's research appear to have a considerable bearing on the mechanics that lie behind "phone calls from the dead" cases. Unbeknownst to us, we had discovered and isolated the paraphysical mechanisms behind these mystery phone calls as far back as 1970—years before we even believed in them or had any idea we would eventually be studying them!

First, though, we should give some background regarding the incredible controversy which the taped-voice phenomenon ignited within parapsychological circles during the early 1970's.

The parapsychological world received quite a shock in 1959 when Friedrich Jurgenson, a Swedish film maker and former opera singer, announced that he had successfully tape-recorded the voices of the dead. A second breakthrough came in 1968 when Dr. Konstantin Raudive, a Latvian scholar living in Germany, announced that he had successfully replicated Jurgenson's experiments and had also established electronic communication with the dead. Both experimenters conducted their experiments in roughly the same manner. They would simply sit with a group of people by a tape machine hooked up to an open microphone, and carry on a normal conversation. Sometimes they would verbally ask the "dead" to speak to them over the machine, or would even address specific questions to them. Both experimenters claimed that extra voices—often fleeting whispers which could be heard darting in and out of the conversation—would sometimes call out the names of people present in the room or answer questions asked during the preceding taping. The voices often claimed to be those of the dead.

Sometimes Jurgenson and Raudive would employ a different recording procedure. They would hook up tape machines to a radio set on a white-noise band between commercial stations and would try to pick up psychic voices *through* the radio. This recording technique has been criticized, though, both by skeptics and by many other experimenters engaged in tape-voice research. When using this technique, it is extremely hard to completely filter out extraneous broadcast interference, and sometimes these signals, if picked up on a tape, can easily be mistaken for genuine paranormal voices.

The parapsychological community had pretty well slept through Jurgenson's 1959 announcement, and the Swedish experimenter's book on his research, *The Inaudible Becomes Audible,* never even appeared in English translation. But the whole topic of paranormal tape-recorded voices evolved into a hot controversy within parapsychology when Raudive's book, *Breakthrough*, was published in English in 1971. Not only was it complete with the testimony of many European scientists and recording engineers who were fully supporting Raudive's discoveries and theories, but it bore a most interesting preface written by its editor, Peter Bander, who had been instrumental in getting the work accepted and translated by the British publishing firm Colin Smythe Ltd. Bander claimed that he had personally tested Raudive to his own satisfaction and that independently, Colin Smythe had replicated Raudive's work and procured voices of the dead on his *own* tapes.

Raudive's book caused a sensation, and the parapsychological community, which is a reactionary body if ever there was one, immediately went in for the attack. Raudive's voices were admittedly faint and were sometimes barely audible over the rumbling background noise of the tape itself. Subsequently, his detractors merely scoffed at Raudive's work and argued that he was "hearing things" or was only picking up commercial broadcast signals. This debate and heated, lasted until 1974, when Raudive died from a heart attack.*

Despite the enormous amount of publicity Raudive received, the discovery of the tape-recorded voice phenomenon predated both his discovery of the tape-recorded voice phenomenon predated both his and Jurgenson's research by several years. The phenomenon was first accidentally noted by Raymond Bayless and Attila von Szalay in 1956; although they published the results of their work in 1959, their claims and results were generally ignored by the parapsychological establishment—thus failing to make the stir, which Raudive achieved some 15 years later.

Their joint endeavors began in the mid-1950's when von Szalay, whom Raymond had met through mutual friends, told his colleague that back in the 1930's he had sometimes heard a tiny voice speaking in the air next to him. Being a natural psychic most of his life, he did not believe that the voice was an illusion, and he firmly believed that it was an actual disembodied voice somehow being produced right in the room with him through his psychic abilities. The first voice Art heard was in 1938, and it simply called out his name, loudly yelling "Art" quite distinctly. He was sure the voice was that of his dead son Edson. These aerial voices were conspicuously common and loud after he meditated or engaged in Yoga exercises, and in 1941 he even tried to record them on an old 78 r.p.m. record cutter. The process was expensive, and Art didn't have too much luck with it.

Raymond was intrigued by von Szalay's story, so in 1956 the two of them decided to renew the experiments. They wanted to determine (a) if von Szalay really could produce objective psychic voices and (b) if they could physically isolate and separate von Szalay from the *source* of the voices. The surprising outcome of the experiments led to the first discovery of the tape-recorded voice phenomenon. They published

---

* For more comprehensive analysis of this phenomenon, the reader might wish to peruse Susy Smith's book, *Voices of the Dead?* (New York: New American Library, 1977). This volume recounts some of the von Szalay work as well as a report on the Raudive and Jurgenson experiments. Raudive's own researchers are chronicled in his book *Breakthrough* (New York: Taplinger, 1977). The incredible controversy the Raudive work ignited in England is fully detailed in Peter Bander's *Carry on Talking* (Gerard's Cross: Colin Smythe Ltd., 1972). For a shorter discussion on the taped-voice phenomenon, see my article, "Paranormal Tape-Recorded Voices: A Paraphysical Breakthrough" in *Future Science*, ed. John White and Stanley Krippner (Garden City: Anchor, 1977).

their initial findings as a letter in the January 1959 issue of the *Journal of the American Society for Psychical Research* (coincidentally, a few months before Jurgenson announced his similar discovery of the voices in Sweden).

Raymond and Art's first experiments were conducted in a Hollywood studio they specifically rented for the purpose. They constructed a special wooden enclosure in which Art would sit while trying to produce the voices. (Sometimes a clothes closet was used instead.) Raymond hoped that Art could get the voices to speak within the cabinet even *after* he had left it. To facilitate recording, a microphone was placed in the enclosure, usually resting in the mouth of a speaking trumpet that was also placed in the cabinet. (They believed that the trumpet might help amplify any voices created in the booth.) The tape machine, however, was left outside the enclosure, where it was attached to a speaker. Thus, people sitting outside the closet could monitor and hear any voices or noises produced within the enclosure while taping them.

Invariably, whether von Szalay was in or out of the cabinet, whispering voices, whistles, or rapping sounds could be heard over the loudspeaker. Only a few words were spoken at a time, and the voices were both male *and* female in quality. Often, they sounded rather mechanical. They were heard over the speaker even when von Szalay was *outside* the cabinet and standing or sitting several feet from it. These tests not only verified the existence of the independent voices, but led to the discovery of the tape-recorded voice effect on December 5, 1956. As Bayless reported to the *Journal* of the A.S.P.R:

> Mr. von Szalay, for the purpose of this particular experiment, sat in the cabinet alone for fifteen minutes. Believing that nothing was forthcoming, he left the cabinet. We then played back the tape recording, expecting to hear nothing, but were surprised to hear a distinct voice say, "This is G." At this time I was sitting on the outside of the cabinet listening to the highly amplified loud-speaker and heard absolutely nothing.
>
> I then decided to make certain tests of the amplifying system, and we both stood a few feet from the closed cabinet door and each other in full light while Mr. von Szalay made single whistles at short intervals. I was listening to the loudspeaker when I suddenly realized that we were receiving low whistles in answer. I then told Mr. von Szalay when to whistle, and each time answering whistles were heard. There were at least six or seven answering whistles, and at the end

of this sequence, double whistles replied. We were standing within three feet of each other and were able to observe each other closely. The room was normally illuminated and fraud, under such conditions, is completely eliminated.

The December 5 experiment demonstrated conclusively that von Szalay was able not only to produce disembodied voices, but somehow to get them to appear directly on tape as well. Consequently, Raymond decided to carry out a more stringent experiment to prove the existence of von Szalay's voices. For the pilot test he procured a large upright cardboard box in which he placed the microphone and trumpet, which in turn led to a recording machine several feet away. The experimenters then sat a yard away from the box, turned on the tape, and replayed it at intervals. Three distinct voices were heard on the tape, but were so garbled that they couldn't be deciphered. (I've encountered this type of reception with von Szalay very often. The psychic voices will be almost as loud as our own, but so "mush-mouthed" that they cannot be understood. Anyone who has had some experience with a bad-quality tape recorder answerphone system will recognize the similarity.)

Raymond carried out a follow-up experiment run under even more stringent conditions. He covered the box containing the microphone with a heavy camel-pile overcoat. This entire setup was placed in another large box. Both boxes were suspended from the ceiling of the cabinet, and von Szalay and Raymond sat outside the enclosure, several feet away. A cable led from the microphone to the tape machine, which was also placed outside the cabinet. The results were just as successful. As Raymond reported:

> During an experiment on July 7, 1957, we placed the upright cardboard "box cabinet" previously described inside the closet-cabinet, closed the cabinet door and remained outside in the main room for 45 minutes. One clear human whisper was recorded.

Later that night, after Raymond had left, Art decided to continue with the experiments himself by sitting in the cabinet with the tape running and replaying it at intervals. He was in for quite a surprise. Since he had not heard any independent voices while sitting in the cabinet, he thought that his test had been a complete failure. But on replaying the tape, he discovered that he had successfully recorded a female voice saying, "Hot dog, Art!" quite loudly. The voice even twittered off with a high-pitched laugh. Von Szalay realized that while this clear voice had bypassed his own ear, it had been impressed on the tape. The voice also had a special meaning for him. Years before, he had dated a young woman in New York. Both of them were trying to sweat out the impoverished Depression years and could only afford to dine at the local hot dog stand where they could buy two hot dogs for a nickel. They often joked about their dinners, promising each other they would always remember them. Art had not seen or heard from his old flame in years, and she was presumably dead.

Was von Szalay recording the voices of the dead? This voice was a definite clue to the identity of these fleeting voices. And it was a possibility that became more and more obvious as Raymond and Art proceeded with their work.

Raymond soon learned that von Szalay's voices, whatever their nature, were endowed with some sort of intelligence of their own. For instance, they would often answer specific questions addressed to them.

During one test, for example, Raymond asked the voice-entities where his brother, who had left town suddenly, was living. Almost immediately after this question had been asked, a voice on the tape blurted out, "Bridgeport." Several days later Raymond learned that his brother was setting up his medical practice in Bridgeport, Connecticut. During another experiment, Raymond asked that the name of his grandmother be given over the tape. This was a name totally unknown to Art, but sure enough, the name "Emma" was correctly imprinted on the tape moments later.

On some occasions, von Szalay's voices even seemed aware of distant events and transactions. The following extremely evidential incident is an excellent case in point.

On September 30, 1971, Raymond sulkily told his wife Marjorie that he would like to cut himself off from the rest of the world. His wife countered by saying that she knew a man who felt that way and had become a "recluse." (The word "recluse" was actually used in the conversation.) Their subsequent conversation, carried out in the privacy of their own home, concerned Raymond's growing disenchantment with the human race. That same day, Art was 15 miles away in his Van Nuys, California, apartment experimenting with a tape machine and recorded a male voice saying, "Bayless is virtually become a recluse."

(Von Szalay keeps detailed notes of all his private sittings. These notes, along with transcripts of any voices he receives, are kept in notebooks which he periodically turns over to Raymond. Raymond saw the written words, "Bayless is virtually become a recluse," before he told Art of his conversation with his wife.)

I began my own work with Art in 1968; I had several informal as well as controlled sessions with him between 1968 and 1971 and sporadically after that. Even during my first experiments I encountered the same effects Raymond had noted years before. Not only could Art produce psychic voices on tape for me, but I could sometimes hear those voices quite audibly right in the room with us. They sounded like whispers produced right out of thin air.

One test I conducted with Art was run at his photographic studio on October 26, 1968. We used his darkroom for the experiment, and I supplied the tapes and recorder and maintained complete control of the apparatus. I also loaded and unloaded the machine myself. To facilitate the recording, I placed the recorder's microphone inside the large end of a speaking trumpet, which I placed right next to me. Von Szalay sat over a yard away.

Fifteen minutes after we began taping and while I was looking directly at the trumpet, I heard a tiny airy whistle emanate from it. Art heard it, too, and we simultaneously shot a glance at each other. Upon replaying the tape, we found that this whistle had been recorded. Unfortunately, Art's results were pretty meagre that time, and although we sat for another hour, we failed to record any voices. The tape was also blank when it was replayed. Eventually we started asking the voice-entities questions, hoping to coax them onto the tape, and made replays at 15-minute intervals. It was only after several such replays that we finally achieved some results. At 9:00 p.m. Art asked who would be elected president during the upcoming election. When we played back the tape, a voice could be heard clearly answering, "Humphrey!"—a definite, though very incorrect, answer to the question.

Later that evening Art and I left the trumpet and microphone in the darkroom and sat outside in the studio work area. We were separated from the recording equipment by a closed door. Nonetheless, at 10:50 we recorded a clear voice, yelling as though from a great distance, "Hi-ya, Art."

During another experiment I was also able to hear an independent voice during our taping session. Art and I were sitting in the darkroom quietly running the tape when suddenly we heard a gruff voice grumble right out of the trumpet. This voice, too, was caught on tape.

The von Szalay experiments have been going on for many years now, and over this time the quality and demeanor of the voices have changed considerably. The voices now seem able to speak for lengthier periods than before. During the 1956 tests, Art rarely received any voice speaking more than 5 to 7 words at a time; yet now he is receiving voices speaking up to 15 words in sequence. He once recorded a spectacular voice which spoke on tape continually for about 45 seconds. The voices have also become more "spiritistic" in nature, and will now often call out their names, answer questions, and deliver short messages.

As we said before, the study of tape-recorded paranormal voices has been extensively criticized. Some have argued that we are only picking up on random radio broadcast fragments or calls from overhead aircraft. This criticism is frankly ridiculous and can be easily rebutted. For one thing, von Szalay's voice (as well as Raudive's and Jurgenson's) clearly answer questions, call proper names, and often even use rather crass profanity! This is hardly consistent with the radio-pickup theory. It is true that Raudive and Jurgenson sometimes procure their voices by plugging their equipment into radio white-noise—an admittedly poor method, but one which we have never used with von Szalay. Most likely this faulty experiment procedure first led critics to argue that many of us were only picking up radio signals. It is a valid criticism, as we are the first to admit. *However,* the radio pickup theory cannot explain the clear human voices that Art, Raudive, and others have received by using the simple open-mike technique. Even Raudive's worst critics were nonplussed when they realized how often the names "Kosta" (a nickname for *Konstantin*) and "Raudive" were called out on his tapes. Similarly, I have heard Art's name often spoken on his tapes.

Critics who advance the radio pickup theory also totally fail to explain why these voices are usually recorded only in the presence of certain people. For example, some would-be investigators we know of have sat for days by their tape recorders hoping to receive phantom voices, all to no avail. Yet von Szalay and others can record a plethora of voices just about every time they experiment.

Of course, some of our more-than-myopic critics have claimed that we, as well as Raudive and Jurgenson, are just imagining that there are voices on our tapes. This argument is usually promoted by people who have never bothered to listen to any of them. Indeed, we certainly do not deny that many of the articulations we have recorded are very indistinct and hard to hear. The same goes for those of Raudive and Jurgenson. But others are extremely loud. Von Szalay's voices are the loudest we have ever heard and are many times the magnitude of Raudive's. Sometimes they are clearer than our own and on occasion will obliterate our voices by speaking over them. On one occasion, as briefly mentioned before, Art taped a voice speaking for 45 full seconds on the tape. The voice was so loud that Art's own voice, which was speaking about four or five sentences into the microphone when the voice was caught, is completely hidden and undecipherable.

Another criticism levelled at Raudive in particular was that many people will interpret the same example of a tape-recorded voice quite differently. This is sometimes true when several people try to decipher some of Raudive's and Art's weaker attempts. One must remember that hearing is a very indistinct and subjective sense. Even clear tape recordings of normal human speech will be interpreted differently by various listeners. But this is not true all the time. This argument is also short on logic. Just because these paranormal voices are often garbled does not mean that they do not exist on our tapes. (For example, several segments of the Watergate tapes could not be transcribed to the total satisfaction of all the people working on them. But we don't dismiss the value of the Watergate tapes on those grounds.) It would certainly be convenient to know what these voices are saying every time they appear; but the fact that many of them cannot be deciphered does not in any way detract from the fact that *any* type of voice, which can be somehow psychically impressed on electromagnetic tape, is in itself a phenomenon of immense importance.

Now, just what does all this have to do with the phantom phone call mystery? The answer to that question is twofold. We feel that the von Szalay research bears on both the nature of the *intelligence* behind the phone call mystery and, perhaps even more important, to the *mechanics* of the calls.

To begin with, the tape-recorded voice phenomenon serves as an *independent line of evidence* that the dead can contact us by manipulating electronic equipment. By far most people who have actively experimented with these voices believe that they are literally communications from the dead. This is certainly the conviction of Raudive, Jurgenson, and von Szalay. There also exists a considerable body of a *priori* evidence that this assumption is correct. These taped voices often call out their names, invariably matching those of people who are dead but who were known to the experimenters during their lives. Von Szalay once received a voice that spoke in the identical timbre of his late father's. Raymond, who knew the elder von Szalay, has also heard this tape and agrees with Art's impression. Jurgenson is likewise convinced that the very first voice he ever recorded was that of his mother.

Our own minds, however, vacillate on this issue a bit. Have von Szalay, Raudive, *et al.* really established some sort of instrumental contact with the dead? Or are these psychics somehow using their own PK powers to *impress* the voices directly onto their tapes or otherwise create them? There is no clear way to resolve this issue, just as there is rarely any way to resolve any problem in parapsychology absolutely. But during the course of our work we have run into definite suggestions that von Szalay's voices are spiritistic in nature. Once Art taped and recognized the voice of a woman he had known some years before. Later he learned that she had committed suicide just a few days before he recorded her voice. He has also recorded the voices of many other people he had known before their deaths. Often there will be a strong resemblance between their taped voices and their terrestrial ones. The voices have given Art advice, personal abuse, and now and then have even offered him instructions on better methods of taping and equipment usage.

All in all, it has always struck us that we have been dealing with an intelligence that is somehow independent of Art's own mind. This is perhaps the one single most important conclusion we have reached from our research into the taped-voice enigma.

Now just how are these voices getting onto tape in the first place? The answer to this question also bears on the phantom phone call mystery.

Back in 1970 Raymond and I often discussed the possible mechanisms responsible for producing psychic voices onto electromagnetic tape. There were two possible solutions. Either (a) somehow the voices are impressed directly onto the tapes via some sort of PK-mediated electromagnetic manipulation, or (b) the voices are being paraphysically created—though inaudible to the human era—directly in front of the tape recorder microphone or in it. Note that this is the same problem we invariably confront when studying "phone calls from the dead" cases. In this instance, too, we began to wonder whether the voice effects are produced by some sort of electromagnetic manipulation of electrical equipment or by voices psychically created within the telephone. If both the taped and phone-voice phenomena are being masterminded by the dead, we might expect to find a similar mechanism producing both effects.

In 1973 Raymond decided to resolve this issue once and for all by carrying out a new series of tests with Art. The experiments were simple in design. Sometimes he would leave the tape recorder mike open and unobstructed; during other tests he would place heavy cloth over it. Raymond discovered that as long as the cloth covered the mike, no voices were ever recorded. This fact tends to prove that Art is not capable of directly manipulating the tapes by PK. Somehow a *physical* voice is being produced within the proximity of the mike. (Of course, this discovery is consistent with the fact that sometimes we have heard these voices quite audibly in the course of our experiments.)

It should be pretty obvious how this finding ties in with our "phone calls from the dead" cases. Raymond's discovery is totally consistent with what we have learned about the probable paraphysical mechanics of these calls. Much circumstantial evidence indicates that many phantom calls are not due simply to electromagnetic manipulation of phone lines, but are produced by voices paraphysically created within the telephone mouthpiece. Our work with Art serves as an independent line of evidence to this effect. His voices also appear to be created paraphysically over the microphone system of the tape recorder. So a similar mechanism seems to lie behind both tape-recorded and telephonically received voice phenomena. This is why we believe that the von Szalay experiments had isolated the general mechanics behind these phone calls years before we ever began studying them seriously.

At this point, though, we should note that at least one experimenter has come to an opposite conclusion about the nature of paranormal taped voice-effects. William Welch, who was a well-known Hollywood screenwriter, carried out extensive research on the taped-voice phenomenon before his recent death. Bill, whom we knew well, once found a voice imprinted on a portion of tape which he had not yet run through his machine. Therefore, this voice must have been an electromagnetic effect. (He gives the details about the incident in his book, *Talks with the Dead*, which was published in 1975.) Bill encountered this odd effect only once during his experiments and believed that it was purely an anomaly. However, this small discovery is still consistent with our phone call data. This electromagnetically imprinted voice may be similar in nature to those phone calls from the dead that are indeed produced by psi-mediated* manipulation of phone lines. So it looks as though the dead—or whoever is producing the calls—can actually employ two different mechanisms in their attempt to use the telephone system, both of which lead to the same result. This self-evident fact obviously relates to taped-voice effects as well.

The von Szalay work also helps us to answer another question about the phantom phone call mystery. In the previous chapter we suggested

---

* The term "psi" refers to any type of psychic phenomenon.

The Mechanics of the Calls

that the dead's attempts to contact us through the phone system may be a product of habit. But could it be that the dead are continually trying to contact us *any way possible?* Telephones, tape machines, and other mechanical equipment that rely on electrical energy could all be natural media over which the dead have some control. Just how or why, we cannot say. But these telephone contacts may be only one element of a concerted effort on the part of the dead to establish contact with the living.

This idea may be pure speculation, but we are certainly not the only parapsychologists who have ever suggested this possibility. C. T. L. Chari is perhaps India's most distinguished parapsychologist. A professor of philosophy and psychology at Madras Christian College in Tamil Nadu, Dr. Chari is a widely respected scholar on subjects ranging from parapsychology to quantum physics. Dr. Chari became interested in our project when we first informed him about our case studies. He wrote to us: "I have a hunch that all information networks used for our normal communications—telephones, telegraph, radar, radio waves, etc.—can also be used paranormally by the ostensible dead as well as the living."

Chari's thoughts have been echoed by Susy Smith, an author of more than two dozen books on the paranormal. She has cogently written in the preface to her book, *Voices of the Dead?*:

> With the invention of every new mode of communication, there is always a flurry of excitement when someone believes he is using it to communicate with the dead. We have heard of a few incidents in which the telegraph rattled out a Morse code warning that prevented disaster to a ship or train when there was no human at the sending end of the apparatus. Occasionally there is an account of someone who is sure he has spoken to a deceased relation or friend on the telephone ... Even television has had one or two flings of producing evidence of survival.

Both Dr. Chari and Miss Smith seem to be correct. The telephone is only one channel over which psychic communications are being received from some unseen dimension. This is a subject to which we'll return in Chapter 8.

7

Further Elements of the Mystery

It was 4:00 o'clock that Thursday afternoon. I knew that I had to put in a phone call to the UCLA Neuropsychiatric Institute, but I was lying comfortably on my living room couch, almost dozing, and just couldn't bring myself to break my inertia and get up. So I just rested there, listening to the radio. Two hours later, at 6:00, I was still right there on the couch, feeling just as snug, and I still had no intention of getting up and doing anything, much less making a call, when the phone rang. To stifle its angry wail, the only thing I could do was answer it. "So much for loafing," I thought to myself as I muttered a few choice pejoratives about being disturbed.

When I picked up the phone, I was surprised to hear the voice of a young research assistant who worked at the Neuropsychiatric Institute.

"I'm answering your message," he said.

"What message?" I asked, a bit puzzled.

"The call you made to us at four," he continued, equally bewildered.

"What do you mean? I didn't call you," I added a bit nastily.

"Oh? I just got in and found a message on my desk saying that you called at four and wanted us to return the call."

To say the least, I was thunderstruck. Indeed, I had *wanted* to phone UCLA at 4:00 that day, and I had actually wanted to speak to this assistant's boss. But I most assuredly had never made the call.

Phone Calls from the Dead

On questioning the assistant further, I learned that someone had called the office and had spoken to one of the Institute's volunteers while most of the regular staff were out of the lab. The caller had left my name and said that I wanted the call returned. And that was the end of the incident.

This little episode took place in 1975, only shortly before Raymond and I began systematically studying the "phone calls from the dead" mystery. In fact, it was this personal incident more than anything else that convinced us that the phantom phone call mystery deserved serious study. Raymond even knew of a similar incident that has occurred in his own family.

Our major project has always been the study of phone calls from the dead, since they appear to be the most common form of phantom call. But as we proceeded with our survey, we started stumbling across accounts of phantom phone calls suspiciously similar to the one in which I had "participated." We started calling these calls "intention" cases, since they usually reflect an *intention* in the mind of a living agent. My own case is a good example. My intention to place a call was somehow actually carried out psychically and without my knowledge.

It didn't take us long to realize that these mysterious calls *from the living* represented a parallel aspect of the phantom phone call mystery. Consequently, we started making a special study of them, hoping that in the long run they would shed some light on the nature of "phone calls from the dead." These two types of calls are too similar not to represent anything but closely related aspects of a wider mystery.

Mr. William Eisenwein of Yarnell, Arizona, reported a similar telephone case to the August 1968 issue of *Fate* magazine. The incident occurred in March 1960. It was 12:30 p.m. He had just finished writing an article for *Audubon* (a wildlife magazine) and was about to phone the magazine's editor, John K. Terras. By the time he got to a phone, though, it was 5:00 p.m. Since the magazine's editorial offices closed at that time, Eisenwein decided to defer making the call until the next day. But, as he explains:

> When I arrived home that evening, I learned that Mr. Terras had left word for me to give him a ring. I went out and did so. I said that I had received his message.
>
> "What message?" he asked.
>
> "Why, didn't you phone and leave word for me to call back?"

"Yes," he answered, "because I found a note on my desk saying that you had called at 12:30 while I was in conference to tell me that the article was ready."

I did not tell the *Audubon* editor the truth of the matter, nor did I ever meet the secretary who accomplished this remarkable feat. I don't know whether the telephone was involved but somehow the message got through.

Eisenwein's experience is virtually identical to the one I had. In both instances, our pains to make phone calls were somehow carried out psychically—as though our very thoughts had directly affected the material world.

"Intention" cases also represent one of the few elements of the phantom phone call mystery that at least a few conventionally oriented parapsychologists have attempted to study. For example, Renée Haynes, a leading British author and parapsychologist, includes a number of them in her book *The Seeing Eye, the Seeing I*. In one case she cites, a surgeon was aroused late at night by his phone's incessant ringing. His nurse was on the line. She hurriedly told the doctor that he was urgently needed at his hospital, where one of his patients was undergoing a crisis. The physician rushed to the hospital just in time to save the man's life, but the nurse later emphatically denied that she had ever placed the call.

Miss Haynes also quotes a similar case about a priest who received a call late at night. The caller, whose voice he didn't recognize, gave him an address and urged him to go there to give the Last Rites to a dying man. The priest asked no questions, but rushed off to the address the caller had given him. There he found the dying man, just in time to give him the Last Rites. But no one present at the house took credit for making the call, and they were totally surprised by the priest's opportune arrival.

While trying to formulate an explanation for these cases, Miss Haynes totally rejects the notion that either the doctor or the priest received *genuine* phone calls. She argues instead that the witness actually experienced bizarre and complex psi-mediated hallucinations. In other words, they only *imagined* that they heard the phone rings and the voices on the line. They really had, she argues, telepathic experiences. Their unconscious minds picked up information or "signals" about the crises in which they became involved, and then imparted the information to their conscious minds in the form of elaborate hallucinations. To support her theory, Miss Haynes quotes the case of an Englishwoman who was about to travel to an Indian province when she received a mysterious phone call instructing her not to make the journey. The woman convinced her husband to forestall their trip and, sure enough, a smallpox plague broke out in the province on the day they would have arrived. To Miss Haynes, the telephone in this case acted as a symbol of communication. "The ringing of the bell and the telephone may have been hallucinatory," she explains, "a means used by the unconscious mind to alert the conscious mind" of the danger.

Miss Hayne's theory is plausible for a few cases. (We have even collected two cases from people who *dreamed* about receiving phone calls from the dead.) But we have personally run into a couple of cases in which the witnesses undoubtedly received genuine, physical, (i.e. nonhallucinatory) phone calls. One extremely well-witnessed episode of this sort was told to us by Jerome Clark, the associate editor of *Fate* magazine. The case is doubly evidential since an independent witness observed the call.

"The incident occurred one Saturday afternoon in June 1975. A friend, Dr. Benton Jamison, and I were sitting in my apartment in Moorhead, Minnesota, and conversing," Jerry told us. "The phone rang. I answered it. The person on the other end, whose voice I immediately recognized, identified herself as Mary, a friend of my wife's. My wife Penny babysat Mary's two young sons from time to time, and Mary asked if she would do so that evening because she wanted to go out. I explained that Penny was out of town visiting her parents and wouldn't be back until the next day. Mary expressed disappointment, and that was the end of the conversation."

Clark's wife returned home in due course and, after learning of the call, called Mary to apologize for not having been able to help.

"Mary was flabbergasted," Jerry continued "and denied she had made any such call. She said, however, that she'd thought about doing so all afternoon but had decided against it. When Penny explained that the telephone 'Mary' had expressed disappointment, the real Mary said she would never have done that. I agree. At the time of the phone exchange, in fact, I had been a little surprised at her reaction."

After receiving Jerry's account, we contacted Dr. Jamison. He verified the incident, saying that he, too, had heard the phone ring and had overheard Jerry telling the caller about his wife's absence.

Since Clark certainly did not imagine the ring, it is very hard for us to believe that he hallucinated this telephone voice. Instead, somehow Mary's intention to call him translated into a *physical effect* that psychically affected his phone system.

The intentions that are sometimes converted into these phone calls are not always conscious, however. On rare occasions, a mystery phone call will be prompted by an unconscious intent or preoccupation. One such call was reported in the December 1973 issue of *Fate* by Robert Ferrara of Napa, California. The events leading up to it had taken place during World War II, when Ferrara had been attached to a Marine artillery unit in the Pacific Theater. In June 1944, his unit landed on Saipan and Tinian to wrest the islands from Japanese troops. During the ensuing battle, an artillery shell landed at the foot of Ferrara's foxhole and exploded. As he lost consciousness, he thought of his mother. At about the same time, Ferrara claims in his story, his mother in Sacramento, California, received a mystery call from him. The voice just kept repeating, "Mom, it hurts," over and over.

Exactly what do these cases have to do with phone calls from the dead? There is probably a very definite connection. For one thing, each group of cases, by their very nature, helps substantiate the existence of the other. And "intention" cases, few though they are, also help make the "phone calls from the dead" phenomenon more credible and understandable in another and more direct way. If the dead can psychically produce these phone calls, then one would expect that a living mind also possesses this same psychic ability. Likewise, one might argue the issue the other way around: If we can produce these calls psychokinetically while we are still alive then there's no reason to assume that we couldn't also produce them after death as well. (That is, of course, if we do survive.)

Our studies, though, indicate that phantom calls from the living are much less common than phone calls from the dead. Why should this be? If both the living and the dead can produce psychic phone calls, shouldn't these two types of cases be equally common? Yet our data indicate the exact opposite.

Now this finding could be an artifact—that is, reflecting more on our methods of research than on the data it collects. People may be simply more willing to *report* "phone calls from the dead" than a phantom call from the living. Also, a person who receives a phantom call from the living might never come to realize that anything unusual has transpired. Clark, Mrs. Ferrara, and other witnesses certainly did not suspect anything unusual about their calls when they first received them. They almost accidentally discovered that the calls were phantom ones. On the other hand, a person who receives a call from a deceased friend or relative has a higher chance—because of the very nature of the call—to eventually discover the paranormality of the experience. Aside from these factors, there are probably psychic reasons, as well, why "intention" cases are rarer than "phone calls from the dead." Might it be, for instance, that the dead can produce these calls more easily than the living can?

I think all these issues will stand in better perspective if we try to figure out the possible mechanisms that lie behind these phantom calls from the living. Determining *how* these calls are produced might help us understand the nature of "phone calls from the dead," their relation to phantom calls from the living, and the entire phantom phone call mystery as a whole.

One simple theory might be that an individual who wishes to make a phone call can, under just the right circumstances, project PK over vast distances and use it (unconsciously) to electromagnetically affect the witness's phone. This theory might seem a little extravagant, but there is some scattered laboratory evidence that PK, like ESP, is not hampered by distance. In 1955, for instance, Dr. R. A. McConnell, a physics professor at the University of Pittsburgh, published a provocative paper in the Journal of the American Society for Psychical Research. He had tested to see if his subjects, while sleeping in their own homes, could affect dice being thrown in his university laboratory. Sometimes the subjects, including himself, were sleeping miles away from where the dice were being thrown. The test was moderately successful, since McConnell himself scored admirably on it!

Similar success along these same lines had previously been reported from England in 1953: G. W. Fisk and A. M. J. Mitchell, two highly respected British investigators and members of the Society for Psychical Research, related some experiments with a subject who could psychokinetically affect dice being thrown 170 miles away. So the idea that PK-from-the-living can function over great distances must be taken seriously.*

However, merely theorizing that these "intention" cases are "PK-mediated" by the living actually isn't saying very much, since we really don't know what PK is! It isn't a "substance" or a "thing." It may not even be a force or energy, although this does seem likely. The term *psychokinesis* is merely a label under which we place many anomalous phenomena, which so far appear inexplicable according to

---

* For discussion of long-distance PK, refer to Louisa Rhine's *Mind Over Matter* (New York: Macmillan 1970, pp. 210-17).

Further Elements of the Mystery

the laws governing the physical world. PK is not really an explanation for anything, merely a categorization. When trying to understand a particular psychic event, it may be proper to ask *who initiates* the PK *process*, but it is not proper merely to assume that we have automatically explained an event by classifying it as PK.

Nonetheless, certain theories about PK can help us explain "intention" cases. Dr. John Beloff, one of Great Britain's leading parapsychologists, argued in his 1975 Presidential Address to the Society for Psychical Research that PK may not be an energy, force, or physical process at all, but may be the unusual outcome of a direct link existing between our minds, the universe, and everything in it. He further posits that PK need not be any type of hyperenergy stored in the mind or body, but may be something that occurs when "under certain circumstances, still to be established, an idea or intention in the mind can automatically constrain a physical system to act in such a way as to express the idea or intention. That this is, in the last resort, an ultimate fact about the world; there is no further 'bridging' mechanism to be invoked to make this fact intelligible."

Of course, one could spend pages debating the relative merits of Beloff's conceptualization. But, in light of this sort of hypothesis, "intention" cases do become somewhat more understandable. The calls may simply be the direct material outcome of the agent's mental intention.

But still, one might ask, why are phantom calls from the living so much rarer than calls from the dead? What is the actual link between these two elements of the phantom phone call mystery?

One explanation might be derived from the realms of quantum physics. What we're about to say is extremely speculative—perhaps even gratuitously so. But some findings being made in quantum physics seem to make the whole phantom phone call mystery (and especially "intention" cases) much more intelligible, while at the same time suggesting a connection between phantom calls from the dead and those from the living.

The world of subatomic particles is vastly different from the world about us. At the subatomic level, some of the basic "laws" of the world governing causality, action and reaction, motion, physicality—and even time—break down almost completely. For instance, some particles within the atom seem capable of flowing backwards in time, while others can apparently exist in the same place at the same instant. Two particles in a beam of such particles, all traveling at the same velocity and in the same direction, may pass consecutively through a pinhole, but strike a screen at two different places. This is physically "impossible," but it occurs at the subatomic level all the time. Very few outcomes from a subatomic process can be predicted. These findings have drastically revised the "lawfulness" of the cause-and-effect relationship, which some physicists regard as a mere "myth" promulgated by classical Newtonian physics. In general, then, physicists today do not talk about the deterministic *outcomes* of subatomic processes, but about the *probabilities* of various solutions eventually occurring.

This all might make more sense if we draw upon some arguments presented by Dr. Erwin Schrödinger, the Nobel Prize-winning physicist. As science writers Michael Talbot and Lloyd Biggle, Jr., point out in the December 1976 issue of *Analog*:

> The implications of an unpredictable universe that can be described only in terms of mathematical probabilities have been dramatically illuminated in problems posed by the Austrian physicist, Erwin Schrödinger.
>
> Take, for instance, the previous illustration of two equal particles passing through the pinhole. Even though all apparent knowledge concerning the particles is identical, they still strike the screen at different points. Schrödinger developed the differential equations that described the development in time of such a physical system. Schrödinger's final equation, however, predicts two equally probable outcomes for the same particle. In mathematical theory as well as in observation, there is no explanation for the unpredictable behavior of the particles. The system therefore seems to have entered into a schizophrenic state of constantly changing values.

In other words, any single quantum process has various probable outcomes, all of which have equal likelihoods of occurring. The actual solution to the process will always be random and unpredictable.

An interesting approach to this very problem has recently been made by Hugh Everett and John Wheeler, two physicists who have proposed what has been called (naturally enough) the Everett-Wheeler interpretation of quantum mechanics. In almost science fiction fashion, they argue that the universe as we see it is only a fraction of what exists in the cosmos, and that it "is constantly splitting into a stupendous number of branches, all resulting from the measurement like interactions between its myriad components. Moreover, every quantum transition taking place on every star, in every galaxy, in every remote corner of the Universe is splitting our local world on earth into myriad copies of itself."

The upshot of the Everett-Wheeler theory is obvious. A quantum event has X number of outcomes, and all occur simultaneously—but in different parallel universes. We see only one outcome because we are chained to only one point of observation. "Not only does every quantum mechanical event in our universe cause an indefinite ... number of divisions, but perhaps all possible realities exist simultaneously," argue Talbot and Biggle. "In such a garden of forking paths," they say, "the solution to the dilemma of indeterminism may be a universe in which all possible outcomes of an experiment actually occur."

These same principles might hold true at the psychic level in our real world. Every act of conscious intention might also have a variety of outcomes. If I *think* about making a phone call, there are two ways the intention can be resolved: Either I make the call or I don't. And there are hundreds of factors, both within my control and beyond it, that will mitigate my final choice of outcome. But arguing from the Everett-Wheeler interpretation, it could be possible that while I don't make the call in one universe, in another universe the intention is followed through at the psychic level and the call is actually made. This possibility cannot be rejected. And could it be that on rare occasions, these psychic channels become confused and a person in *this* world actually witnesses the outcome of the intention as it takes place in a psychic dimension? This idea might form a theoretical model that can explain some PK actions—actions which often seem to reflect the conscious and unconscious intentions of a human mind.

But what about phone calls from the dead?

The dead, by existing in a different psychic dimension altogether, might be in a better position to monitor or experimentally manipulate these psychic cross-channelings. They might therefore be able to produce phone call effects more easily than we can.*

---

* We are sure this theory and conceptualization will strike the reader and probably other parapsychologists as novel and daring, if not extravagant. The fact remains, though, that this theory is not new. It is so old, in fact, that it has been forgotten. A vaguely similar theory was first proposed in 1880, long before the emergence of quantum physics, by Dr. Johann Zöllner of the University of Leipzig. He theorized that PK was possible if one postulated the existence of a fourth dimension. On the basis of some PK demonstrations he had himself witnessed, he argued that beings existing in a psychic plane

But can this theory be proved? Perhaps not experimentally, but on the basis of it we might expect to find that the intentions of a living person will sometimes be transmitted by a phone call from the dead, imparting by proxy the idea behind the intention.

One case of just this sort is recounted by psychic and author Ursula Roberts in her book *The Great Tomorrow*. The call came during a time of particular trial for Mrs. Roberts. She was unhappy, her husband was dying, and the strain of living was becoming too much for her. She had no one to turn to, and her closest friend, a foreigner named Rog-Til, had moved. She couldn't get in touch with him even though she needed him desperately. One night things got so bad that she wanted to phone somebody to come over and help her out of her depression, but she couldn't think of anyone to ask. So she just sat at her husband's desk, playing with the phone, before eventually dropping off to sleep. Her husband died that night.

At 8:00 o'clock the next morning a loud knock resounded on her front door. It was Rog-Til. She was puzzled by his sudden and opportune appearance and immediately asked him what prompted his visit.

"Last night," he explained to her, "about ten past midnight, apparently you telephoned the police station at Norwich. You asked them to find me, giving my old address, and saying that you had lost the new one. They came right round to me fairly quickly, and woke me up. They said that you were in great trouble, and I must come to you at once because Arthur was dying. I shot into my clothes, caught the milk train to Colchester, and here I am."

Mrs. Roberts just couldn't buy the story since she hadn't made any calls the night before, even though she had thought about doing so. As she explains in her book:

---

might be able experimentally to manipulate this fourth dimension and thereby produce psychic phenomena. Zöllner explained these ideas in his book, Transcendental Physics. Although his theorizing was perhaps a bit naive, it was no more so than much that goes on in parapsychology today. It has often been argued that Zöllner, who was a highly respected man of science, was insane and senile when he developed his theories. That is simply not the case. He was only 43 when he began his psychic experiments, and he died at the age of 48 from a cerebral hemorrhage. He taught at the University of Leipzig right up to the day he died.

Further Elements of the Mystery

Rog-Til and my own doctor did not understand the story at all, and Rog-Til, who was a very persistent man, got hold of the telephone operator who had taken the call and asked him to come round and see him in my house. At the time I knew nothing about this, but they told me later on, when I had recovered and was feeling better.

The operator said that the message had come from my house at about ten minutes past midnight, and I had asked for the police station at Norwich. I admit that I believed this to be possible, for I have the greatest faith in the police, and in any grim emergency would turn to them. They would have been the very people whom I should have called.

The operator said to Rog-Til that the woman who had spoken to him was not myself, whom he knew quite well, and he was used to my voice, especially during the last few days when I had been telephoning all the time. He said that it was the voice of a quite calm, but he would have thought a much older, woman, someone who was a stranger to him and whom he would have believed to be middle-aged. She was not worried and spoke quite clearly. She said that she wished to speak to the headquarters of the police in Norwich, and he had put her through.

He thought that she was a bit disturbed, but certainly not distracted in any way. She did not muddle her words. He was later called off on other business, so did not hear all that she said.

The operator also told them that the voice was quite controlled and had told the police that she was *speaking for her daughter*, whose husband was dying. The caller wanted them to get in touch with Rog-Til and said that her daughter needed to deliver an urgent message to him.

The police had subsequently checked into Rog-Til's whereabouts, contacted him, and sent him to the Roberts's residence. It was a happy ending, except for one strange fact—Mrs. Roberts's mother was dead!

This case is hard to explain as the result of PK-from-the-living. If Mrs. Roberts had produced the call herself, psychokinetically and unconsciously, why didn't she produce it in her own voice? In a typical phantom call from the living, the telephone voice usually resembles that of the person whose intention is being acted upon. But in this case, the voice specifically identified itself as Mrs. Roberts's mother. So it really does seem as though the psychic's deceased mother had placed the call. Somehow, it would appear, her mother's Theta-agent acted as a mediary, produced the call, and delivered the message by proxy. One can only conclude that, for some reason, the discarnate woman found it easier to produce the call than did Mrs. Roberts's own unconscious mind.*

Before leaving the subject of "intention" cases altogether, we would like to discuss one other even more bizarre aspect of the phantom phone call mystery. These are cases where a person receives a *precognitive message*—that is, cases where a witness receives a phone call which matches the caller's *future* intention!

Since we have only two cases of this nature in our files, we'll discuss them only briefly. In one instance, a northern California woman wrote to us about an incident that had occurred in the small country town where she had grown up. While our correspondent was a young woman still living at home, she had been friendly with a young woman whose parents were constantly fighting, literally at each other's throats. One day while the couple's daughter was visiting our correspondent and her mother, a frantic phone call came in. It was the town doctor, who explained that the girl's mother had been battered by her husband and that he was taking her to the hospital.

The three women rushed off to the doctor's office, only to find that the physician adamantly denied ever making such a call. Everyone was puzzled until the next day—when the girl's mother was seriously beaten by her husband, and the doctor did have to get her to the hospital—and call her daughter.

Our correspondent gave us the name of the doctor and the town in which she thought he still practices, but so far, our attempts to trace him have failed. We have therefore been unable to corroborate this fascinating case.

Our only other precognitive phone call case was reported in the March 21, 1978, National Enquirer by Melvin Belli, the celebrated attorney. Belli told the Enquirer that in July 1960 he had received a phone call from an Oakland mortuary informing him that a dear friend, Suey Ng, had died. The funeral was set for the next day, the caller explained, and Belli offered to be a pallbearer. The next day, however, the funeral

---

* We are currently investigating a similar case. The witness was desperately trying to locate some family friends who had moved. She tried reaching them in every way possible, but failed. Nonetheless, these acquaintances received a mystery phone call during that time. The voice, speaking as though from a great distance, cried that it was "lost" and "needed help." They immediately recognized the voice as that of our witness! They eventually tracked her down, and all ended happily. So the living as well as the dead can produce these special types of calls.

home was quite dismayed by Belli's appearance at their doorstep, since they had never heard of Suey Ng much less knew anything about a funeral for him. The attorney immediately called Ng's phone number and, indeed, found him quite alive and well. A week later, though, Ng died unexpectedly—and his funeral was held at the same mortuary that had prompted the psychic call a week prior.

There is really no theoretical reason to reject these two accounts. As we've pointed out before, both distance and time can be transcended at the psychic level. If a living person's intention to make a call can be translated into a material event miles away, why couldn't this intention also transcend time? This idea has been called "time displaced" or "retroactive" PK, and recently a number of parapsychologists have been experimenting to determine if a person's future intention can psychokinetically affect a present event. They are finding that it can!

A classic experiment along these lines was reported by Dr. Helmut Schmidt to the 18th Annual Convention of the Parapsychological Association, held in Santa Barbara, California, in August 1975. Dr. Schmidt is a former Boeing Laboratories physicist now engaged fulltime in parapsychological research at the Mind Science Foundation in San Antonio, Texas. He was the first parapsychologist to postulate the theoretical existence of retroactive PK, and has since run several sophisticated experiments demonstrating this mind-boggling form of psi.

Schmidt's experiments hinge largely on the use of a machine called a random number generator (or RNG for short), an apparatus he introduced into parapsychology several years ago and which is now commonly employed in PK and ESP research. A binary RNG might best be visualized as an automatic coin-flipper. Inside the machine is an oscillator that can "flip" to either of two positions. These positions might be termed either "heads" and "tails," or +1 and –1. The oscillator's speed can be set so that it makes hundreds of flips per second. The flipper is also randomly set. In other words, during any given large number of trials, it will flip 50 percent of the time to the +1 position, and 50 percent to the –1 position. Schmidt, however, has discovered that some subjects can cause the oscillator to depart from randomness by merely willing (or "PKing") it, causing the flipper to generate more +1's than chance can account for. For these experiments, the subject is allowed to watch a panel that tells him how many +1's and –1's he is producing per run (runs of 100 or 1000 trials per second are common) and is instructed merely to "will" the generator to produce whatever outcome he wishes. Some people actually seem to do better with practice.

For one "time-displaced" PK test, Schmidt generated a series of "flips" on his RNG, which he simultaneously recorded on magnetic tape. He didn't try to influence the outcome of the RNG, nor did he play back the tapes at the time. Theoretically, then, the RNG output as recorded on the tapes should have shown a 50 percent division between the number of +1's and −1's generated. Moments later, Schmidt tested a subject for PK on his RNG. The subject was asked to make the machine generate more +1's than −1's.

But Schmidt had a surprise up his sleeve. Although his subject didn't know it, the machine was not merely generating new targets. Before the actual experiment, Schmidt took random sequences of targets from the prerecorded tape, and stored them in the RNG's memory banks. These sequences of prerecorded targets were subsequently mixed in with the targets being generated at the moment. (These sequences were, in fact, played over several times during the course of the experiment so that the subject would have the chance to "reinforce" his PK on them.) So in order to do well on the test, the subject had to affect the number of +1's on the prerecorded and presumably unaffectable targets!

Schmidt eventually tested 20 subjects with this procedure. Sure enough, the subjects succeeded at the task. Somehow, Schmidt theorizes, the prerecorded sequences had been biased to produce more +1's than −1's when he originally recorded them. In other words, each subject's *future intention* to use PK on the RNG had affected the generator when Schmidt originally made the tapes.

One could argue that Schmidt merely used his own PK on the RNG at the time he made the tapes. Schmidt's note that *all* his subjects contributed to the collective extra-chance scoring he obtained in his test would also tend to indicate that Schmidt himself contributed the PK. However, he has run even more complex experiments in hopes of circumventing this problem, and the "time-displaced" PK effect has now also been replicated in Europe.

These results tend to confirm our phone call data. Notice that, in both cases, the future intention of the subject is seemingly translated into a PK action in our present-time reference. The fact that a living person can produce these phantom phone Calls also throws some interesting light on a phenomenon well known to UFOlogists. Many people who have witnessed UFO landings or experienced other "close encounters" often receive harassing phone calls shortly after. Sometimes the calls will start as soon as the witness returns home after his experience, or within a day or two. Many UFO witnesses have complained that

Further Elements of the Mystery

the calls were made to their unlisted numbers, and often *before* they had told anybody about their experience. The "callers" always impart the same basic message: they instruct or warn the witness to "forget" about what he has seen and to keep quiet about the incident. Usually only one call is received, but on occasion there will be a series of them.*

Most UFOlogists maintain that these calls are somehow produced by the same intelligence that operates the UFOs. However, it is also possible that the witness is actually producing the calls himself through some form of PK. And, from a psychological perspective, the reason is not hard to fathom.

Many people who have had UFO sightings find their experiences stressful and anxiety provoking. For instance, suppose an average man-in-the-street has a close UFO encounter. On the one hand, he probably wants to tell everyone he knows about his experience, or at least he feels he should report it to *someone*. On the other hand, our UFO witness also realizes that (1) probably no one will believe him, and (2) his claim might subject him to ridicule. Yet these negative emotions are equally balanced by the witness's excitement over his experience.

Dual emotions such as these are often hard to resolve and lead to what psychologists call an "approach-avoidance" conflict. An approach-avoidance conflict arises when, in order to resolve a single problem, a person can take either of two contradictory actions ("should I or shouldn't I?"), both of which are equally appealing. Now, how can our UFO witness resolve his dilemma? The phantom phone call neatly solves it for him. A "higher authority" conveniently comes into the picture, intimidates him into silence, and then vanishes. Since the witness has now had his course of action determined for him, he no longer has to take further responsibility for his experience, and the conflict is thereby immediately resolved. While we're not suggesting that all these UFO-related phone calls are PK-mediated, it does look as though some of them are psychically produced by the witnesses themselves in order to resolve personal conflicts.

Whether or not there is a connection, we know of one case in which a UFO sighting may have prompted a phone call from the dead. Since the call came in several days after the family's sighting, the synchronistic timing may have been purely coincidental, however.

---

* Space does not permit us to cite any specific examples of this phenomenon, but they are so common that we could spend a whole chapter on them. Examples of these phone intimidations can be found in most books on the UFO mystery.

The case was supplied to us by Dr. Berthold Schwarz, whose help we acknowledged earlier.

A middle-aged woman, who was an acquaintance of Schwarz, saw a UFO as she was driving in the country with her husband. The object followed her car for several hours before disappearing. Some time later, the witness received a phone call from a man who said his name was Roger. When she said that she didn't know any Roger, the voice said that he was a family secret and was her brother!

The woman chalked up the call to a prank, but later learned that years before she herself was born, her mother had given birth to a stillborn child who would have been named Roger had he lived. This sad event had been kept a secret of sorts and the witness had never been told about it. If nothing more, this report certainly gets the blue ribbon for being the strangest case in our files!

As we've pointed out before, it seems logical that, if we can produce these calls after death, we should also be endowed with the same ability while we are alive. The cases we've presented in this chapter also lend added support to our contention that "phone calls from the dead" are indeed produced by the dead and not by the surreptitious activities of our own minds *en masquerade*. If indeed we are psychokinetically producing these phone calls by ourselves, we should also expect to find phantom calls from the living (such as "intention" cases) are every bit as common. But they aren't. In our case collection, phantom calls from the dead outnumber "intention" or related cases about eight to one.*

There is yet another aspect of the phantom phone call mystery that is just as perplexing. This aspect consists of what we call "answer" cases—that is, cases in which a person makes a call that is *answered* by a person who either (a) is dead or (b) couldn't possibly have been home to answer it. The Marie D'Alessio case recounted in Chapter 3 is a classic example of this phenomenon. It is also an experience that has occurred in my own home on at least two occasions.

The first incident took place in 1974, shortly after I had moved into my present home in Reseda, California. At the time I was renting the

---

* Of course, the critic will claim that this ratio was caused by a sampling basis—that is, that we were mainly interested only in phone calls from the dead and did not encourage people to report other types of mystery calls to us. This is not the case, however, for in the course of our work we actively encouraged people to tell us about any unusual phone calls they had received or knew about.

Further Elements of the Mystery

back bedroom to a college student named Gary. I had met Gary through his brother, Tony, with whom I had gone to college. One evening as I was fixing dinner, Tony called.

"Didn't you give Gary my message?" he asked indignantly. He was obviously vexed, and I didn't have the slightest idea why.

"No, what message?" I asked in a voice which must have struck Tony as painfully naive.

"The message Bob was supposed to give you," he responded.

By this time I was totally confused. Who the hell is Bob? I thought to myself. I told Tony that, quite frankly, I didn't know what in blazes he was talking about. After cooling down a bit, he explained that he had called my house earlier that afternoon trying to contact Gary. He said a man had answered the phone, explained that Gary and I were not at home, and volunteered to take a message. The man said he was a friend of mine and that his name was Bob.

By reconstructing the events of the day, I was able to determine that Tony had called me at about 2:00 that afternoon. That's when the surprise came. I had been home all day, working at my desk. I had left the house only once, for about half an hour, and that was at about 2:00. Now, I always lock the house securely when I leave, and it was still locked when I returned. (To the best of my knowledge, burglars do not usually answer phone calls made to the houses they are robbing.) And where had I gone? I had driven to a friend's house, so we could call another friend who had just arrived in San Francisco that day—whose name was, naturally, Bob.

Coincidence, you might say. But the very same thing happened a few months later.

On this occasion I was home reading when Raymond called. "Didn't Gary give you my message to call back?" he asked brusquely. He sounded quite peeved, and once again, I didn't know what was going on. I had been home all day, except for about twenty minutes during which time I was out running an errand. No phone calls had come in, and Gary had left that morning for neighboring San Bernadino. He left at 7:00 a.m. and didn't return until evening. Yet Raymond kept insisting that he had called that afternoon and had spoken to my tenant. As he states in his deposition about the episode:

> I telephoned Mr. Scott Rogo about noon about a matter of some importance. I heard the receiver lifted and the voice of Gary, a student who was renting a room from Mr. Rogo, answered. He did not give

115

his name, but said that he was not Scott after I had asked if Scott was there. He replied that he was not at home, and when I asked him more than once to tell Scott that I had called and that the matter was important, he said that he would. I even suggested that he write my message down, but he answered that it was not necessary. As time passed no return call came.

Later that evening I again called, and Mr. Rogo answered. I was fairly angry and after I had asked, "Didn't Gary give you my message to call me back?" ... I was told that no call had been received.

As we started comparing times, it became apparent that Raymond had called during the precise twenty minutes that I was gone from the house. Yet there seemed to be no doubt that someone, imitating Gary's voice in an uncanny way, had intercepted the call. According to Raymond's report:

> The voice that answered me was in every respect like that of Gary's. I was familiar with Gary's voice, having spoken to him several times on the telephone. When he continued speaking to me, there was absolutely no doubt in my mind that he was answering me. In fact, I at first found it hard to accept that he really hadn't answered me, so realistic was the "voice."

Facts are facts, though. Raymond couldn't possibly have spoken to Gary, who was out of town that day. He had gone with a friend to donate blood to a blood bank operated by one of his friend's relatives. Just to prove all of this to Raymond (who was still miffed) and myself, I made Gary show me the dated receipt he had picked up in San Bernardino at the blood bank. Gary's friend also confirmed that they had spent the whole day there together.

So who answered the phone? We don't know, and we probably never will. Maybe it's more than coincidental that my friend Bob was due to arrive in town within a few days. In fact, I had left the house that afternoon in order to make arrangements for his arrival.

These two incidents certainly had an impact on Raymond and me, eventually prompting us to explore this aspect of the phantom phone call mystery in greater depth. To date, we've turned up relatively few "answer" cases. They seem even rarer than "intention" cases, but we did stumble onto two excellent cases in which normally placed phone calls were answered by the *dead*.

Further Elements of the Mystery

Gus Torkildson, a Wisconsin physician, reported a classic "answer'" case to the October 1976 issue of *Fate* magazine. The incident had occurred in February 1976 while he was driving cross-country with his wife and another couple. At 6:30 p.m. on February 12 the group stopped at a Benedictine Monastery in northwestern Missouri. As Torkildson explains:

> Since it was after six I felt the offices most likely would be closed and I went alone to the anteroom of the main building while the others waited in the car.
>
> There was no one around so I picked up the phone and dialed the business office, thinking that by some chance there might be someone there. The call was answered by a pleasant male voice.
>
> He asked to whom I wished to speak and I told him I was looking for the abbot.
>
> He answered, "This is Father Clement. You must call number 44 to reach the abbot."
>
> I called the number given me and the abbot appeared very soon and inquired how I had located him so quickly. I told him that I had dialed the business office and Fr. Clement had given me his number.
>
> He looked quite startled and asked again who I said had answered the phone.
>
> Again I told him, "Father Clement."
>
> He said, "Well, Father Clement used to be in charge of the switchboard but there is no one there now. Father Clement has been dead for several years."
>
> There was no other Father Clement in the monastery and although the abbot questioned all those persons attached to the office no one had answered the switchboard during that hour.

We immediately contacted Dr. Torkildson and he verified the *Fate* account for us personally. Unfortunately, the abbot at the monastery had been reassigned, so we couldn't get a statement from him about the incident. Dr. Torkildson is presently attempting to track him down, hoping to substantiate his story further.

What intrigues us about this case is the self-awareness possessed by the entity who answered the phone. "Father Clement" was apparently not locked into the time frame of years past when he lived at the monastery. He seemed well aware of what was going on at the monastery, knew where the abbot could be reached, and took on very human responsibilities quite naturally. In other words, the ghostly monk was well oriented toward *present* time.

It is also provocative that, to all appearances, the switchboard was not activated by Torkildson's call. This would indicate that somehow the call was intercepted by the answerer before it was connected. In other words, "Father Clement" didn't actually answer the call. Somehow, some force manipulated the phone lines as the doctor placed the call and produced a paraphysical voice inside the phone mechanism itself.

Many of these same features crop up in another case we investigated. The report was sent to us by Dr. Gertrude Schmeidler, one of this country's top parapsychologists who presently teaches psychology at the City College of the City University of New York. The incident had been reported to her by one of her students, for whose integrity Dr. Schmeidler was willing to vouch. The witness, whom we'll call Nora, was a little hesitant about discussing the experience and wished to remain anonymous, so Dr. Schmeidler interviewed the witness and passed her account on to us. It is a fascinating story, and in many respects matches some of the same phenomenology found in the Torkildson case.

Here is Nora's account, in all its bizarre detail:

> In the fall of 1969 my family moved to a farm in upstate New York. The farm was built in 1822 by a Swedish immigrant named Hansen, and had remained in the Hansen family until sold to us. Our neighbors, Ray and Barbara Rose [pseudonyms] had moved in eight years before. The houses are about a quarter-mile apart, and very similar in style. The Rose house was built in 1818 by the Duncan family, and the private burial ground was used by both Hansens and Duncans until 1893. Between 1969 and 1971 I spent very little time at the farm, since I was in college and worked during the summers.
>
> During the summer of 1971, I decided to stay in the country for a month while the rest of the family was away.
>
> With a friend, I spent a good deal of time getting acquainted with the neighbors and the countryside. The Roses were a great help, since Ray was a doctor and Barbara taught at the local school. We also spent several evenings with them, discussing theatre, since we had all worked in it at one time or another. We didn't discuss our houses or their histories.
>
> One morning, I came downstairs to find that the Roses' German shepherd was loose and was chasing our ducks. I dialed the Roses' number—the line was busy, so I hung up, checked the number, and

Further Elements of the Mystery

dialed again. This time the phone rang and was answered by an older woman's voice. I asked if Barbara were home, and the woman said no, she had gone to town.

At this point, I thought that Barbara's mother had probably come for an unexpected visit. Although Barbara had spoken of her mother, I had never met her, so I introduced myself, saying that I was next door at the old Hansen farm, and could she please call the dog, since he was attacking the ducks. The woman replied that the dog was with her, at her feet. I said that this was definitely Barbara's dog, the German shepherd. "But, dear," she answered, "Barbara doesn't have a dog. I have the dog, and he is a schnauzer, not a shepherd."

Not knowing what to do, I said that I'd call the other neighbors and check. As we hung up, she asked me to give her regards to Eliza and the girls, and to have Lavinia go over to pick up some preserves.

The reference to Eliza and Lavinia Hansen was disturbing, since Eliza had died many years before, and Lavinia was now 50—living in Washington State, where she had moved at the tender age of seventeen. There were few people in the valley who could have been contemporaries of Eliza Hansen and none were near enough to consider themselves neighbors.

I called the Roses again, thinking that I must have dialed the wrong number. Barbara answered at once. I told her what had just happened, and asked if she knew of anyone that I might have mistakenly reached who would fit the conversation. Barbara said that as far as she knew, there was only one person in the vicinity who might have known Eliza Hansen, and that she was a widow who had three German shepherds, and so was out of the question. The other real "old-timers," who lived much farther away, had avoided the Hansens because Mr. Hansen drank and had been known to become quite violent.

Barbara added that the conversation was particularly disturbing because the last owners of the Rose house had been the Duncan sisters, Mary and Barbara. According to the Duncan niece, from whom they had bought the house, the sisters had been very close to the Hansen women, and had been particularly fond of Eliza and Lavinia. Mary had had a schnauzer, who had been her constant companion, and whose remains were buried in the cemetery behind the barn. The coincidences between my phone call and the peculiar circumstances of the Hansen and Duncan households interested us both.

Since then, we have tried to discover anyone else in the vicinity who might have known the Hansens, had a relative named Barbara, and a pet schnauzer, but no one has turned up. It remains a coincidence that we can't explain.

Notice how Nora's call—just like Torkildson's—never reached its destination. Barbara was home when the call was made, yet her phone didn't ring. Instead, the call was intercepted and our witness carried on a lengthy and coherent conversation with a deceased woman who had once lived in Barbara's house. (Again, notice the overt similarities to the Torkildson case.) All the "coincidences" Nora cites in her report lead us to suspect that the deceased Mary Duncan did, in fact, answer the call. Unlike the voice of "Father Clement," though, "Mary" seemed wrapped up in the past of her own life. She thought Nora's call to Barbara was meant for her sister, and still thought of her little schnauzer as being "with her."

The phantom phone call mystery is composed of several elements, each just as puzzling and mind-boggling as the others. Since these "answer" cases are extremely rare, we don't have enough data to formulate any theory that can account for why or how they occur. But they do indicate that the intelligences behind the phantom phone call mystery can *selectively* affect electronic equipment in order to produce whatever effects or outcomes they wish. And if the dead can manipulate phones, there is no reason why they couldn't manipulate telegraphs, radios, amplifying equipment, and so on. We pointed this out in the preceding chapter, so perhaps now we should discuss the case for electronic communication with the dead and see how this wider perspective relates to the phantom phone call mystery.

8

Electronic Contact with the Dead: A Wider Perspective

There is a considerable log of evidence on hand substantiating our general theory that the dead can contact the living by simply manipulating electrical equipment. During the early years of the telegraph and wireless telegraphy, for instance, several operators in England discovered that spontaneous communications "from the dead" sometimes came over their equipment. Some of these messages were one-time occurrences whereas some operators apparently received long series of communications. Sometimes these phantom messages imparted information which no living person could have known. Reputedly, there were even frantic distress signals received from San Francisco throughout the United States a few hours *before* the devastating earthquake of 1906.

One can unearth many instances of instrumental contact with the dead by digging into parapsychology's rich history and literature. These cases, in turn, will help keep the phantom phone call mystery in proper perspective. If nothing more, they indicate that the "phone calls from the dead" phenomenon is probably only one of many mechanical ways the dead can reach us.

One of the first investigators ever to experimentally study electronic communication with the dead was David Wilson, a London solicitor who issued a number of reports on his experiments in 1915. Wilson was an amateur psychic investigator of sorts, as well as an amateur wireless operator. (A wireless is similar to a telegraph, except that it receives Morse code signals by radio waves instead of over wires.) He first became interested in the subject in 1913 when a friend of his mentioned that he had received curious signals while toying with his own wireless. Wilson's friend had apparently received intelligent signals over the device, which sometimes spelled out messages directly alluding to himself or to his family, *even after* he had disconnected its aerial receiving wire.

Eventually Wilson became so intrigued with his friend's report that he designed and built an apparatus that he felt might be particularly sensitive to the "ether waves" that were possibly mediating these mystery signals. In essence, it was a battery hooked to a detector sensitive to electrical influences which, in turn, was attached to a galvanometer—an apparatus that registers the presence and strength of an electric current. (Any current affecting the machine is registered by a needle set against a gradient chart.) After constructing the device, Wilson monitored it day after day to see if it would start registering any inexplicable influences.

He didn't have long to wait: "One day," Wilson reported to the March 13, 1915, issue of *Light*, "for no assignable reason the needle of the galvanometer gave a pronounced jerk. As the time went by and no other movement occurred, I supposed that perhaps in some way the table on which it stood had been shaken. When the evening came, however, the needle was again deflected on this occasion sharply and several times in succession."

Wilson did not immediately jump to the conclusion that the signals were any sort of psychic communication. His first suspicion was that they might have been due to any of several normal causes, including: (a) some subtle vibration in the room which he had not perceived; (b) an interference effect from a wireless unit transmitting in the neighborhood; (c) some bizarre effect caused by light waves; or (d) perhaps some undiscovered physical wave. Unfortunately, Wilson was not able to isolate the source of these needle movements, since after this initial success the unit lapsed into a blissful quiescence for over a week.

Several days later, however, the needle again started registering the mysterious signals, but this time it moved in patterned responses. It would successively deflect four times, with the fourth jerk noticeably longer than the preceding ones. These group deflections kept recurring one after another in rapid sequence for six minutes before the machine deactivated itself. Since random tremors in the room could not account for

Electronic Contact with the Dead: A Wider Perspective

the consistency of these deflection patterns, Wilson naturally concluded that something rather unusual was going on! And it was at this stage of his research that he made his major breakthrough: He began wondering if the deflections he had witnessed constituted Morse code signals.

Wilson's suspicions were confirmed three days later (on June 10, 1915) when the needle of his galvanometer activated for eight continuous minutes, deflecting in a series of short and long movements. Translated into Morse alphabet, they spelled out the message, "Great difficulty; await message, five days, six evenings." In his report, Wilson readily admitted that "this was [given] in a very mutilated form, of which, however, I have given the general sense." Wilson also realized that he should have an independent observer at hand who could verify reception of this promised message should it actually come through. As he writes in his report:

> Before the time arrived I invited to my house a very reliable witness, whose testimony could be trusted to carry weight, and suggested that between then and the time appointed the witness should learn the Morse alphabet, at any rate to be able to check letters if they were given slowly by the deflections of the galvanometer.
>
> When the day arrived I felt extremely dubious as to the outcome of the affair, because the vibrations of the needle seemed to have degenerated into utter incoherence, such as one might imagine would be created by vibration from ordinary causes if such a thing had been feasible.
>
> I was astounded, therefore, when at 6.4 p.m. [sic] by my watch the dial once more recorded slowly and unmistakably the Morse call signal, which it continued to do for nearly half an hour.
>
> At 6.31 the dial recorded the following letters by Morse, which were taken down independently both by myself and the witness to whom I have referred, and of which the following are word for word versions:—
>
> Version by witness:—
> TRZELIOININAMEVIVRATIMNS.
> 2. My version:—
> RYELIMINA-E-BRA-IONS—ARTK
>
> These two versions were taken down quite independently of each other. From a comparison of them both it is obvious that wherever the message came from it could only mean one thing, namely:—
>
> "Try eliminate vibrations. ARTK."

The fact that the observer recorded a somewhat different version of the message does not strike us as strange. Wilson was apparently only an amateur wireless operator, and his friend had learned the Morse alphabet only in the brief days before the experiment. Under these conditions, one would expect a certain amount of imprecision from the witnesses.

Wilson was at first confused by the message, but eventually got the gist of it (that his methods were too unfocussed) and modified his apparatus by linking it to a human subject. As he explains:

> I inserted into the circuit a Morse key which was to be operated by someone after the manner of automatic writing. This it seemed to me could in no wise affect the origin of messages given by the galvanometer because the person, so to speak, inserted in the circuit could himself do nothing by depressing his key, for the circuit would be still broken at the detector which would be absolutely beyond his power of affecting. At the same time any chance or incoherent atmospheric disturbances which might affect the detector would accomplish nothing, for then the circuit would be broken at the Morse key. It could not possibly happen that the person should depress his key consciously when the detector was affected because he would know nothing about it. Therefore, the only possible way in which the message could come through the receiver would be by means of an agency which could *not only affect the new detector but also the brain of the (so to speak) "circuit person."* Moreover, these actions would have to be synchronous before the needle of the galvanometer would deflect.

Wilson procured several lengthy communications by using this method. Their contents, though, were usually banal, and Wilson gave only a few examples of them in his first 1915 report.

During the next several months Wilson reconstructed his apparatus several times and made two important modifications. He did away with the deflecting needle of the galvanometer, and instead hooked the apparatus to a device that translated all incoming signals into audible "bleeps" representing Morse dots and dashes. By this time, he also fully realized that somehow he was communicating with at least some sort of independent intelligence, but was far from sure that he had established communication with the dead. He was more prone to believe that perhaps he was picking up telepathic signals from some anonymous source that were registering on the "psychic ether" to which his machine was particularly sensitive.

Electronic Contact with the Dead: A Wider Perspective

To test his theory, Wilson had a friend in Paris construct a duplicate apparatus in order to determine if both machines, properly attuned though separated by a considerable distance, would pick up the *same* psychic messages. And on occasion, indeed they did. At 11:10 p.m. on March 19, 1916, Wilson's machine spelled out the message: "Nyet leezdyes Kogoneedbood kto govoreet poroosky." Translated from Russian, the message reads: "Is there anyone who speaks Russian here?" Six minutes later, the machine in Paris picked up a distorted fragment of the same message. Wilson's friend, knowing nothing of what his colleague had received, recorded: "Nyet ... lee ... (incoherent) ... kto ... porooski."

After publishing his experiments in *Light*, Wilson dropped from sight. He never published another word about his experiments, nor did any of his contemporaries or critics ever attempt to replicate them.

Wilson's experiments were a strange combination of the scientific and the bizarre. Judging by his reports, he was certainly a keen and careful experimenter. But was he really receiving communications from the dead? That is one reasonable solution to the mystery, but it also seems possible that he may have been psychic and capable of affecting his own equipment psychokinetically. This was a possibility that Wilson never considered in his reports. Remember that Wilson carried out his novel experiments before and during World War I, long before parapsychologists discovered how widespread PK abilities are. In Wilson's time, most people believed that only rare and gifted individuals possessed this unique and wonderful power. We now know differently. We know that many people without any overt psychic ability can use PK to random number generators, oscillators, magnetometers, projected light beams, and other delicate instruments. It doesn't strike us as too unfeasible, then, that Wilson may have been psychically contaminating his own experiments without even appreciating the possibility.

The results of the London-Paris experiments are harder to explain so simply, though. There are, nonetheless, two ways Wilson could have produced the results himself. He might have: (1) used PK to affect his own machine and then affected the Paris apparatus by long-distance PK, or (2) affected his instrument psychically and then telepathically infected his Paris friend, who thereupon used his own PK to influence the duplicate machine. All this, of course would have been transacted at an unconscious level.

While possible, both these theories strike us as grossly unparsimonious! Both pose more questions than they answer. Why were some of the messages received in Russian? Did Wilson understand or speak this difficult language? If not, this particular message could not have emanated from his own mind.

It is hard for us to accept either of the above explanations for several other reasons as well. First, PK is a very imprecise faculty over which most of us have very little control. It is hard to believe that Wilson could have had enough unconscious control over his PK to "send" it to Paris, set up a series of electrical signals capable of affecting his friend's apparatus, and then make it spell out precise letter sequences that matched those he had produced over his own machine. Admittedly, his friend's signals were weak and fragmented. But notice that *all* the letter sequences received in Paris were virtually identical to *portions* of the message transcribed in London. It is also hard to believe that Wilson's friend merely received a telepathic message from his colleague and then translated it by PK over his own machine. ESP signals, are, again, usually very imprecise and usually fragmented, symbolized, and distorted, and often are converted into mental imagery as they are processed by our minds and brains. Unless Wilson was a super psychic, it is improbable that his friend could have so consistently picked up specific words telepathically.

Despite the complexity of the messages he received, Wilson himself never concluded that they emanated from the dead. Apparently, most of the messages were never "signed," nor did they specifically appear to be coming from the dead. Though obviously addressed to him, they were just random but intelligent messages, and Wilson continued to believe that he had merely stumbled onto a way by which telepathic signals traveling through the air could be monitored mechanically.

Wilson's theory leaves several aspects of his own data unexplained, though. Why, for instance, were the messages obviously addressed to him? And if Wilson wasn't himself producing the signals, who was? One clue may have come during the Paris-London test. Wilson's friend received his communication six minutes after the matching communication was registered in England. To all intents and purposes, it looks as though some *independent* intelligence was first trying to influence Wilson's machine and then, after completing the task, proceeded to influence the Paris machine. These messages could well have come from the dead, but the ultimate solution to the Wilson mystery will always remain a question mark.In the 1960's, however, one partial confirmation of the "Wilson effect" was announced. In September 1962 Mark Dyne, a technical editor for a major British electrical company, gave an interview to the Manchester (England)

Evening Chronicle in which he admitted that he had been investigating telegraphic contact with the dead for several years. His techniques were roughly similar to Wilson's. "With a Morse buzzer and lamp," he told reporters, "and with 'Positive' and 'Negative' panels of copper gauze wired into an amplifier, we set about detecting psycho-physical forces, or the movement of spiritual energy in the atmosphere. On the panels we got a series of tremors." The flashing light, Dyne said, spelled out "Good Luck" and "A new age has commenced." He also told reporters that he was just then completing a major report on the project, but to the best of our knowledge, none was ever issued.

During the early years of telegraphy there were many similar instances published by radio operators who believed that they had received communications from the beyond. These incidents apparently were so frequent that they gave one writer an idea for a most enterprising hoax. In 1918 the prestigious Boston publishing firm of Little, Brown issued a curious and anonymously written book entitled *Thy Son Liveth*. (The author was a Mrs. L. N. Geldert, but this fact wasn't revealed until 1927.) The book consisted chiefly of transcripts made from Morse code communications which the author claimed she had received from her deceased son, Bob, over a *disengaged* wireless. The lad had been killed during the Great War which was still raging in Europe at the time. The story line of the book was sentimental, if somewhat corny. According to Mrs. Geldert, the boy had always been an avid wireless enthusiast, and after his induction she had kept his set intact (though disengaged from operation). Then, she claimed, one day while reading some letters from her son the inoperable wireless began signaling. It spelled out a message from the boy in Morse code announcing that he had been killed at the front. Mrs. Geldert claimed that afterwards she received dozens of such messages.

The book created quite a sensation, but was heartily condemned by two prominent psychical researchers of the day. Soon after its publication Professor James H. Hyslop, the director of the American Society for Psychical Research, and W. Franklin Prince, his assistant and later his successor, both wrote scathing attacks on the book. Although their conclusion that the book was a hoax was no doubt correct, much of their reasoning was less than fair, and was based on several personal biases. Hyslop's critique is a good case in point. Shortly after the book appeared, Hyslop sent Little, Brown a series of questions about the book, requesting that they be forwarded to the author. When Mrs. Geldert declined to answer his queries, Hyslop apparently became infuriated, and his review, more a cry of righteous indignation than a reasoned critique, talks more about the refusal than the book itself. This was typical of Hyslop in many respects. Although a great pioneering figure in American parapsychology, he had his shortcomings. If a psychic wouldn't cooperate with him, or if he couldn't gain entry into a case, he easily became annoyed.

Prince's major points are hardly any better than Hyslop's. Prince had a keenly analytical mind, but had a propensity for tossing off armchair criticism in an *ex cathedra* manner. The crux of his argument against the book was that it concerned instrumental contact with the dead—a possibility which he just couldn't buy!

Despite their often misguided criticisms, though, both Hyslop and Prince did make one valid point: The alleged communications from "Bob" were blatantly ridiculous. They pointed out that his descriptions of the European war contained a horrendous amount of inaccuracies and absurdities. For instance, Bob described nurses tending the wounded at the front. This was hardly the case, since the gallant Florence Nightingales of World War I were always kept safely behind the lines. Several other similar ridiculous communications could be cited. The descriptions of the war contained in the book actually seem to be nothing more than the author's patchwork guesses about how she *expected* a battle to look. Unfortunately, she was wrong more often than right.

Of course, it is possible that Mrs. Geldert had produced the messages by unconsciously activating her son's wireless psychokinetically. Hyslop and Prince never considered this possibility, even though it does seem quite unlikely. The sheer volume of the communications would tend to indicate a hoax and as more than one skeptic pointed out, the messages received from "Bob" were written in a literary style virtually identical to those sections of the book authored by Mrs. Geldert herself.

We don't really know very much about Mrs. Geldert, nor even if she had a son killed in the war. But if she did, she was certainly able to mourn her way to the bank. Her book sold over 31,000 copies when first issued and it was republished during the height of World War II.

The grueling years of World War I also encouraged quite a bit of genuine experimentation into the possibility that electronic contact could be established with the dead. Several researchers even claimed to have successfully made contact with the *voices* of the dead over a host of odd equipment. Most of these claims were dismissed as fraudulent at the time, but can we be so sure? Our research into the "phone calls from the dead" mystery indicates that there may have been more fire under the proverbial smoke than anyone has ever suspected.

In 1921 F. R. Melton, a Nottingham (England) inventor and psychic investigator, kicked up a considerable stir in the pages of *Light* when he claimed that he had actually invented a "psychic telephone." The instrument was simple in design—merely a telephone apparatus hooked to an amplifier and placed in a small box. Yet Melton claimed that time and time again, he had received voices directly from the dead over his machine. He contributed three articles to Light in 1921, and later that year issued a short, illustrated booklet, *A Psychic Telephone*, in which he gave more details about the device and its construction.

Melton's articles were enthusiastically published, and the British College of Psychic Science, a privately run spiritualist organization, publicly encouraged other would-be experimenters to replicate Melton's work. But very few psychic researchers of the day took him seriously, even though Melton himself states in his booklet that he had "received letters from all parts of the world" about his invention. The only attempt that we know of to replicate these experiments were conducted in the United States by Hereward Carrington over ten years later. Carrington was one of this country's most talented psychical investigators and was the founder of the New York-based American Psychical Institute. (The Institute later moved to Los Angeles, where it was ultimately disbanded because of a lack of funds.) Carrington built a partial replica of the Melton telephone but, as he reports in his *Laboratory Investigations into Psychic Phenomena*, "no results were obtained as the result of repeated experiments." In all fairness to Melton, though, it should be pointed out that Carrington's phone was a revised version of the original instrument, and not an exact replica.

Carrington never really took Melton's work seriously, a fact that is obvious from the tone he adopts when discussing it. Neither did we ourselves, at first. But, after stumbling across the phantom phone call mystery, we began to suspect that perhaps Melton was neither the crackpot nor the charlatan history would have us believe. It was with considerable interest that we started collecting copies of all Melton's published work, and, as a result of our research, we made some curious historical discoveries.

First of all, Melton did not invent his spirit telephone entirely on his own, as historians have always assumed. The initial impetus came from his son George, who had been a wireless operator during World War I. While out in the field, George had often received odd, disjointed messages over his instrument, and although he had never been able to isolate their source, the young soldier had often wondered if these messages were emanating from the dead. After young Melton sustained battle injuries, he was relieved of active duty but continued to serve his country as a lecturer in wireless and telephone operations at a military training school. During this time he once again became interested in the possibility of instrumental contact with the dead. But not until after the war did the Meltons decide to explore this possibility in any depth. Their interest was reawakened in 1920 when several British newspapers started reporting that wireless stations across the country were picking up "strange and unaccountable" signals. Outer space communications were at first suspected. Around this time, too, young Melton discovered that he had mediumistic powers. While attending a seance, he unexpectedly went into trance himself. An entity named W. G. announced his presence and began communicating details about the design for a "spirit" telephone that would help amplify one's psychic abilities.

It has also been assumed that Melton believed his telephone was a "mechanical medium", not dependent on any human operator. Yet in his writings Melton states quite clearly that his psychic telephone was not a mechanical medium, nor did he really claim that just *anyone* could procure results through it. He maintained only that the instrument could *amplify* psychic voices otherwise beyond the sensitivity of the human ear. Melton's first device, for instance, was designed especially to *amplify his son's independent voices*, much the same as Raymond Bayless accidentally discovered that the tape recorder helped amplify von Szalay's.

It is rather clear in reading Melton's booklet that George's presence was necessary before the telephone could function, at least at first. Melton soon revised his instrument, however, hoping in part to circumvent this problem.

Melton's original telephone was merely a 23-inch-long aluminum tube, three inches in diameter at one end and eight at the other, in which was placed a receiver and an amplifier. A telephonelike headset was attached to the receiver, over which the voices could be heard delivering faint messages to the experimenters. (Note how similar this apparatus is to the one Raymond used when first testing von Szalay. The parallel is so close that we are tempted to believe that through the agency of his son's psychic abilities, Melton was in fact receiving psychic voices similar to the ones von Szalay can produce.) It was later that Melton

Electronic Contact with the Dead: A Wider Perspective

constructed his famous "spirit telephone" which he described in such detail in his booklet. The key ingredient was a balloon, which was blown up with a medium's breath and placed within the circuitry of the device. Melton believed that the "psychic ether" contained in the balloon would automatically help amplify the voices or act as a "sounding board" for them so that anyone, psychic or not, could receive these faint voices in the comfort of his own home. Melton ultimately did away with the original metal tube, and the transmitter and balloon were placed instead in a small 12-inch-square box, where the transmitter was attached to a telephone receiver and several batteries.

Melton maintained, though, that the telephone still worked best if a psychic were present and touching the box. He claimed that through the agency of his son's psychic abilities he had received very distinct voices over the instrument.

Although Carrington failed to replicate these results, we don't feel that Melton's work should be merely dismissed. His methods and results were very similar to those Raymond achieved and used with von Szalay. The parallels are too close to be ignored. In all likelihood, Melton probably did produce some genuine results with his apparatus, just as von Szalay, Jurgenson, and Raudive have today. But the mitigating factor was probably George Melton's psychic abilities, not the telephone itself.

At around the same time, another psychic telephone was developed in the United States by the well-known author Francis Grierson. Few people (including his biographers) know that besides being an important American literary figure, he was also a psychic and medium who gave many demonstrations in Europe under the name of Jesse Shepard. After his retirement, Grierson invented some sort of telephonic device over which he apparently received several postmortem communications. These tests are described in a short book, *Psychophone Messages*, which he privately published in Los Angeles in 1921. (Since we have not yet been able to locate a copy of this publication, we can offer little information about his work.) Grierson lived the rest of his life in Southern California and died there in 1927. His huge Victorian home in San Diego is now a city monument open to the public; but his psychic work is nearly forgotten.

Below is a diagram of the telephone adapted from Melton's booklet:

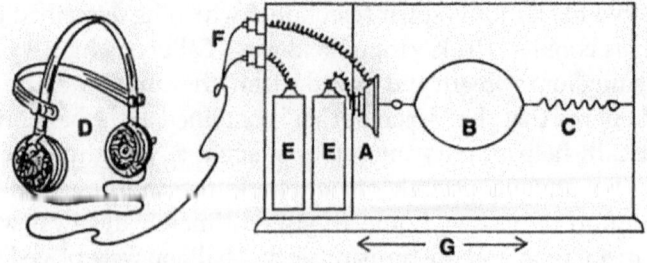

A—Transmitter
B—Balloon.
C—Tension Spring.
D—Receivers, with Head Piece.
E—Dry Cell Battery.
F—Terminals, or Connections for Receivers to Transmitter.
G—Box or Cabinet.

Yet another psychic telephone showed up in the 1940's. In 1957 *Psychic News*, a British spiritualist weekly, reported that a Dutch experimenter by the name of N. Zwann showed up in England in 1947 with plans for a spirit radio. Zwann claimed that he had received the plans and circuitry for the device through mediumistic communications. Having little personal background in electronics, he had come to England hoping that someone there would help him construct the instrument. An apparatus was allegedly built and, according to the *Psychic News* report, the experimenters achieved considerable success with it. However, no public demonstrations or reports were ever made or issued, and nothing has been heard of Zwann's psychic radio again. He, like so many other would-be inventors, disappeared from the psychic scene as mysteriously as he entered it.

A device similar to the Melton telephone also surfaced during the 1940's. It was developed by Harry Gardner and his associate, J. Gilbert Wright, who was for years a researcher for the General Electric Company. Gardner was a spiritualist of sorts and believed he had developed an instrument that could amplify psychic voices. Like Melton, Gardner did not maintain that his apparatus was a mechanical medium, but claimed that it could nonetheless act as a *channel* for paraphysical voices when placed in the presence of a suitable psychic. The device was simple enough, consisting of a 24-inch by 7-inch box, lined with soundproofing. A small hole was drilled in one side, and inside was placed a microphone that led to a loudspeaker. Later, Gardner revised his working model by adding finely reduced iron along with a puttylike substance to the lining of the box to make it magnetic. Some initial experiments were conducted with a psychic by the name of Margaret Lewis. Gardner and Wright claimed that even though the device was placed several feet away from the medium, voices immediately issued through the loudspeaker.

It really isn't hard to believe that the Gardner-Wright experiments were successful. Once again, their methods and findings seem almost identical to Raymond's early work with von Szalay. Unfortunately, Gardner and Wright never continued with their experiments, and Wright retired from the psychic scene altogether before his death in 1959.

When Melton, Grierson, Zwann, Wright, and others invented their machines, they all apparently had the same goal in mind. Each wanted to develop a method by which imperceptible paraphysical voice-effects could be amplified and made audible. A few psychics, however, can produce psychic voices of such volume that no complex apparatus is needed to intensify them. Some of von Szalay's voices are quite audible to the human ear, but a few psychics have had powers even more astounding. It appears that any type of simple device, such as a metal enclosure or tube, will help generate these voices as long as a suitable psychic is in attendance.

The American Society for Psychical Research became interested in one such case in 1906. The psychic was an elderly, crippled woman named Elizabeth Blake, who lived in the small rural town of Broderick, Ohio. Mrs. Blake could produce the von Szalay type of voices in daylight by merely taking two aluminum cones (wide at one end and narrow at the other), placing their large ends together, and holding the tubes in her hand and up to her ear. Voices would sometimes emanate from them which could be easily heard by anyone in the room. The case first came to the A.S.P.R.'s attention through the efforts of David Abbott, one of the foremost magicians of his day. Aside from being an expert conjuror, Abbott was also harshly skeptical of psychic phenomena and even wrote a scathing book, *Behind the Scenes with the Mediums*, which remains today a classic volume on psychic fraud. Unlike many magicians, though, Abbott did have an open mind. In March 1906 he received a letter from another well-known magician describing his own experiments with Mrs. Blake. Abbott was so impressed by his colleague's testimony that he decided to organize an investigation and recruited James Hyslop of the A.S.P.R. and his own cousin and fellow skeptic, George Clawson, for the project. The results of their amazing investigation were published by the A.S.P.R. in 1913 in a 200-page report.

The investigators carried out their first tests with Mrs. Blake the very day of their arrival at the elderly woman's country home. All of them visited her together under assumed names. Mrs. Blake asked a few questions, and immediately proceeded to give them a demonstration by taking her two trusty aluminum horns, placing them mouth to mouth, and holding them in her hand. She then encouraged the experimenters to listen through the opening at the far end of the tube. Clawson was the first to test the psychic. To quote Abbott's account:

> Mr. Clawson now seated himself beside the lady, and she instructed him to take one end of the trumpet in his palm, while she did the same with the other end.
>
> In a moment Mr. Clawson remarked, "How heavy that is getting!" and as he did so, I thought I heard a faint whisper in the end of the trumpet that Mr. Clawson was holding. It was, however, so faint that I could not be certain of it. It was more like a single syllable, the drawing of a breath, or like a hissing sound, but it was very indistinct. In a moment the trumpet began to rise toward Mr. Clawson's ear, and the lady said, "Someone wants to speak to you, sir; place the trumpet to your ear." He did so, and she placed the other end to her ear.
>
> Whispered voices in the trumpet now began to address Mr. Clawson, but from the outside I could not understand what was said. Mr. Clawson seemed unable to do much better, and it appeared that the sitting would prove a failure on this account. Mrs. Blake now spoke and said, "Please try and speak plainly, dear friend, so that the gentleman can understand you." The voice now seemed to become more distinct, and Mr. Clawson asked the question, "Who are you?" He did not appear to understand the reply; for he repeated his question a few times, as one does at a poorly working telephone. Finally I heard him say, "You say you are my brother Eddie?" Mr. Clawson seemed confused at being unable to understand the many whispered words in the spoken sentences; and turning to me, he said, "You take the trumpet and see if you can understand any better."

Abbott watched Mrs. Blake's mouth carefully all through the demonstration and was sure she never opened it while the voices were speaking. Although he didn't understand the allusion to the name "Eddie," he later learned that Clawson had a deceased brother by that name.

Abbott himself took up the trumpet immediately afterwards and heard a voice speak in a loud whisper. "I am your brother and I want to talk to Mother. Tell her ... " Abbott encouraged the failing voice to speak further, and it continued, "Tell her that I love her." A few more sentences were uttered from the horn, but Abbott could make little sense of them. But then:

> I now handed the trumpet to Mr. Clawson, and the voice kept repeating, "I want to talk to my brother," so he gave the trumpet back to me.
>
> "Whom do you want to talk to?" I asked.
>
> "I want to talk to my brother Davie—brother Davie Abbott," responded the voice. I could hear the name "Abbott" repeated several times after this, and then the voice finally ceased.
>
> Mr. Clawson now took the trumpet. I may remark that although Mr. Clawson's parents, and also a little son who was never named, were dead, his whole heart was set on obtaining a communication from his daughter Georgia, who had recently died; and unless he could do this, the whole sitting was a failure as far as he was concerned. This daughter had been very affectionate, and had always called her mother by the pet names of "Muz" and "Muzzie." She also generally called her father "Daddie," in a playful way. She had recently graduated from a school of dramatic art, and while there had become affianced to a young gentleman whose Christian name is "Archimedes." He is usually called "Ark" for short. Mr. Clawson had these facts in mind, intending to use them as a matter of identification.
>
> A voice now addressed Mr. Clawson, saying, "I am your brother."
>
> "Who else is there? Any of my relatives?" asked Mr. Clawson.
>
> "Your mother is here," responded the voice.
>
> "Your baby."
>
> "Let the baby speak and give its name," requested Mr. Clawson.
>
> This is followed by many indistinct words that could not be understood. Finally a name was pronounced that Mr. Clawson understood to be "Edna." He had no child of that name; but in what followed, although his lips addressed the name "Edna," his whole mind addressed his daughter, "Georgia."
>
> "Edna, if you are my daughter, tell me what was your pet name for me?" he asked.
>
> "I called you Daddie," the voice replied.
>
> "What was your pet name for your mother?"
>
> "I called her Muz, and sometimes Muzzie," responded the voice.

"What is my name?" asked Mr. Clawson, but the reply was so indistinct that it could not be understood.

These prolonged conversations continued over the several sessions Abbott and Hyslop had with the psychic. Often the voices became so loud that they could be heard clearly across a large room, and on rare occasion they even *sounded exactly like* the voices the "communicators" had possessed while still alive!

Abbott, Hyslop, and Clawson witnessed some of these spectacular effects during the second day of their investigation. For this particular demonstration Mrs. Blake sat in a darkened room, since she felt the dark helped conserve energy. The procedure seemed to work; her voices were louder and able to sustain themselves for longer periods of time. They were not whispered articulations, but often powerful tonal voices. They seemed very well aware of who Abbott and Clawson were, called them by their proper names, and communicated details about both their living and deceased relatives. But the major surprise of the day came when the "voices" announced that one of Abbott's deceased uncles was present and wished to communicate. Again, to cite Abbott's eyewitness testimony:

> "Well, I am here," spoke a man's voice near the table top in a few moments.
> "If you are our uncle, give us your name," I requested.
> "Dave, I am Uncle Dave," now spoke the voice. We had an uncle whose Christian name was "David Patterson," and who was dead.
> "If you are Uncle Dave, tell me your second name," I requested. The voice pronounced a name that resembled "Parker." It began with the letter "P," but we could not understand what followed.
> "Dave, you were named after me," continued the voice.
> "What is your last name?" I asked. This was "Abbott"; but the voice replied with an inarticulate sentence, in which we distinguished the name "Harvey." My uncle Richard Harvey and the uncle whose voice this purported to be, were quite intimate many years ago.
> One remarkable feature of the voice which claimed to be that of my uncle David, was that it resembled his voice when alive, to an extent *sufficient to call to my mind a mental picture of his appearance;* and for an instant to give me that inner feeling of his presence that hearing a well-known voice always produced in one.

Hyslop and his co-workers sat with Mrs. Blake several times over the next few days. The more they sat, the better the results they achieved, and by the end of their stay, the voices were issuing one after the other from the trumpet in rapid succession. Sometimes the investigators would even challenge the "voices" with test questions—about their deceased relatives or friends about whom Mrs. Blake could have no normal knowledge—and the voices would often answer correctly within moments. For instance, the following communications addressed to Clawson constitute some of the most impressive records transcribed during the experiments. Even though he was skeptical of mediums in general, Clawson had hoped to receive some communications from his deceased daughter, Georgia. He was beginning to get downhearted at the course of the tests when Georgia finally did communicate, and it would appear that her fiancé Archimedes was still very much on her mind. To quote from Abbott's account once again:

When next he raised the trumpet to his ear a whispered voice said, "'Daddie, I am here."
"Who are you?" asked Mr. Clawson.
"Georgia," replied the voice.
"Georgia? Georgia, is this really you?" asked Mr. Clawson, with intense emotion and earnestness.
"Yes, Daddie. Didn't you think I knew my own name?" asked the voice.
"I thought you did, Georgia, but could not understand why you would not tell it to me. Where do we live, Georgia?"
"In Kansas City," responded the voice, and then continued, "Daddie, I am so glad to talk to you, and so glad you came here to see me. I wish you could see my beautiful home. We have flowers and music every day."
"Georgia, what is the name of your sweetheart to whom you were engaged?" now asked Mr. Clawson.
"_ _ _." The reply could not be understood.
"Georgia, spell the name," requested Mr. Clawson.
"A-r—c, Ark," responded the voice, spelling out the letters and then pronouncing the name.
"Give me his full name, Georgia," requested Mr. Clawson.
"Archimedes," now responded the voice.
"Will you spell the name for me?" asked Mr. Clawson who wished to prevent a misinterpretation of sounds.
"A-r-c-h-i-m-e-d-e-s," spelled the voice.

"Where is Ark, Georgia?" now asked Mr. Clawson. The reply could not be understood, but an inarticulate sentence was spoken ending with a word which sounded like "Denver."

"Do you say he is in Denver, Georgia?" asked Mr. Clawson.

"No, no," responded the voice loudly and almost vocally, and then continued, "He is in New York." This, Mr. Clawson afterwards informed me, was correct; but he thought the gentleman was at the time out of New York City, though somewhere in that state.

Remember that these voices were issuing from a simple tube in full light, while Mrs. Blake was being carefully watched for ventriloquism by one of the most famous magicians in the country.

Hyslop and Abbott left Ohio both excited and puzzled by their investigations. Hyslop readily conceded that Mrs. Blake had communicated information that she could not have possibly possessed normally, but he could never resolve to his own satisfaction whether her voices were truly paraphysical effects. Although he had not detected Mrs. Blake making any ventriloquist-like movements during her feats, he did notice that at times the psychic's throat muscles tensed when the voices were speaking. Abbott tended to concur with him. Although initially impressed by the quality of Mrs. Blake's voices, he eventually developed the rather curious theory that the psychic had ventriloquized the sounds by talking out of her ears! Abbott never offered any evidence supporting his rather farfetched theory; nor did he ever explain how these "ventriloquized" articulations were so ingeniously produced that they actually mimicked the voices some of the communicators possessed while alive.* Abbott did, though, end his report by admitting that he could not explain how the voices knew so much about his personal life and his relatives.

The strange case of Mrs. Blake does not, of course, represent an instance of *instrumental* contact with the dead, but we've discussed it in some detail because it bears intimately on the whole problem of tape and telephone-voice phenomena. If a psychic such as von Szalay or Mrs. Blake can act as a channel through which paraphysical voices

---

* Mrs. Blake was not the only psychic of yesteryear who could apparently produce these paraphysical voices in full light. There were several others in the United States and in Great Britain, though few of them were ever tested as comprehensively as Mrs. Blake. For a history of this curious form of mediumship, see a Bayless's Voices from Beyond (Secaucus, N.J.: University Books, 1976).

are able to precipitate out of thin air, why couldn't they manifest spontaneously over tape recorders and telephones as well? The case of Mrs. Blake serves as another line of evidence that direct-voice contact with the dead might be more common than anyone has ever believed.

Paraphysical voice-effects do not occur merely over telephones and on electromagnetic tape. During our investigations we ran into cases of similar mystery voices speaking over radio receivers, TV's, a CB radio in one instance, and even over record player amplifiers. We collected no fewer than three instances of these record player voices, which constitute even further evidence that the dead can communicate with the living by producing "prints" of their own terrestrial voices over electrical equipment.

Zoë Richmond is a grand old lady of parapsychology. Now a stately, white-haired woman of 90, she retired from the psychic scene years ago. During her prime, though, she was an active investigator for the London-based Society for Psychical Research and author of a classic book on survival after death, *Evidence of Purpose*. Her husband, Kenneth Richmond, was a highly respected psychical investigator in his own right. Mrs. Richmond has harbored a lifelong interest in the subject of instrumental contact with the dead; in the 1920's she even received plans for such a machine through a medium she was studying. She built the device, but it didn't work. One day several years later, however, both Mr. and Mrs. Richmond suddenly witnessed a spontaneously established momentary contact with at least *something* over their Gramophone.

"My husband and I were listening to a solo singer on the Gramophone singing a well-known song which we had often heard before," Mrs. Richmond wrote us in answer to a query about her research. "Suddenly the singer was joined by another most beautiful soprano voice, singing a part with him to the end—to our great astonishment! We immediately put the record on again, but no voice came [through] ever again. My husband, Kenneth Richmond, had a correspondence about all this with Sir Oliver Lodge** and the makers of the record, but no explanation was forthcoming."

Mrs. Richmond's experience is not an isolated incident. In their book, Beyond Biofeedback, Dr. Elmer Green and his wife Alyce describe a similar incident. Dr., Green is director of the Voluntary Controls

---

** Sir Oliver Lodge was a celebrated physicist and also one of Great Britain's leading psychical researchers. See W. P. Jolly, Sir Oliver Lodge (London: Constable and Co., 1974).

Program at the Topeka-based Menninger Foundation, where for several years he has pioneered research into biofeedback and autogenic training techniques. In their book, the Greens also discuss their early involvement with psychic studies. As a young man, while studying the psychic abilities of Dr. Will Erwood (a psychic and spiritual teacher in Minneapolis), Green and a small group of acquaintances ran into paraphysical effects similar to the one Mrs. Richmond described to us. Their weekly get-togethers usually began with music, provided by records played over an old wind-up Gramophone.

I was responsible for winding it up," writes Green, "and handling the one record we used at the beginning of meetings. On occasion it would emit voices in addition to the instrumental music, sometimes with oddly distorted music as a background, sometimes alone, and sometimes the voices were distorted."

In a letter to us dated May 3, 1978, Dr. Green verified the account in his book and explained that the voices came directly through the amplifier, although they were often distorted. Dr. Green told us that the voices explained that they were basically interested in demonstrating how they could affect electronic devices. The theory that these effects are merely *demonstrations*, rather than seriously planned or urgent communications, is totally consistent with some of the viewpoints Raymond and I have developed as a result of our own research.

Dr. Green is by no means the only investigator who has witnessed an entire series of these "demonstrations." His experiences are almost identical to some reports included in a strange little book entitled *The Blue Room* published in 1927. The book, written by Clive Chapman, a New Zealand businessman, chronicles his experiments with his niece, Miss Pearl Judd, who was a gifted psychic. Chapman, like Green, notes that when the girl sat down to play the piano, psychic voices often emanated from the horn of her Gramophone.

While we have little to say about this curious phenomenon, it does seem as though these articulations are somehow produced through the manipulations of sound waves generated by music. Just how, we'll probably never know.

A related incident was once reported by the secretary of the late Edgar Wallace. Wallace was one of the most popular mystery writers of his day, perhaps rivaled only by Arthur Conan Doyle of Sherlock Holmes fame. In his work Wallace used an old 78 r.p.m. record cutter. Shortly after his death in 1932, his secretary cut a disc on it. While replaying the disc she was shocked to hear her late employer's voice speaking a

Electronic Contact with the Dead: A Wider Perspective

few words. No one took her story seriously at the time, but the incident may have been a precursor of the taped-voice effect.

While on the subject of anomalous voice effects, we might as well answer one question we are often asked: Have any of these telephone-like voices ever been recorded over an automatic answering device? So far, we have heard of two such cases. One instance was, in our estimation, a hoax, but the other case is more interesting. A British investigator of our acquaintance claimed that a friend of his once found a "telephone message from the dead" recorded on his answering machine, but he refused to give us any further details about the incident.

Apart from those using telephonic devices, there were several other attempts made during the early years of parapsychology (roughly, 1900-1930) to prove that the dead could manipulate electrical or mechanical gadgetry without the mediary of a gifted psychic. One of the most concerted efforts to achieve purely instrumental contact with the dead was carried out in Holland by Dr. J. L. Matla and Dr. G. J. Zaalbert van Zelst, both trained physicists, who initiated their research in 1904. Both scientists had spent considerable time investigating psychics and mediums in their hometown of The Hague, and their various inventions were the direct outcome of their field investigations. Apparently, most of their equipment was designed from rough blueprints actually given them through the psychics they were studying. Matla and van Zelst carried out their first experiments in a specially prepared room measuring 6 by 6 by 9 feet. It had a concrete floor and only one door with a glass window set in it. This chamber could be monitored from a control room outside this window. Their first "test device" was a small 20-inch by 10-inch cylinder with a capacity of 22 liters, hermetically sealed with sheets of tinfoil. A rubber tube, through which air could escape, was attached to one side of the cylinder and was connected to a device they called a "manometer." This invention somewhat resembled a carpenter's level, complete with an alcohol bubble that floated along a glass tube. Matla and van Zelst planned to see if they could encourage some unseen "entity" to displace the air in the cylinder and thus register a concurrent reading (i.e., a movement of the alcohol bubble) on the manometer. The tubes and manometer were constructed right in the experimental room. Since the room constituted a sealed and controlled environment, the physicists believed that no normal influence (such as drafts, tremors, etc.) could possibly influence the manometer's readings.

They were apparently successful with their first trials, and in their book, *La Mystére de la Mort* [The Mystery of Death], they report that the manometer registered a deflection as soon as they began mentally invoking the dead from the control room. Sometimes two cylinders were used, one stationed next to the other. Their book describes how they were able to mentally command the "dead" to manipulate one tube while leaving the other unaffected. Both scientists felt that no normal explanation could possibly account for these consistent results.

During the second phase of their research, Matla and van Zelst invented an even more complex device, which they called the "dynamistograph." It consisted of three working parts—an indicator, a key, and a register. The indicator was merely an electrically driven wheel, which rotated sequentially when activated, and around which were written the letters of the alphabet. The wheel, in turn, was connected to a very delicate key. When it was depressed, whatever letter was at the top of the wheel would be printed by and on the register. The apparatus was often powered by static charges produced by an old-fashioned Wimshurst machine, and for over a year, recorded messages were systematically received over the dynamistograph. The machine, like the manometer, was often left in the empty experimental room, yet it would type out messages. It would type out meaningful communications even when the physicists were totally absent from the building.

One of Matla's most intriguing discoveries was that atmospheric conditions had a noticeable effect on the machine. Humid and rainy weather seemed to inhibit good results, while the best communications were received during the drier seasons. He also discovered that certain types of electrical currents channeled through the device helped generate stronger results. In fact, he came to the conclusion that *the very element of our personality that survives death is partially electrical in nature and has an affinity for manipulating electrical energy.*

The Matla-van Zelst work was replicated only once. In the 1930's, Hereward Carrington built replicas of the manometer and dynamistograph in his American Psychical Institute and carried out several experiments with them. (These are carefully chronicled in his *Laboratory Investigations into Psychic Phenomena* in which, as mentioned earlier, he also discusses his replication of Melton's experiments.) Carrington always maintained that the parapsychological community of his day had never given Matla and his co-worker a fair hearing. He even wrote in his book that "one cannot dismiss with the wave of the hand the work of Dr. Matla, of The Hague, as being merely a series of errors. His results were startling in the extreme and have never been 'explained.' Matla's critics have never attempted to duplicate his experiments, using the same apparatus which he employed; they have merely stated or assumed that he was wrong." Nonetheless, Carrington's attempts to replicate Matla's successes were a complete failure.

At least, that was his *own* opinion. In reading his report, it seems to us that Carrington did achieve some small success with the Matla cylinders which even he himself never quite appreciated. He notes that, on occasion, the cylinders did, in fact, react via the manometer when they were verbally "addressed." In other words, the alcohol bubble moved when Carrington and his co-workers "invoked" the dead as Matla and van Zelst had done. These movements occurred, Carrington points out, only when several people were standing near the tubes. Later, he also learned that the tubes were very sensitive to heat, and that any temperature change in their vicinity would cause the manometer to activate. Carrington therefore assumed —without any concrete evidence—that the movements of the manometer were reactions to body heat generated by the observers. It seems to us, though, that these readings could very well have been genuine PK effects produced by the experimenters.

We know that PK can influence the surface temperature of small objects. In the October 1973 issue of the *Journal of the American Society for Psychical Research*, Dr. Gertrude Schmeidler, a psychology professor at the City College of the City University of New York, described a series of tests she conducted with a subject who was able psychically to alter the temperature of Bakelite and graphite fragments at will. Since her report was issued, other experimenters have discovered that many unselected subjects possess this same curious type of PK ability. Carrington's curious results with the Matla cylinders could therefore have been genuine psychic effects, since either he or one of the observers could easily have manipulated the surface temperature of the manometer psychokinetically. In retrospect, it also seems likely that Matla may have been Pk-ing his own machines, unwittingly producing the very deflections, messages, and phenomena that he so readily attributed to the dead.

Only one other independent investigation was ever made into the Matla-van Zelst affair. Soon after Matla announced his discoveries, the Dutch Psychical Society investigated the dynamistograph and issued a cursory report stating that the experimenter had not taken into account such physical factors as earth tremors, which might have affected the machine. But the Society did not explain just how these random tremors succeeded in spelling out intelligent messages!

Phone Calls from the Dead

Matla and van Zelst failed to make any lasting impact on parapsychology. Yet 25 years later the Belgian government actually issued a patent for a machine designed to bring through signals from the next world. Its inventor was Henri E. G. B. Vandermuelen, who had been given the plans through some Ouija board communications allegedly dictated by his deceased son. The apparatus consisted of two glass prisms, one coated with resin; an electric bell; and a dry cell. All these components were connected by various wires. A light metal triangle was balanced between the prisms, next to one of the connecting wires. The bell would activate when the metal triangle was pushed (psychically, that is) into contact with the positive connecting wire, thus closing a circuit between the component parts. The device was never meant to bring through communications from the dead *per se*, and Vandermuelen himself felt that it could be best used as a signaling device. As the patent papers explained:

"The purpose of the signaling device lies in informing persons who are busy otherwise that an entity desires to make communication ... and if the person has the required faculty of taking a message by Ouija or automatic writing, the latter may be received. If while a person is present the bell does not ring, it is because the entities do not wish to communicate."

Since Vandermuelen never marketed his invention commercially, no one knows how many of these devices were ever built. However, Mrs. Gwendolyn Kelly Hack, an American investigator and a psychic in her own right, experimented with the device in Italy during the 1930's. She later told J. Gilbert Wright that it had "worked lustily."*

It almost seems that during these years there were more machines that could contact the dead than there were gifted mediums. Even Thomas Edison got into the act. Edison's parents were spiritualists of sorts, and he himself harbored a lifelong interest in life after death, psychic phenomena, and related subjects. He consequently spent several years toying with the idea that some sort of telephone between the living and the dead could be developed, making no secret of his interest in the matter. When *American Magazine* printed a story in 1920 claiming that the inventor was already at work on such a project,

---

* Mrs. Hack's testimony cannot be taken lightly. Aside from being psychic herself, she was a diligent and trustworthy investigator. Even the normally cynical W. F. Prince, who had so forthrightly condemned Mrs. Geldert's claims, once described Mrs. Hack as "estimable, charming, sincere, and ardent" in her investigations, though he considered her incautious in her research.

Edison publicly verified the rumor a week later during an interview he granted *Scientific American.*

Edison was 73 in 1920, and that year the death of Walter Dimwiddie, his close friend and associate, apparently renewed his interest in designing a psychic machine. Unfortunately, since Edison was absolutely paranoid about his inventions and kept them strictly secret until they were patented, we know very little about the project. Since he apparently never completed it, no one today has any idea what kind of machine he was trying to construct. Norman Speiden, his associate and later the supervisory museum curator of the Edison National Historic Site, searched through the inventor's notes after his death, but found nothing that shed any light on the matter.

In 1941, however, an alleged blueprint of Edison's machine surfaced in New York. The apparatus consisted of an aluminum speaking trumpet connected to an aerial. The aerial wire dangled down into the middle of the trumpet which, along with the side of the aluminum cone, formed the opposite poles of a battery. Potassium permanganate attached to the wire in the trumpet served as an electrolyte between it and the cone. The machine allegedly amplified any "ether waves" generated inside the trumpet and directed against the aerial.

It is impossible to say whether these blueprints were actually Edison's own design or just a hoax. Chances are, they were frauds. Some of Edison's former associates built an operating model of the machine, but it didn't work.

Few researchers today have ever attempted to follow up the leads offered by Matla, Melton, Wilson, and others. Even Raymond's work with von Szalay and their joint discovery of the taped-voice phenomenon was completely ignored by the parapsychological community of the 1950's. Parapsychology today is an experimental science, and most researchers would probably look upon the work of these pioneers with the same type of cynical humor usually reserved for someone trying to build a perpetual motion machine. Nonetheless, we hopefully have shown that their work constitutes an unduly neglected chapter in the history of psychical research. Their work was most likely a curious mixture of malobservation, PK-mediated experimenter effects, and probably a great deal of genuine success.

The idea of electronic communication with the dead did have a renaissance, in the late 1960's, though, when Raudive's work burst upon the psychic scene. Although the parapsychological establishment attacked him bitterly (and often unfairly), Raudive did make a lasting mark on psychic research. If nothing more, he encouraged many investigators, both amateur and professional, to reconsider the issue that Melton and others raised in the 1910's and 1920's. For the first time in over 50 years, a few parapsychologists began to wonder once more if electronic contact with the dead could be established. Since we already discussed the taped-voice phenomenon in Chapter 6, we won't consider it again in any depth here, but we would like briefly to bring this area of research up to date.

Ever since the 1960's, experimenters in just about every Western country have been attempting to replicate and extend Raudive's work. Some have even gone on to invent revised gadgets to electronically monitor taped-voice articulations. Von Szalay is still active, though he has somewhat retired from the psychic scene, and there are dozens of other amateur researchers experimenting with taped-voice research throughout the United States. Jurgenson is continuing his work in Sweden; in Switzerland and Austria, Professor Alex Schneider and Dr. Franz Seidl, two of Raudive's original collaborators, are now developing new methods of taping the voices. Dr. Guiseppe Crosa is conducting taped-voice research in Italy, and Richard Sheargold in Great Britain has attained outstanding results. Since the researches of Seidl and of Sheargold are probably the most innovative, we should discuss them in some depth.

Franz Seidl and Richard Sheargold have developed recording techniques that open new dimensions in the controversy over the taped-voice effect. Both have departed in many ways from the methods Raudive first developed. For instance, while attempting to receive paraphysical voice effects on electromagnetic tape, Seidl no longer uses the open mike or radio plug-in technique. An electronics engineer by profession, he has invented a device called the *psychophone*, a primitive type of radio receiver with a wide frequency range combined with an amplifier. A tape recorder can be attached directly to the instrument so that any voices coming over the receiver will be recorded automatically. Seidl describes this device and his work in *Phänomen Transzendentalstimmen (The Phenomenon of Transcendental Voices)* published in 1971.

Seidl achieved some recognition with his device in his native Austria when he publicly admitted during a 1970 newspaper interview that he had attempted to get information about a recent kidnapping via the taped voices. A girl had disappeared while camping and was never seen or heard from again. Later, the girl's family learned of Seidl's experiments and verified that at least one proper name given over the psychophone matched that of a young man who was at the campsite when the girl vanished. The case, however, was never solved.

Richard Sheargold has been replicating the work of Jurgenson and Raudive in an even more innovative way. He is currently trying to prove that the taped voices are not acoustical in nature, as we believe, but are produced by a psychic "reordering" process affecting the sound waves emitted either by a radio attached to a recorder or by the background noise of the tape recorder itself. He is testing his theory by taping the background noise of a radio set on an interband white-noise frequency. He then retapes the broadcast onto another machine while attempting to make contact with the voice-entities. He is finding that voices often appear on the second tape, but not on the first.

Except for those engaged in taped-voice research, very few present-day researchers are experimenting with instrumental or electronic survival research. Nonetheless, one unique approach is currently being made by Julius Weinberger of Huntington, New York. Weinberger, probably one of the most qualified investigators in this country, spent 41 years directing research for RCA Laboratories before his retirement in 1958. He holds 40 patents in the field of radio communication, acoustics, motion picture and television production and the like. Weinberger began his research in 1941 and at one time got J. B. Rhine, the dean of American parapsychology, interested in his claims, methods, and results. He also feels that he has developed a semi-electrical method by which the dead can be contacted. His research may be controversial, but it represents some of the most carefully designed and systematic approaches to instrumental contact with the dead ever published.

During his first experiments with various inventions, conducted over 30 years ago, Weinberger began noticing an odd tingling sensation in his scalp. It felt as though some force were stimulating the nerve endings on his head. His eventual conclusion—that these sensations were being produced by the very entities he was trying to contact—gave him the general idea for a research project that ultimately proved extremely fruitful. If the dead can stimulate human nerve endings or hair receptors, he theorized, they should also be capable of affecting other types of living tissue. So for his subsequent tests, Weinberger used Venus flytraps as psychic detectors. The plants were attached to a variety of indicators, thus forming a receptor unit for the dead to manipulate much as they had apparently affected his own hair. As he explains in his report on these experiments:

A vacuum tube amplifier was designed to obtain electrical indications of very minute changes in the bioelectrical potential between two points of one of the trap units (a unit is a leaf and trap connected together by a joint which possibly contains some specialized mechanism that closes the trap when the hairs are stimulated. ...) The points finally chosen for the two electrodes were, a point along the midrib of the leaf (for a "grounded electrode") and a point inside the trap, close to the little connecting joint (for the "active electrode"). The resting or steady state DC potential between the two points in a healthy plant is usually between fifteen and forty millivolts. The apparatus could detect changes in the potential of the order of twenty microvolts, that is, less than one part in a thousand.

Weinberger also shielded the setup by placing it in a grounded steel container which kept the unit as stable as possible. He also tested to make sure that the electricity in his house, lighting, and other possible contaminants did not affect the setup. In short, after considerable pilot studies he proved to his own satisfaction that the plant would react only if an external stimulus was applied to it. For recording purposes, the setup was attached to a pulse amplifier that intensified the fluctuations of the leaf's electrical potential. Two other amplifiers were hooked up to the leaf, and the shifts in its electrical potential were graphed out on a recording chart.

Weinberger carried out most of his experiments in his cellar. First he activated the unit, and then mentally "invoked the dead" to make contact with him and waited to feel the then-familiar scalp tinglings. As he had hoped, he often found that his apparatus simultaneously recorded deflections of the leaf's electrical potential. Sometimes the chart recorder would register a single pulse signal, and at other times double or multiple pulses were graphed out. Of course, Weinberger wanted to know if he could make *intelligent* contact with whatever force was causing the deflections.

"To settle this question," he states in a recent report on his experiments, "one evening I watched a series of pulses being recorded during the first twenty minutes of the half-hour session. At this point I said, 'Will you please stop transmitting for the next five minutes?' ... at the moment the request for 'silence' was made, these ceased. The next five minutes shows only small pulses, which were obviously part of the plant noise."

His report continues: "Further evidence of intelligent control of the phenomena came from time to time in the form of responses

Electronic Contact with the Dead: A Wider Perspective

to questions or remarks. That is, the writer might say something, or ask a question, perhaps at a time when there was little activity, and immediately the recorder pen would swing over to a deflection well above the noise level, as though to indicate or to lend added emphasis to what was said."

Weinberger issued his first detailed report on his experiments in 1961, and in 1969 he presented some of his data to Dr. J. B. Rhine at the Institute for Parapsychology of the Foundation for Research on the Nature of Man (this is the old Duke Parapsychology Laboratory, which became autonomous in 1965). Rhine was impressed enough by Weinberger's report that he sent Bob Brier, a research associate at the Institute, to carry out a series of controlled tests with him. Even under independent supervision and controlled conditions, Brier was able to verify that Weinberger could get intelligent signals through his plant-apparatus.

Because of his advanced age, Weinberger has recently deferred from further experimentation, though he feels he has adequately proved his premise that man can communicate with the dead electrically. While he admits that PK-from-the-living could also feasibly affect his apparatus, he rejects the suggestion that he himself might have unconsciously produced the results of his flytrap experiments. We, however, feel that this possibility cannot be easily dismissed.

By way of conclusion, then, what can be said about these various attempts to contact the dead through psychic telephones, telegraphs, hermetically sealed cylinders, electrically driven Ouija boards like the dynamistograph, and even Venus flytraps? Can studying these experiments help us understand the phantom phone call mystery? We think we can indeed make a series of general statements about their possible importance to our work:

- First, it does appear that some of these experimenters— Matla, Melton, Wilson, and the others—successfully established contact between themselves and *some* sort of psychic force. It is hard to determine, though, whether this force was being generated by the dead or by the experimenters themselves.
- Second, the most successful of the apparatuses we've been discussing were either electrical in nature or electrically powered.

- Third, the plans to many of these instruments were not actually designed by their earthly inventors: they were *communicated* through mediums or psychics. In this category we can place Melton's psychic telephone, the Matla cylinders and dynamistograph, the Vandermuelen signal detector, and so on. Even experimenters such as Wilson and Wright received ideas for improving their apparatuses by way of communication received over their own inventions! The same goes for many researchers engaged today in taped-voice research. (Von Szalay, for example, often received helpful hints from the "voices" on how to improve his techniques.)
- Fourth, most of these machines worked best when operated by certain individuals who were probably extremely psychic.
- And last, it would seem that all the instruments we use in the course of normal communications operation—the telegraph, telephone, radio, and so on—can be manipulated by some form of psychic force. This conclusion, needless to say, has a direct bearing on the phantom phone call mystery.

We also have our own personal conclusions about all these psychic machines and their inventors. Although many of the experimenters we've discussed in this chapter were probably using their own PK to unconsciously "rig" or "load" their results, it is hard, in the more global sense, not to believe that on occasion these pioneers actually succeeded in establishing instrumental contact with the dead. Wilson's London-Paris successes and Melton's achievements are especially hard to explain any other way. It is also difficult to understand what force, other than the dead themselves, produced the curious voice-effects that Mrs. Richmond and Elmer Green witnessed over their phonographs. PK-from-the-living seems a farfetched explanation for many of the other results chronicled in this chapter. All of these research findings and spontaneous occurrences are more easily explained on the assumption that under certain circumstances, the dead can *and* do make contact with the living by manipulating electrical power.

But why would the dead want to contact us by such cumbersome means instead of by direct mind-to-mind communication? We think there are a number of answers to this question. To begin with, gifted psychics are rare. It may be that the dead can make purely psychic (mental) contact with a living mind only when certain psychic conditions

Electronic Contact with the Dead: A Wider Perspective

prevail, or that they can contact only certain types of individuals. When they are trying to establish contact with the living, electronic communications *might* be an alternative method or strategy, which the dead can rely upon. For instance, both Raudive and Jurgenson believe that it takes no special psychic ability to receive paranormal voices on tape. Their point is well taken, since many people without any discernible psychic talent have been able to receive these mysterious and fleeting voices. Likewise, most people who receive phone calls from the dead do not, as far as we have been able to determine, seem to possess any remarkable psychic ability.

Electronic contact might also be an easier and less complicated method of communication than direct mental contact. The incident we quoted from Patrick Mahony's *Who's There?* in Chapter 5 serves as an excellent confirmation of these points. The witness received her husband's postmortem call only *after* he had unsuccessfully tried to make mental contact with her in the form of an apparition.

As we also pointed out earlier, the desire to make contact with our deceased friends and relatives seems to be a natural human need. But why should one conclude that only we the living are interested in establishing two-way communication? The dead might also possess this same human drive. This is a theme we've constantly emphasized throughout this book. The dead might be actively experimenting with different methods in order to contact us, just as we are continually experimenting in the hope of contacting them. This is probably why the designs for so many instruments described in this chapter came through mediumistic communications, and why some experimenters have received instructions for improving their methods over their own equipment.

All of these factors lead us to one main conclusion. A person who receives a "phone call from the dead" or a telegraph signal from the next world or a psychic voice printed on his electromagnetic tape might be witnessing the end result of an organized experiment on the part of the dead as they continually try to make contact with us. These experiments are bound to continue.

If nothing more, then, the phantom phone call mystery indicates that perhaps one day, direct-voice or other forms of electronic communication with the dead will be a common occurrence. Each witness whose story we've included in this volume probably had more than merely a personal psychic experience. He or she may have been previewing what might eventually be the technology of the future ... the technology of psychic communication.

APPENDIX

Some Critiques of the Evidence

Whoever reads this book will be left at a certain disadvantage. That's an awful thing for an author to say, but it's an admission we're obliged to make. Every author approaches the subjects discussed in his book with a set of biases, and these he invariably passes on to his readers no matter how objective he tries to be. This problem is even more acute in parapsychology than in most other areas of science, since there are few "final authorities" on ESP and PK whose judgments can be unhesitatingly relied upon. This volume is the first ever written on the phantom phone call mystery. No other parapsychologist or writer has ever studied these cases in any depth. So the reader of this volume will have nowhere to turn should he wish to read another viewpoint or evaluation of this strange phenomenon. Frankly, you are all "stuck," so to speak, with our data and interpretations.

At the very beginning of this project, we realized that we were treading on controversial ground and that other parapsychologists would probably approach the types of data we were collecting from very different viewpoints. We were, however, quite heartened to find that many of our more conventional colleagues were showing a great deal of interest in our work. So, during the actual writing of this book, we decided that it might be wise to show our manuscript to selected colleagues for comment, and to print their critiques along with the text. This way, potential readers of this volume would get an idea of what other researchers think about the phantom phone call mystery. It would also give our readers an opportunity to see what types of criticisms might be leveled at our work—criticisms which you might have formulated yourself—as well as our rebuttals.

After completing the first major draft of this volume, copies were sent to three well-known and highly respected parapsychologists, each of whom agreed to write some comments for us. Our "panel of experts" included Dr. Gertrude Schmeidler, Dr. John Palmer, and Dr. John Beloff. Dr. Schmeidler, presently a professor of psychology at City College of the City University of New York, has been an active experimental parapsychologist for over 25 years. Dr. John Palmer, also primarily an experimental parapsychologist, is currently the Eileen J. Garrett Lecturer in Parapsychology at John F. Kennedy University in Orinda, California. Dr. Beloff, as mentioned earlier, is one of Great Britain's most prominent parapsychologists and a faculty member in the psychology department at the University of Edinburgh. Each of our colleagues was asked to comment on the validity of our study and on the cogency of our interpretations.

Here, then, are the evaluations we received from our panel of experts.

All three agreed that our study was of legitimate and important concern to parapsychology and worthy of scientific attention. For example, Dr. Schmeidler wrote to us:

> This is a provocative book. Its style is chatty and entertaining; its ideas are mind-boggling; its arguments are often persuasive. It would make a good conversational topic for a dinner or cocktail party or a late evening get-together.
>
> Is it a scientific document too? My answer to that must be a hesitant, 'Well, yes and no." I'll list the yesses first.
>
> One reason to take it as scientific is that it is intended to be. The authors are devoted contributors to psychic research. We can disregard the possibility that it is a spoof or a fraud. A second reason is that Rogo and Bayless have facts to report. Even though their data base consists mainly of anecdotes collected after a long delay, some cases were investigated quickly, some are supported by other witnesses or records, and many come from people of known good reputation. There is a central core of claims that seem well authenticated, with a periphery of weaker ones. This is the usual pattern of such collections, and the book resembles other sets of spontaneous cases which deserve to be examined seriously.

Some Critiques of the Evidence

A third reason is that the claims of psychic telephone calls or recordings fit well with a prior body of knowledge (though they represent an extraordinary extension of it). Good experimental research has shown that PK occurs, i.e., that mental processes can directly cause changes in physical objects. It is plausible that telephones or tape recorders should be good instruments for registering PK because they amplify weak physical effects. And once we grant that PK can produce a sporadic change to express a person's intentions, it is only a short further step to posit that a verbal intention can produce a short meaningful PK voice effect, like a single word or a phrase. Half-hour conversations are another matter, of course; but at least the nose of the camel can be allowed to come into the tent.

Both Dr. Palmer and Dr. Beloff address this issue in a different way. In their remarks they pointed out that it is all too easy to dismiss oddball facts out of bias. After all, psychologists dismissed the existence of ESP for years because the phenomenon did not accord very well with their views about man and his mind. The apparent rarity of psychic interactions didn't help matters either. Parapsychology today has its own orthodoxy as well, and parapsychologists—who are a rather conservative lot—also tend to dismiss cases and facts which seem too "far out." However, Palmer and Beloff agreed with us that the inherent rarity and oddity of phantom phone calls shouldn't keep us from studying them seriously. As Dr. Palmer wrote on this issue:

> "Death call cases" (as I will hereafter label them, hopefully without theoretical commitment) represent another class of ostensibly paranormal phenomena that have been ignored by parapsychologists, at least partly because they don't quite fit our stereotype of what psi is. Somehow, phone calls from the dead seem too complex to fit under the rubric of psychokinesis or "PK," the label we apply to such relatively simply "physical" phenomena as making dice come up the way we want and bending spoons. This kind of exclusion can't stand up to critical scrutiny.

Dr. Beloff similarly states:

Before I read my Rogo and Bayless, the only instance of a phone call from the dead which I had come across was a fictional one, namely that described by Anthony Burgess in his recent novel *Beard's Roman Women*. Since I can, I think, claim a fairly extensive knowledge of the psychical literature, this would suggest to me that such cases must be extremely rare. Of course, such cases may not be quite as rare as we might suppose. It could be that reports of them have been systematically suppressed precisely because they are so bizarre that they invite incredulity and ridicule even more than the traditional kinds of survivalist evidence. If so, then the authors are to be congratulated on ferreting out so many instances and perhaps, now that the phenomenon has come to light, others will be encouraged to speak out. Certainly the rarity of these cases should not be taken as a reason for dismissing them out of hand. They will stand or fall on the strength of the testimony that can be adduced in support of them.

But what of this "evidence," of which Beloff speaks? Our commenters had differing opinions on this matter. Dr. Beloff simply stated that " ... while all human testimony is suspect, these cases are in no worse position, evidentially, than any other spontaneous psychic phenomenon." This issue was addressed more fully by Dr. Palmer, who writes:

> The cases that compose the meat of the book ... strike me as being rather weak from the standpoint of evidence for psi.
>
> The weakness is attributable in large part to the very nature of this type of phenomena. Like most cases of spontaneous psi, "death calls" occur infrequently and at times when they are unexpected. People usually do not wait around for a phone call from a departed relative! Thus, in contrast to laboratory experiments and certain *recurrent* spontaneous phenomena such as poltergeists, there is unlikely to be a trained investigator on hand when the phenomena occur. This puts a tremendous burden on the memory and interpretational skills of generally untrained witnesses who must accurately report, not only the event itself (which was probably quite traumatic), but any other events that might bear upon its interpretation. Witnesses are customarily asked to recall these events weeks or even years later, which only increases the burden. I found that the cases in this collection depended almost exclusively on the retrospective testimony of those who received or initiated the calls, or who were present at the time. While these case reports are certainly suggestive and worthy of serious scientific attention, they are not the kind of "hard evidence" that the game of science requires.

Some Critiques of the Evidence

What criteria spontaneous cases must meet before they can be considered evidential has been debated by parapsychologists since the nineteenth century. Many parapsychologists, most notably Louisa Rhine, have concluded that even the best spontaneous cases can be no more than suggestive from the scientific viewpoint. Other researchers are not quite so pessimistic, but they do adopt rather rigid standards of evidentiality or "authenticity" for spontaneous cases. (Incidentally, it is not only "death call" cases that have trouble meeting these criteria.)

Among the most important criteria applied to spontaneous cases of the "ESP" type is that the percipient make a written record or contact an investigator about his experience prior to his knowledge of the verifying event. Of course, not all "death call" cases convey information unknown to the percipient, so this principle does not apply universally. However, in those cases where, for example, the recipient suspects at the time that the call is paranormal and that it conveys information (e.g., about the deceased state of the caller) not known to him normally, he would render parapsychology a great service by writing down the experience, sharing it with a trustworthy friend, and (if possible) contacting an investigator, *before* seeking the verifying information. In any case, the recipient should immediately contact the phone company, switchboard, etc., to determine if a "real" call had been put through.

If this type of case were to be fully documented and published in a respectable scientific journal, it would go a long way toward increasing the credibility of death call cases, a credibility I am inclined to think they deserve. Indeed, one of the important contributions this book can make is to alert people that such cases are of scientific interest, that people who experience "death calls" are not "crazy," and that such experiences should be reported to qualified investigators as soon as possible.

Dr. Palmer's points are interesting, but we can't simply quote them without some comment. First of all, many parapsychologists—like Palmer—believe that the value and evidentiality of a spontaneous case of psychic phenomenon (such as a precognitive dream, apparition, or "phone call from the dead") is strengthened if the incident is committed to writing within a day or so of the incident and when the facts are still fresh in the witness's mind. People who relate from memory experiences that occurred years ago, they argue, are prone to exaggerate their experiences and/or unconsciously distort them to make them seem more impressive than the true facts would warrant.

This is, of course, all good common sense; but there exists little empirical evidence that this actually occurs when people report about psychic experiences, which they may have had years before. One pioneer in parapsychology, W. Franklin Prince, demonstrated this point in 1919. In 1902 he had experienced a vivid psychic dream, which had been witnessed by his wife. Both of them had made written accounts of the incident and eight years later Mrs. Prince rewrote her account from memory. By comparing the three versions, only one minor discrepancy could be found. Prince also published an account of a psychic experience written by the witness, some ten years after it happened, who then wrote an independent version of the same incident twenty years later. The two versions were almost identical. Relatively recently, Rosalind Heywood, a British investigator and psychic, deliberately carried out an experiment along these same lines. She once wrote out an account of a personal experience, sealed it, and then wrote an independent version of the same event ten years later. Only minor discrepancies could be found between the two written accounts.

In short, it doesn't seem that the delay between the time one of these phone calls is received and when it was reported is as important an issue as Dr. Palmer would have us believe.

Nonetheless, we are certainly aware of this problem and have a ready-made solution to it. Years ago, J. B. Rhine, who pioneered the experimental study of ESP and PK, pointed out the value of what might be called "pattern recurrence." While his skeptics were criticizing him for everything from sloppy methodology to fraud because of the successful outcome of his ESP and PK tests, he countered by pointing out that many researchers were finding similar patterns in their data. For instance, many independent researchers were finding that their subjects scored better at the beginning of a test, but did progressively worse as the test continued on. This pattern and those like it, Rhine argues, have cropped up in the work of many researchers and cannot be explained away as the result of fraud or experimental error. In other words, these patterns constitute strong evidence that these researchers were procuring genuine ESP results in their tests and that ESP seems to be guided by inherent principles and behavior characteristics.

All through this book we have made a similar point. We have shown that many of our phone call cases share common characteristics and seem to conform to a few general, but predictable, patterns. (The fact that extended phone contacts occur only when the witness does not know he is speaking to a psychic entity is a good case in point.) These patterns should not have occurred in our data if phantom phone call cases were merely the result of hallucination, lying, or cribbing. Yet these patterns do emerge—and impressively so. So while each of our cases can be faulted on evidential grounds, our entire case catalog is so inter-corroborative and content-consistent that we can rule out most normal explanations for our cases. These factors tend to override the specific evidentiality problems that each case, taken alone, is plagued by.

Nonetheless, we do think that some of our cases meet the criteria for evidence Dr. Palmer outlines, or fall only a fraction short of it. We have several cases on record (i.e., the Karl Uphoff and John Medved cases) where two witnesses agreed on the nature and content of the experience; and although incomplete, our report on Ida Lupino's phone call does constitute a case where (a) information was given to the witness which was unknown to her at the time, and (b) which was communicated to an independent party before it was proven correct. We also have several cases on file where multiple witnesses have observed a phantom phone call before they learned that their caller was, in fact, dead.

Only one of our authorities directly challenged the completeness of our reporting. Dr. Schmeidler wrote to us:

> The book falls sadly short of scientific standards for reporting. Again and again we are given evaluations rather than facts. We are told, for example, that two events occurred at the same time. What time? "Same" to the second, or the minute, or the hour, or the afternoon? We are told that two reports are identical. Word for word? That would be cause for suspicion. If not that, then how "identical" are they? ...
>
> The analyses as well as the reporting are also incomplete. One example is the statement that 10 percent of the cases occur on anniversaries. This sounds impressive until we wonder how many anniversaries there are; and obviously it would lose interest if the number approached 10 percent of the days in the year. I began to make a quick list, starting from examples in the book, and included as a starter the birthdays of the listener and the dead person; their marriage day(s); personal dates like first meeting or engagement day; date of injury, death, funeral; national holidays like New Year's Day, Memorial Day, July 4, Thanksgiving; informal days like Valentine's or Mothers' or Fathers'; and many religious holidays like Easter and Christmas. And Christmas Eve? Then what of the eve of the other

days? Including all of them could bring the total even above 36%. Until the authors state their criterion for an anniversary they have made a meaningless statement, not a careful analysis.

In short, this stimulating and readable book is not a scientific report. It is rather a bird's-eye view of what may become important scientific data. We must hope that the authors will publish their scientific statement later.

We think we can rebut Dr. Schmeidler's criticisms. First, we do not mean to imply that any two cases are perfectly identical. What we are saying is that, on many occasions, we have come across two or more cases which contain several characteristics in common. What we should have said was "virtually identical" or "identical with a margin of expected error."

Dr. Schmeidler's comments about our "anniversary cases" is probably the most direct challenge any of our commentors made. She makes a valid point in this regard, since we did not define what we meant by "anniversaries" or "emotionally meaningful days" when we discussed these cases. However, Dr. Schmeidler's list is much more extensive and inclusive than the working definition we used (but which we did not state in the text) while compiling these reports. We took a very limited view of what would constitute an anniversary day. To us, these psychologically meaningful days would include only the birthday of either the caller or the witness; the anniversary of the day of his death; major public holidays on which families usually gather such as Christmas, Thanksgiving, and Easter (and not Labor Day or Arbor Day); marriage anniversaries, Mothers' and Fathers' days; and maybe one or two others that had a private significance for either the caller or the witness. The days before these anniversaries would not under any condition constitute a meaningful date, and no such cases are quoted in the text. Thus by our count, these potential "anniversary" days only number between 10 and 12. That's only a fraction of the number of days in the year, and considerably less than Dr. Schmeidler's calculation. In this respect, then, the fact that 10 percent of our cases occurred on emotionally meaningful days is extremely significant. It was only by oversight that we did not spell out what constitutes an anniversary date more clearly in the text.

Despite these problems, all of our experts agreed that we were no doubt "on to something," so to speak. However, not all of our colleagues felt that our conclusions about the nature and *modus operandi* of these

Some Critiques of the Evidence

calls could go unquestioned. Two commentors specifically promoted the view that these calls might not be physical, but subjective events. Dr. Beloff explains:

> Granted that these phone calls are precisely as described by the informants, exactly the same question arises as arose with any other form of ostensible post-mortem communication; namely, who or what is responsible for the events observed? On whose initiative do these phone calls take place? Is it indeed the deceased individual whose voice or whose apparition, as the case may be, is perceived who undertook to make contact with us in this way? Or is it, perhaps, the bereaved person who unconsciously stages the entire incident by duly hallucinating the appropriate voice or appearance? Certainly, the mere fact that the communication is received by means of the telephone cannot per se demonstrate that the initiative comes from the "other side" as it were, especially when the authors admit that "the vast majority of phantom calls are rather brief, and only a few of them contain information of a sort that could not possibly have been known to the recipient."
>
> In the light of these considerations it seems to me that the authors are much too hasty in dismissing the idea that the entire telephone conversation as well as the ringing of the bell which precedes it might, at least in a large proportion of the cases, be a complete hallucination. This suggestion, which they attribute to Renée Haynes, is dismissed because, in certain of the cases, more than one witness reports hearing the bell ring. And yet, as with apparition cases, we cannot rule out the possibility of collective hallucination. Hence, unless the call is tape-recorded, we cannot be sure that an actual physical event is involved. We might be dealing with an elaborate hallucination of the sort which can readily be induced under hypnosis with a good hypnotic subject. Most of us have had the experience of thinking we heard the telephone ring only to discover a few moments later that it was just our imagination. Given the right conditions plus a little prompting by our unconscious it is conceivable that we might go all the way with some of those whose experiences are described here and carry on a pseudo-conversation with a nonexistent entity! The authors, on the other hand, prefer to interpret the typical case—from the ringing of the bell to the sound of the voice coming through the receiver—as a physical event emanating presumably from the discarnate communicator. Such a view certainly accords better with their own preferred survivalist standpoint, and is, indeed, the more straightforward interpretation

of the phenomenon. But, rightly or wrongly, the usual convention in parapsychology is not to invoke a physical effect if what is observed can be explained in purely mentalistic terms. But, even if we grant that a PK effect is involved, there is still the problem as to the source of the PK, whether it derives from the living or from the dead. For, after all, the authors include among their case studies instances in which a call is received from some living person who, though he may have intended to make such a call, never in fact put through the call!

In other words, Dr. Beloff is suggesting that some of these cases are psychic hallucinations, while others might be just plain imaginary. These are the exact explanatory models we suspect most parapsychologists will entertain after studying these accounts. However, it would be hard to make a very strong case for them. *If* these calls were either imaginary or psi-mediated hallucinations (such as a "psychic voice" that might be heard clairaudiently), we would expect to find, apart from collective cases, at least a few cases in which one witness heard the phone ring (and subsequently engaged in a conversation) while another witness in the room heard nothing. Yet no such cases have been reported to us. This is inconsistent with the data parapsychologists have collected about apparitions. *Sometimes* apparitions are collectively seen, but these cases seem to be exceptions to the rule. Should an apparition appear in a crowded room, it will *usually* remain invisible to all but a single witness. We would expect to find this same pattern cropping up in our phone call data too if, as Beloff suggests, the calls are psychic hallucinations.

Neither is Dr. Beloff's analogy to the common illusion of hearing a telephone ring applicable to our data. This illusion, which no doubt everyone has had, occurs only when the illusion can be projected against background noise. Hearing a phone ring while one is taking a shower or shaving is a common experience. These experiences, though, are only *illusions*, not *hallucinations*. The sound is not actually hallucinated, but is a misinterpretation weakly projected over an undifferentiated background noise. This illusion is certainly not analogous to the experiences of our witnesses, who were just sitting around quietly when their phones rang loud and clear.

As for Dr. Beloff's suggestion that some of these calls might be "pseudo-conversations with a nonexistent entity," we have only a brief reply. Anyone who could hallucinate such a conversation over the phone in such a manner would be quite insane and need immediate

Some Critiques of the Evidence

institutionalization! Such hallucinations simply do not occur to mentally healthy people and would be a prime symptom of paranoid-schizophrenia. The only exception would be if the phone conversation were some sort of *telepathic* hallucination. We will return to this possibility in a moment.

Dr. Beloff is certainly correct that in parapsychology it is "conventional" to explain a psychic experience as a mental event before accepting it as a physical one. For instance, it seems more reasonable to believe that apparitions are immaterial telepathic hallucinations than immediately to accept them as physical objects. However, this convention came into being only because the early S.P.R. investigators were biased against the possible existence of PK. The existence of this power has been better authenticated today than it was when the S.P.R. leaders began their work. So while an historical "convention," it is probably an incorrect one to work from. Simply speaking, it's an antiquated principle.

Convention it is, nonetheless. Dr. Palmer also seems to respect this principle and wrote to us:

> I think too short shrift is given to the hypothesis that the voices could be impressed directly on the mind of the percipients telepathically, rather than being physical sounds heard normally. This theory was discussed in Chapter 7, but I think it should have been discussed in Chapter 6 alongside the two physical theories. It is true that it is awkward as an explanation for some of the cases, but then so are each of the other two theories. Also, it is possible in some of the cases that the phone actually rang, the caller hung up right before the percipient answered, and the conversation was then conveyed telepathically, blocking out the buzz tone.

Dr. Palmer's point, suggested also by Beloff, is a clever one, but strikes us as unlikely. First of all, we have collected some good examples of collectively heard telephone voices. The McConnell case (see Chapter 3) is one case in point. To explain the phantom phone call mystery along the lines Dr. Palmer suggests, we would have to postulate that the agent making the call somehow telepathically affected two witnesses in the exact same way or that one witness telepathically "infected" the other. There is little evidence that telepathy works in this way.

Dr. Palmer also fails to take into account just how very imprecise ESP is as a communicating channel. ESP is basically a pictographic, not a linguistic channel. If we were to think about an apple and then tried to send this thought to you telepathically, you would probably not mentally receive the specific *word* "apple." You would probably get a mental *image* of an apple, or the vague image of a red ball from which you would deduce the nature of the ESP message. Even great psychics do not try to pick up specific words or phrases when they attempt to "tune in" on telepathic messages. They usually try to receive mental pictures or symbols about the targets. What they do receive, though, is usually not a precise image of the target, but an abstracted, symbolized, and fragmented version of it. In other words, ESP is not a very good information carrier. For that reason, when psychics give a reading or telepathy demonstration, they often have a rough time picking up specific names and dates—linguistic constituents that are not easily converted into mental imagery.

This model for the way ESP works is accepted, in one way or another, by most parapsychologists. This model also stands in striking contrast to the type of channel which would have to exist to make Palmer's theory work. At the present time, there is simply no evidence that anything so complex as a specific conversation could possibly be communicated by telepathy.

Despite all this, all three of our colleagues did agree that the *physical* reality of these calls was not unlikely and could represent a form of PK. As quoted earlier, Dr. Schmeidler points out that telephones and tape recorders might be natural PK amplifiers. In this same respect, Dr. Beloff writes:

> I will admit that the idea of the phantom calls being real physical events is not as preposterous as it may sound. A number of recent poltergeist cases involve a paranormal interference with electrical appliances of one sort or another; the celebrated "Rosenheim" case from Bavaria involved extensive interference with the functioning of the telephone system at the lawyer's office in which the disturbance took place, although no phantom calls were reported. More to the point is that there now exists a new type of paranormal phenomenon which has come to the attention of parapsychologists in recent years, namely the tape-recorded voice phenomenon which the authors discuss in Chapter 6. This first attracted widespread publicity with the work of Konstantin Raudive in Germany and Friedrich Jurgenson in Sweden although many years before then, it was being studied by Raymond Bayless himself through the mediumship of Art von Szalay. Now, if the tape-recorded voice-phenomenon is a valid analogue of the phantom phone-call phenomenon, this would imply that the latter, too, must be

Some Critiques of the Evidence

a real physical phenomenon for the tape-recorded voices are certainly not hallucinations, although where they come from and whether they are indeed genuine voices uttering coherent phrases is still very much a matter of controversy among the experts.

Dr. Palmer obviously shares Dr. Beloff's sentiments, but did not think that our analogy to the tape-voice phenomenon was necessary. As he wrote to us:

> I don't think one needs to resort to the controversial taped-voice research to find an experimental model for "death call" cases. As parapsychologists are now coming to realize, such simple and relatively easy to control PK phenomena as influencing dice or the output of Dr. Schmidt's random number generator would require for their normal reproduction a detailed knowledge of the forces involved and an exacting manipulation of them. The complexity of the required process would seem to closely rival that needed to make a phone ring or even to mimic a voice electronically. A recognition of this complexity has led some parapsychologists, including Dr. Schmidt himself, to describe psi as "goal directed" rather than mechanistic.
>
> The general point I want to stress, though, is that I think it is important for us to keep our options open and not prematurely close on any one theory, or even on the conclusion that the origin of the "calls" is a discarnate entity.

Dr. Palmer is quite correct. PK is not hindered by the complexity of the task it is asked to perform. Dr. Schmidt has himself proved this point by carrying out an ingenious experiment that he summarized in the *1977 Proceedings of the IEEE International Conference on Cybernetics and Society*. For this test, Schmidt's subjects had to use PK to disrupt the functioning of two different random number generators. The internal structure of the machines was different, one simple and one complex; yet no matter which machine the subjects focused on, they were able to exert the same *magnitude* of PK. So it seems that once PK goes into action, it can carry out any goal, no matter how complex.

It is, however, a moot point whether PK could electronically mimic a human voice, although this seems to have occurred in some of our cases. But since the existence of the "direct voice" seems well established, there does not seem to be any reason why these telephone voices could not be further examples of this interesting phenomenon.

Also, one might ask, how can PK electronically mimic a voice over a phone that has been disconnected? Since writing the body of this volume, one such case has come to our attention—and it is an extraordinary one, even though it occurred some years ago. In August 1978, we received a letter from a gentleman in Chicago who, years before, had witnessed a phone call from the dead meant for his grandmother. The call was apparently long-distance from West Virginia, and from a friend known to both witnesses. The caller told our correspondent's grandmother that she was "going away," but that "everything would be all right" and that the witness would understand everything in a few days. The voice was unusually hollow and distant sounding, and stated that it could speak for only a few moments. The phone call perplexed our witnesses since their phone had been disconnected the day before! The phone company assured the two witnesses that their phone had indeed been cut off before the time of the call, and even sent out a linesman to the house that evening to show the witnesses the disconnected wires. A few days later, just as the voice had predicted, the witnesses received a letter informing them that their friend had died on the day the "mystery" call had been received. The death and the call had occurred at approximately the same time.

In this case, the "voice" could not possibly have been an electrical effect at all.

And do these calls indicate survival after death? They certainly indicate it, but according to our colleagues, they don't prove it. As Dr. Palmer forcefully concludes:

> The cases are fascinating, and the phenomena they represent are potentially important. Specifically, they have the potential of providing better evidence for survival of death than most other physical phenomena, because they suggest intent and intelligent planning on the part of the ostensibly discarnate communicator. I hope this book will mark the beginning of a serious interest in "death call" cases among parapsychologists who study spontaneous cases and PK generally.

Dr. Schmeidler simply stated that our data, " ... fit well with a body of respected but inconclusive material suggesting survival."

Dr. Beloff had a more complete set of statements to make about how our research related to the survival controversy.

Some Critiques of the Evidence

If people do survive death and if, in their discarnate state, they have the power to communicate with the living, then the question arises as to what form such communication may take. Long before there were any professional mediums there were accounts of telepathic dreams, of apparitions, and of hauntings which were taken to be manifestations of deceased persons. Nowadays, post-mortem communications are usually associated with mediums who convey their messages either by automatic writing or by word of mouth. However, other forms of psychic contact as between the living and the dead are still reported, and in principle, there is no reason why any mode of communication whatsoever that is in use among the living should not be exploited by discarnate entities, if such exist, as a way of getting in touch with those whom they knew in their lifetime.

Later in his comments to us, Dr. Beloff even went so far as to speculate on the motivations the dead might have for communicating with us over the telephone:

> Why the departed should wish to communicate with us through mechanical devices rather than by inducing in us clairaudient perceptions is another question which arises from a study of this book. Perhaps the most plausible answer is that one needs to be a very special kind of sensitive to experience clairaudience. Those of us who are not psychically endowed have to be taken off our guard before a psychic impression can get through. This is why dreams are such a common source of ESP-type experiences, but sometimes such experiences might penetrate the mundane events of daily life. In the case of these phantom phone calls it is only after some little while or indeed after the incident is over that we realize with a shock that anything paranormal has occurred. It may be just because the telephone has become for us such a routine way of communicating with our friends in this life that it affords a convenient point of entry for would-be communicators in the afterlife. But all this is speculation rather than fact.

In conclusion, perhaps the most pertinent statement made by our colleagues is Dr. Beloff's suggestion that at this point in the game, anything said about the phantom phone call mystery must remain as pure speculation. We agree totally. We have no vested personal interest in the theories and interpretations we have presented in this volume. Although we feel that they do account for our data better than

any other, we will unhesitatingly abandon or revise them as new (and possibly contradictory) evidence comes in to us. There is no room for dogma in science. It is our plan to continue collecting phantom phone call cases of every magnitude and variety. Eventually, we may even be able to solve the mystery definitely. But that day is far, far away.

Postscript: 45 Years Later ...

A year after the release of *Phone Calls from the Dead*, Raymond Bayless published an article concerning "electronic communication" with the dead in the *Journal of Religion and Psychical Research*. In this article, he proposed that as time and technology progressed, people will continue to report what they perceive to be strange communication—presumed to be from the dead in most cases—via tape recorders, radio, television, and indeed, the telephone. His assumptions were correct! In the forty-five years since their original investigation of the "phantom phone call mystery," people world-wide continue to make these claims. And yet, so much has changed technologically since that time.

Phone Calls from the Dead was arguably the best seller of Rogo's and Bayless's books, and the only piece they had co-authored in the twenty-four years that they had been friends and colleagues. The book ran for three separate editions between 1979-1980, in the United States and United Kingdom, with translations such as the Spanish edition in 1981 under the title *Llamadas Telefónicas Del Más Allá* —"phone calls from the afterlife."

Even though they regularly appeared in the media as experts on strange occurrences—with Rogo regarding October and Halloween was his "busy season"—the "phantom phone calls" saw them both appearing in newspapers, radio and on television numerous times. Journalists and presenters would state that "phone calls from the dead" was their favorite title.

For example, on the radio show *Hour 25* with host Harlan Ellison, October 31, 1986, Rogo was interviewed alongside David Alexander, a professional magician, private investigator, publisher and on the board of directors of the Southern California Skeptics. Rogo introduced himself, after David, and mentioned he'd written twenty-six books to date:

Harlan interjected "including... the one... the title I love?!"
To which Rogo replied "... *Phone Calls from the Dead.*"
"You got it, that's the one I love!" Harlan exclaimed excitedly, with laughter from all three guests.
Rogo quickly responded "we're doing the sequel now, *Phone Calls from People you Wish were Dead!*" further laughter erupted.
"We walked into that didn't we?" said David.
"And the Saturday Night Live version, *Phone Calls from the Dull,*" Rogo quipped.

Rogo and Bayless continued to receive letters from people about experiences involving the telephone, even years after *Phone Calls from the Dead* was released. Such cases and correspondence are now housed in the University of Virginia's Division of Perceptual Studies archive (Raymond Bayless) and the California Institute of Integral Studies' Laurence S. Rockefeller Library (D. Scott Rogo).

Although Dr. Gertrude Schmeidler states in the appendices that essentially the authors would do well to submit their work to peer-review—a journal article for publication—they never actually did. Beyond 1979, Rogo responded to a book review of *Phone Calls from the Dead* by Rodger Anderson in 1981 in the *Journal of Religion and Psychical Research*, in which he intensely disagreed with several of Anderson's assertations. And both Rogo and Bayless went on to publish in separate books, chapters on the topic but without any new developments beyond new cases. Rogo's chapter can be found in the 1986 publication: *Life After Death: The Case for Survival of Bodily Death*. And Bayless's chapter, in the 1981 publication: *The Case for Life After Death: Parapsychologists Look at the Evidence*—co-authored with Dr. Elizabeth McAdams, a former president of the now defunct Southern California Society for Psychical Research. The S.C.S.P.R. transitioned into the Life After Life Club.

There was, however, a further study in Italy, which the authors missed—perhaps due to the language barrier. In the early 1980s, Dr. Massimo Biondi, a medical doctor and parapsychologist from the University of Rome, had become interested in the book *Phone Calls from the Dead*. He placed adverts in newspapers, magazines and on

Postscript: 45 Years Later...

radio shows, for anyone to come forward regarding strange experiences with the telephone. He received around forty or so such cases. After thoroughly exploring conventional explanations for each case, and interviewing witnesses, twenty of these appeared hard to explain. He presented a paper in 1984 to the journal, *Quaderni di Parapsicologia*, outlining his findings. It appeared that Dr. Biondi's Italian sample of cases showed the same features of call types as identified by Rogo and Bayless. Dr. Bondi's thoughts on the origins of such cases, were more in line with psychological error and fraud through to potential psi, but he was highly doubtfully of them supporting the notion of survival beyond death.

In a further article he published in 1996 in *Luce e Ombra*, Dr. Biondi spoke of the methods by which he approached these cases and how mapping them so far had at least begun to demonstrate the nature and circumstances of "phantom phone calls." They take time to gather, investigate, thoroughly check, and personal finances will need to be invested in all of that or grants sought. He concluded that there *are* various cases which lack reliable explanations, therefore, is it not worthy to go on with the research?

Douglas Scott Rogo (preferring Scott over his first name, and the initial 'D.' in correspondence and interviews often mistaken for 'Dr.') reached an untimely end in 1990 at the age of forty. He had written thirty books to that point, numerous papers and reviews, and had been an active attendee at international conferences—particularly for parapsychology. Aside from his faculty status at John F. Kennedy University, lecturing on a master's degree program in parapsychology, his main income and consistent role was as a consultant editor for *Fate* magazine. He had also begun reading as much as he could about the developing research on AIDS between 1988-1990, while contributing to a voluntary hotline (AIDS Project L.A.) for those worried about, or suffering with the syndrome, during what was seen by many as an AIDS epidemic of the 1980s.

In August 1990, issues around funding from *Fate* magazine led to Rogo not attending the annual Parapsychological Association convention in Chevy Chase, Maryland, at the National 4-H Center, held 16th-20th. The PA was an event he normally attended every year to collect notes on the latest research, which would typically turn into monthly editorial pieces for *Fate*. He was last seen on 14th August at a bar in Van Nuys Boulevard, California, with an acquaintance. The bar tender recalled Rogo and the other man being there.

On 18th August, a neighbor alerted the police to the fact that Rogo's lawn sprinkler had been running for two days continuously. A senior police officer, Lieutenant L.A. Durrer, was sent to investigate and found the back door to Rogo's home ajar. Upon entering, he found Rogo's slain body on the floor of the living room in a pool of blood. It was a most violent murder. Various parapsychologists around the world heard the news on the radio, word even got back to the attendees at the PA conference as the event was in full swing. Dr. Keith Harary—a close friend of Rogo—was called to the telephone at the National 4-H Center and he relayed the shocking news back to the various parapsychologists in attendance.

Various efforts went into the tracking of the murderer at the time, even "psychic detective" efforts. Two years later, the evidence led to the conviction and custodial sentence of a Mr. John Battista, who also matched the description of the person Rogo was seen with on the 14th and was a known friend—if not closer—of Rogo's. However, Battista was later released on technicalities in 1996, and Rogo's murder went unsolved for some 30 years.

However, I began working on his autopsy report in 2021 and then with a cold case detective in Los Angeles, who re-opened the case. The murder is now solved, and *case closed*. The details are discussed in his biography—*Rogo: The Life and Tragic Death of an Outspoken Parapsychologist*.

Raymond Bayless lived on a further decade and a half, but his writings and involvement in parapsychology beyond this point was practically non-existent, having already slowed down from the mid-1980s. He continued avidly reading on the topic and stayed in touch with various parapsychologists, particularly Dr. McAdams, given their long association with the Southern California S.P.R. He lived a retired life from parapsychology throughout this time, still focusing on his main profession of landscape painting and also turned his hand to fictional writing. His final books, published posthumously and edited together by his supporters, were of such story writing. Bayless died peacefully at home in his wife's arms in 2004.

The late Dr. Carlos Alvarado, wrote the obituary for Bayless, published in the *Journal of the Society for Psychical Research*. In it, he wrote of a personal visit he made to the Bayless household, spending time with Raymond, and his wife Marjorie. Dr. Alvarado notes that following Raymond's passing, Marjorie believed she had had repeated after-death communication experiences. Bayless had apparently said he would return to her after his death. Marjorie said that she'd experienced his apparition five days after he died, in later months, touches, footsteps, doors opening and closing, and raps.

Skip forward a few years and that's where I came in.

I'd always had a fascination with reports of anomalous experiences, particularly ghosts and hauntings. I'd had many all-day and all-night investigations at various properties since 2004 purporting such activity. As a schoolboy, my fellow classmates and I would digest any books we could get our hands on regarding local ghost reports and the supernatural at large (bigfoot, UFOs, stigmata, etc.). My teachers for Science and English, were also encouraging of me exploring the subject of parapsychology, while my passion at the time was mainly found in performing arts.

In 2007 I began my undergraduate degree in psychology at the University of Northampton, UK, where I had chosen to specialize in parapsychology. The university had gained parapsychologists such as Professor Chris Roe, Professor Deborah Delanoy, and Dr. Simon Sherwood around 1996, setting up a 3rd year module for parapsychology and a research team. Dr. Richard Broughton joined a few years later. Today, in 2025, it is arguably the largest research institution for parapsychology with a team of near twenty people involved in parapsychology. The Exceptional Experiences and Consciousness Studies research group.

While carrying out my usual studies in cognitive psychology, child psychology, biological psychology, evolutionary psychology, research methods and so on, I was forever finding myself in long chats with the parapsychologists or immersed in the library section for parapsychology. I even became a research assistant for Prof. Roe on a remote viewing project and for Dr. Broughton on a psychokinesis project. I was keen to learn anything I could about this field of science.

Among the books in the library, I found a copy of *Apparitions and Survival of Bodily Death* by Raymond Bayless, with a foreword by D. Scott Rogo. I checked it out of the library and took it back to the halls of residence. I read it cover to cover, often while waiting for my laundry to finish—perfect reading time! I was very impressed at the level of historical knowledge for psychical research that Bayless demonstrated, and his writing style was not held back with any unnecessary complex terminology. It was a writing-style I'd call 'accessible' to all, and I'd extend that compliment to Rogo, also.

As I trawled the internet and purchased more and more books for myself, and searching for others by Rogo and Bayless, I stumbled

Phone Calls from the Dead

across *Phone Calls from the Dead* in 2008 and bought it. The title didn't particularly capture my imagination, although I knew I'd not heard of such reports anywhere else in the literature. When it arrived, I just placed it on the shelf with a number of other books I intended to read. And there it stayed for several months.

In September of that same year, I saw on MSN news and other outlets, reports of a train collision, specifically, a Metrolink and Union Pacific freight train, in the Chatsworth district of California. Many people lost their lives. The part of the story that caught my attention focused on one particular passenger, Mr. Charles Peck, who was travelling home to family. At the time of the crash, Mr. Peck's son received a call from his father. There was no voice on the line, his son simply asked, "are you okay?" and "where are you?" to which there was no reply. The immediate family began to receive calls from Mr. Peck's cell phone, all during the time that rescue-workers were trying to recover people form the train carriages. When the family answered their phones, all they could hear was static. When they tried to call him back, their calls went straight to voicemail, as if his battery had died or the phone were switched off.

The family became aware of the crash from the news. When Mr. Peck's wife received the next call, they believed he was trapped in the wreckage, just able to reach his phone and press the buttons. They yelled words of encouragement, "hold on, rescuers are coming, we love you" and words to that effect. Calls were even made to Mr. Peck's landline phone. Rescuers became aware of this and worked even harder to find him—a potential survivor in the wreckage. On tracing the calls, they appeared to be coming from the first carriage. All calls ended at 3:28 a.m.; half an hour later, Mr. Peck's body was found. He'd died on first impact and been dead for hours. A total of thirty-five calls were made from Mr. Peck's phone to family, from the time of the train crash to discovery of his body. His phone was never recovered.

Now, even then, as a budding psychology undergraduate, I thought the most likely explanation for this case was that Mr. Peck's phone was thrown in the wreckage, was pressed against something and was calling the last people in his call register, over and over again. Travelling home, he likely made calls and texts beforehand, and that would be to his family. The phone then called the last people in the phone's register until the battery finally died.

What caught my attention the most, was the popular interpretation of events and the technology. It was perceived as a "phone call from the dead" and the media widely published it as such. But there was no

Postscript: 45 Years Later...

conversation? Just actions of the phone linked to crisis and personal loss. Comforting? That certainly seems to be the case, and such "after-death communication" experience have been known to be of such benefit, especially thanks to Dr. Rees pushing such findings in the *British Medical Journal* in 1971 and highlighting the decades of research behind him from the S.P.R. Even so, surely *Phone Calls from the Dead* by Rogo and Bayless had more to it than ringing phones at the time of loss? Like the stopping of a clocks when someone dies, as was noted by many at one time and written into the children's song *My Grandfather's Clock*.

I turned from the news reports and reached for *Phone Calls from the Dead* from the pile of books and began reading. Sure enough, it was full of examples of actual voices on the line and even conversations. With the Type 2 *Prolonged Calls*, I realized that there *were* extended conversations, ten or twenty minutes at a time, and recipients to the calls discovering afterwards that the caller had died sometime before. I knew the parapsychology literature quite well at this point, but this did perk my interest. Cell phones were rapidly developing in their capabilities and the iPhone had only just been introduced in 2007. It took a few more years to see many people with them, and using them for the internet and satellite navigation when driving.

I was hooked. I read every page of the book, cover to cover, made notes and then trawled through every parapsychology journal I could find post 1979 to find any new material, other articles, mentions, and book reviews of *Phone Calls from the Dead* by parapsychologists, and any other scholar that saw fit to review it. We were now in the age of baby monitors, text messages, emails, and starting to use webcameras for internet calls. What was the state of play now for such strange experiences? As Bayless said in his "electronic communication" article in 1980, as technology developed, people would continue to report strange experiences. He believed ninety-nine percent of it was misinterpretation, psychological errors, and technological faults, but "that one percent" remaining, would be difficult to explain—as Dr. McAdams has often reminded, of Bayless. Had such experiences with the telephone continued with mobile technology?

I trawled the library and I trawled the Internet. I found very little to begin with. The Internet was providing me with fresh material and links, mentions of text messages, and of emails. A few people approached me about such cases when I asked out on social media. I gained a bit of national fame in 2009, when the BBC announced that I'd been awarded the Eileen J. Garrett Scholarship from the Parapsychology Foundation to help support my studies. Suddenly, I had emails and letters posted to my supervisors—Prof. Roe and Dr. Sherwood—offering congratulations and accounts I might be interest in. This led to my first article on the topic simply entitled "phone calls from the dead" which came out in *Anomaly*, the journal of the Association for the Scientific Study of Anomalous Phenomena.

In writing this postscript, I've returned to that article to read it. It contains an account of perhaps one of the longest "phone calls from the dead," whereby there were repeated calls, two to three times a week, for some three years. It was reported to me by a doctor of social science, and I referred to him as Dr. Jones. He'd never been involved in parapsychology, but had shown an interest when the Koestler Parapsychology Chair (a full professorship position for parapsychology) was being offered at the University of Edinburgh in the 1980s. He said to me:

> Ok, the Scott Rogo and Bayless book I have. I bought it a number of years ago when I was doing my Ph.D. I must admit I toyed then with the idea of doing some research myself. My Ph.D. supervisor at Bath, Prof. Harry Collins, had already done some work on 'spoon bending' (in the psychology department) and written a book on the subject (with Trevor Pinch). Moreover, Harry was also one of the panel involved in determining who would get the 'Koestler Bequest' and in appointing Robert Morris to the post at Edinburgh. I met him when he came down to Bath at that time. However, as I have indicated, I felt unable to tell my story in those days … and anyway I was already working in the Social Studies of Science doing my Ph.D.

His story was essentially this: as a child in the winter of 1958, Dr. Jones lived in a complicated but manageable home. His parents had split up but were living under the same roof, still, each going about their daily business without any obvious tensions mentioned. His mother had taken regular calls of up to fifteen minutes at a time, two to three times a week, from an old childhood sweetheart. One day, her heart was broken as she learned of his hospitalization, and soon after, having passed away. But about a week later, at a regular time for him to call, the telephone rang. She went to answer it and was gone for a while and then returned, as white as sheet. "Who was it?" the young Jones asked. His mother was stunned into silence, but then said, "it was him!" Her sweetheart, Richard, had called. More and more calls came through, just as regularly as when Richard was alive.

On one occasion when Dr. Jones's mother was out, and at a time when a call would normally come through for her, the telephone rang, and Dr. Jones somewhat reluctantly answered it. He heard the sound of wind and rushing air on the line and shouted "she's not here" slamming the handset back down on the receiver. Years later, the social scientist in him, wished he'd just been patient and inquisitive enough to hear whatever would have come next. The calls decreased and finally stopped in 1961. This was either a very longwinded prank, that the prankster was highly committed to, or something else. The family didn't know what to do, they just accepted the uncanny.

Many years later, after Dr. Jones's mother had passed away, he discovered her extensive personal diaries from that time. He thought they would hold the answer to what was *really* going on with those phone calls all those years ago. They did nothing of the sort; they just added more questions. Weekly records of those calls had similar wording, over and over again:

> Sunday morning my darling phoned to say that he loved me, and now I must be happy. I had been good, and soon he would come again to talk with me. I ask him to help me sleep, and he said, "now you will sleep." Goodbye darling, I'll be back soon to talk with you.

I wrote more articles on the topic as I found more material. Skeptical breakdowns of cases with cell phones and answering machines, trying to explore the conventional mechanisms involved. I published in *Anomaly* again, the *Australian Journal of Parapsychology* for some international reach, and the S.P.R.'s magazine to share modern accounts of "text messages from the dead."

For example, on April 2nd, 2008, the *Blackpool Gazette* reported on the case of a British man, claiming to have received strange calls and text messages from his deceased wife. Just after Frank's wife had died, and tragically losing his thirty-two-year-old son three months later, he entered the family home to find a missed call on his cell phone without the phone having rung. Now, there are plenty of conventional explanations for that, but *this* missed call to his phone had come from *his house telephone*—the landline. And yet, he was the only one in the house, having just returned from work. He could smell perfume and cigarettes associated with his late wife in the house. Five years on,

Frank's daughter, who no longer lived at the house, reported the text messages. She'd received them to her phone, words and phrases her mother regularly used, but no sender number, date, nothing. There was no information as to where the messages came from. Frank told the *Blackpool Gazette*, that the most eerie and ironic thing was that his wife had been buried with her mobile phone!

After my graduation, and while doing my master's degree, I spent a lot of my time in Portsmouth, on the south coast of the UK. I have fond memories of spending some evenings in The Dolphin pub, co-owned by a Mr. Alan Dale. We'd chat and go on drives around town, talking about the world and ghostly experiences. With the topic of "phone calls from the dead" he knew it would be of wide interest. He put me in touch with his friends at Tricorn Books, and that was that. Deal done. I was writing what I wanted to be considered a second volume to the Rogo and Bayless book—simply called *Telephone Calls from the Dead*.

I presented on the topic at the S.P.R. conference, at the University of Edinburgh, in 2011. It was my first ever conference presentation, and I remember being very nervous. I'd befriended Mr. John L. Randall a few years prior, and he visited the University of Northampton on a couple of occasions. He'd encouraged me to explore the topic and find explanations. Mr. Randall had never been interested in tape-recorded voices (electronic voice phenomenon, EVP), but found phone calls somewhat different. He passed away in 2011, and it spurred me on to write and take these next steps. I spoke of his passing at the conference, and I spoke of the Rogo and Bayless book and where we are now. I got through the talk and people were very interested. I'd clearly hit on a topic that had not been discussed in a very long time and was of popular interest. I had also got in touch Dr. McAdams, and then, Rogo's father—Mr. Jack Rogo—which led to his telling me of the archive of his son's material at the California Institute of Integral Studies, and he gave permission for me to use it. The library staff were very kind. They went through the forty-two boxes of material and a folder of "phone call" cases, scanning them all for me. This included new cases, post 1979! My new book was to be a further analysis of fifty cases (old and new), much like that of Rogo and Bayless, but with added discussion of where technology was going, text message cases, emails and beyond.

Telephone Calls from the Dead came out in January 2012. It was the strangest of feelings having a lorry bring boxes and boxes of material that I'd written and with a cover I'd helped design. I was in Egypt at the time so was not the first to hold or set eyes on it. On my return to the UK, interest peaked, with radio interviews, newspaper articles, and *Coast to Coast AM* with George Noory.

I travelled out to Southern California—on Rogo's birthday, 1st February, coincidentally—to meet Dr. McAdams and speak to her group on the topic. Later on that trip, I met Rogo's father. He showed me around the family home in Hollywood where Scott had grown up. He kept all his books in the dining room, published in various languages. He showed me photos and the painting, above the fireplace, by Raymond Bayless in gratitude to Mrs. Rogo. We remained friends and in communication from then on. Incidentally, I went back out to Hollywood in May 2019 and interviewed Mr. Rogo at length about his son. I was just in time. Two weeks later he passed away peacefully at the age of 98. It felt as if he'd waited for that meeting to help me complete his son's story.

My writing of *Telephone Calls from the Dead* and traveling out to California was my first major stepping-stone in parapsychology, beyond the haunting investigations, the laboratory work, and the reading I'd done. This was traveling, meeting people connected to Rogo and Bayless, trying to understand their perspectives and goals, and taking the next step.

Back in the UK, after a brief spell at Sheffield Hallam University, I returned to the University of Northampton for my Ph.D. I looked at how anomalous experiences around death can promote the emotion of hope (goal attainment and motivation) and aid in bereavement recovery. This was my life for four and a half years. I'd forever get reminded of "phone calls from the dead," indeed, the book remained popular as I put my hand to other work. I assisted with other projects, established myself with the Alex Tanous Foundation, and now and then, did radio and television work as a featured parapsychologist and voice of skepticism. I went on to answer the original desires of Dr. Schmeidler, in that Rogo and Bayless could have strengthened their study, which existed only in book form, by publishing a peer-reviewed report on their methods and findings. Everything I did for *Telephone Calls from the Dead*, the data, the methods, the analysis, was summarized, peer-assessed and published in the *Journal of Parapsychology* in 2014.

Other parapsychology researchers have turned their attention to the "phantom phone call mystery" too. In 2016, French sociologist, Dr. Laurent Kasprowicz, launched a survey into these experiences, having had a strange experience with the telephone himself. He collected approximately thirty cases of substantial quality, and like Dr. Biondi, he found comparable characteristics to the Rogo and Bayless sample. Dr. Kasprowicz published his findings in the book *Des Coups De Fil De L'Au-Delà?* (Phone Calls from Beyond?). Uniquely, Dr. Kasprowicz, has favored a Jungian approach to these strange calls, by exploring the "trickster archetype" because of the *elusive* nature of the phenomenon and the *high strangeness* of the cases with so few recordings. He argues that due to the mechanical involvement of the telephone, and some instances of recordings, it would not be a fair skeptical assertion to say these are purely subjective experiences. Something objective, *is happening* for the witnesses.

Clinical psychologist, Dr. Renaud Evrard, from the University of Lorraine, took examples of cases from Dr. Kasprowicz work and explored the question of how might therapists, dealing with parapsychological experiences (known as clinical parapsychology), support people who have these experiences which involve technological elements? Part of his conclusions focused on the lack of documented cases, and the fact that the focal point is often a telephone, and an objectiveness to the experiences, where many psi type experiences could be seen as subjective. And yet, aside from the issue of the source of the calls, the experient reports a *very real* and *impactful* set of events, which often demonstrates to be of great benefit to mourning and coping.

That same year, 2017, things took a turn on these cases in the media. I had received emails from a Mr. Danny Robins. I'm sorry to say I had got into the typical academic problem of mountains of email traffic. I believe what happened was this. Danny asked to come and interview me and colleagues at the University of Northampton about our work in parapsychology—strange experiences of everyday people to laboratory research of psi—and we set a date. I must have agreed to it… and forgot!

Weeks later, I was going about my duties, Ph.D. research and giving lectures in parapsychology, and on my leaving the main doors of, what was, the Fawsley psychology building, a man with dark hair and a big smile was outside with his colleague, Mr. Simon Barnard.

"Cal!" Danny approached me with that big smile and an outstretched hand to shake mine as though I'd dashed outside ready for a meeting with him. I'd totally forgotten and was begging my brain to give me a clue as to who these people were with recording equipment to hand. And then "brain" helped me, along with the announcement of "I'm Danny, and this is Simon". I dropped everything I was doing—I honestly couldn't remember what I was meant to be doing anyway—and assisted these gentlemen in their podcast and introduced them to

Postscript: 45 Years Later...

other parapsychologists in the department. And so became the episode 'death is not the end' in the podcast, *Haunted*.

I mention this memory of my sometimes being completely unorganized in my social diary—and I'm so glad it actually went well—because it led to the next big jump of interest in the "phantom phone call mystery."

Danny moved on to other podcasts which gained a lot of public interest, *The Battersea Poltergeist*, and now, *Uncanny*, through BBC Radio 4 and BBC Sounds. The latter, has a large fan base, with the show discussing a single case during every episode and bringing in a skeptic (normally a parapsychologist / psychologist) and a believer, to help Danny break down the events that occurred stage by stage.

As voted by fans in 2024, the number one favorite episode is "Harry Called"—a telephone case. It involves a man called Will, who reluctantly got involved in a Ouija board séance with friends. (A self-professed skeptic and non-believer in ghosts.) He decided to watch over what they were doing instead being directly involved. The name "H.A.R.R.Y." was spelt out, they asked what the spirit wanted, to which "W.I.L.L." was spelt out. He asked his friends to stop and thought it was nonsense.

Back in his student residence, and long before mobile phones, there was a payphone at the end of the corridor, which the students on that hall shared. Everyone had a sheet of paper on their door for phone messages: in case you missed a call, a roommate could write down the message. Will returned to see the message "Harry called..." He assumed it to be a prank from his friends, calling the payphone and leaving that message with someone. This continued, more of the same message as he returned, and yet, *he didn't know anyone called Harry.* He asked his friends repeatedly and they categorically denied making such calls.

One day, a fellow student knocked on Will's door and said, "Harry is on the phone." Will rushed to the phone to find out who the "prankster" was, but the man on the line just talked over Will, "talking gibberish" as Will described it, and it certainly wasn't one of his friends:

> It's a very strange thing to say, but the sound seemed *out of time:* this was the 1990s; this voice did not sound as if it was from the 1990s talking. I didn't like it at all. It was the type of voice that unnerved me.

These experiences continued for Will: sometimes notes on his door that "Harry called" and on another occasion he was called to the phone again, but was not hearing a voice, only the distant sounds of wind on the line, whooshing and clatter, which Rogo and Bayless had noted as a common audible feature of many documented calls. Will's case included apparitional experiences, which he attributed to this "Harry" figure, and following one such experience of seeing the figure in his room, he never received the telephone calls again.

This case has become so popular that actor Reece Shearsmith has provided the introduction to the BBC Sounds recording, as one of his personal favorites. I first met Reece in 2012 at a conference at the University of Bath. We shared our love for old devices of the séance room and for the writings of the English ghost hunter, Harry Price. I gave him a copy of *Telephone Calls from the Dead* during this first meet and we've remained friends ever since, often sharing on updates in parapsychology. Indeed, with his popular television series *Inside No. 9*, the Halloween episode "Dead Line" begins with what you think is going to be a "phone call from the dead." An elderly man returns home with a mobile phone he has found and wants to return it to its owner. But the plot twists, in classic *Inside No.9* style—with the viewer feeling confident the story will go one way then takes another route. Often, an eerie and dark one...

Uncanny featured a couple more cases in later episodes. The next time in series 3 with a child's toy, a classic Fisher Price Retro "Chatter" telephone, being a focus of poltergeist activity. Amanda, from Manchester, UK, reported that as a ten-year-old child, her brother Elton was forever using this toy phone one Christmas and irritating the family with the constant ringing.

Elton came into the bedroom one night to wake his sister and said, "Mandy, Mandy, I can hear the telephone ringing, it isn't me, it's scaring me, I don't like it." She invited her brother to sleep in the bunkbed with her, and Elton didn't return to his room. The grandmother, who was round regularly to babysit, complained to the mother of hearing what she thought were the children out of bed at night, footsteps running up and down the landing and stairs. But, on checking, the children were fast asleep. Such experiences continued, with this toy telephone being a focal point. There were independent ringing sounds, which Amanda even encountered herself late at night on going to investigate Elton's room, which had become so cold she could see her own breath. On her flicking the light-switch on, the phone stopped ringing immediately. She found Elton cowering under blankets on his bed and the telephone was found under the bed, and nowhere near his grasp to be manipulating the toy himself. So much more besides happened in this fascinating case.

Postscript: 45 Years Later...

This type of account might even spark memories for many people of the 1986 movie *Poltergeist 2: The Other Side*, where, following the grandmother dying in her sleep, the child—Carol Anne Freeling—awakens in the middle of the night to her toy telephone ringing. She gets out of bed and answers it, to hear comforting words of goodbye from her grandmother before sinister voices take over. Incidentally, Rogo, was featured in a promotional trailer for the first film!

I'd been an expert in series 2 of *Uncanny*, but returned again for series 4 when it went to the USA. The episode "Dad's Phone" involved the case of a deceased father, who had not had a particularly good relationship with his daughter, Wendy, from Austin, Texas. Her Dad had stalker type qualities, owing to his job as a secret agent, and had sophisticated equipment in his house, including a telephone system. On sorting her late father's belongings in the house, Wendy received calls from this device only to hear what seemed to be responsive static. A friend, Brian, who had gotten on well with Wendy's father, was told about these experiences sometime later while in the house. He was very skeptical of their claims, and said it couldn't have happened without it being wired up. He picked it off the wall to show the family, and then when he placed it back on the wall, the phone began ringing! He was shocked at such an impossibility. He'd worked with electronics for a living. Wendy and her children told Brian to pick it up. He did so and could hear the responsive static, yet again, just as it had been described to him. Dumbfounded, Brian decided to speak words of comfort, telling the static, as if it were Wendy's father, to go, be at peace, in an attempt to stop the ringing. He placed the handset down and then picked it up again and it was dead—as it should have been.

Stories like this really capture people's attention, and make you wonder, what is going on? Everyone loves a mystery and many of these phone calls present one where a conventional answer is not forthcoming. It has led to inspired fictional writing as Rogo and Bayless mentioned with Alfred Hitchcock and then exploring whether it was based on truth. Indeed, in the *Book of Ghost Stories* for children, the writer Roald Dahl, even included a telephone-based story; and then there's Daniel Cohen's *Phone Call from a Ghost*. There are countless examples now in fiction writing and motion picture, and like the Hitchcock case, some apparently have been adapted from purportedly true accounts.

Things have advanced in forty-five years—massively in some ways, but with slow progression in others. Dozens more people have completed doctorates, at various universities around the world, in parapsychology since 1979. In the UK alone, there are over a dozen universities with taught modules of parapsychology, and more besides, conducting research. Journals with focus on the topic of death have expanded. Rogo mentioned *Omega*, which is still going to this day, but we also have the *Journal of Near-Death Studies*, *Mortality*, and *Death Studies*, all of which have accepted many parapsychology themed papers. More and more studies have ended up in medical themed journals. As a follow on from Dr. Rees, and his publication in the *British Medical Journal*, I have been involved in the next steps. Dr. Rees surveyed two hundred and ninety-three widows and widowers on their after-death communication experiences. With colleagues, I engaged in another survey of just over *one thousand people* which we published in the *British Journal of Psychiatry Open*, showing how common these experiences are and their common characteristics.*

We've learnt so much more about what the human brain is capable of, especially, what appears "paranormal" when, in fact, it's not. We've learnt a lot about the benefits these experiences can bring, especially to the bereaved in coping with loss and recovery. Research shows that they are highly beneficial, perfectly natural, with rarely ever a sign of psychosis, and have been documented since ancient times. And yet, there are a few, which to seem to be hard to explain by conventional mechanisms. Some might even support the notion of survival of death, where we can find no obvious technical fault, fraud, and no one knew of the death of the caller until after the call had taken place.

Again, Bayless was right: technology has advanced with the times; so too, have our experiences with the technology, including what we *perceive* to be out of the ordinary when it comes to its typical operation.

Dr. Kasprowicz, and I, independently, continue to be interested in these cases and actively collect them where possible. The latest academic interest has come from Professor Imants Barušs, a psychologist at King's University College at Western University, Canada. His study explores after-death communication experiences—whereby people believe the activity was focused on their cell phones—initially by distributing a ninety-five item questionnaire to twenty-one participants. This project is still in its early days, but increasing in participant numbers and now moving into one-to-one interviews for the next phases. The project has also received substantial funding from BIAL Foundation,

---

* To access and read all of our publications to date and media engagement, visit: www.adcrp.org

Postscript: 45 Years Later...

where the 2024 interim report details one hundred and eighteen people who were surveyed on after-death communication experiences, with fifty-six claiming "they had experienced apparent after-death communication with cell phones." That is a very high number of such claims, in my skeptical view. It is, however, due in part to the research team focusing on Facebook interest groups for EVP and Instrumental Trans-Communication (ITC). I eagerly await further developments and findings from Professor Baruss and his team—especially their conclusions.

It should be clear by now that there has been very little systematic research into these very specific forms of anomalous experience that parapsychology can explore. More cases with cell phones need carefully exploring, including text messages, video chat, and now, artificial intelligence implications. I have been asked about all of these in recent times at public talks and on radio shows and I don't have all the answers, because I haven't explored any large sample of more modern cases—yet! I can only offer educated guesses, and some healthy skepticism thrown into the mix, when tasked with explaining such modern cases away as "the voice of healthy skepticism." But that can often be easier said than done.

Are people now claiming the dead are intercepting Zoom meetings? Or sneaking into WhatsApp chats?

"I'll just put you on hold," as the research continues ...

Callum E. Cooper, Ph.D.
January 2025

Bibliography

CHAPTER 2

Harlow, S. R. (1961). *A Life After Death*. Doubleday.

Owens, D. B. (1969). The telephone call. *Fate,* 22 (9), 104-106.

Rogo, D. S. (1977). Phone calls from the dead? *Fate,* (10), 85-90.

Tollen, V. (1974). Phone call from beyond. *Fate,* 27 (7), 94-96.

CHAPTER 3

Harlow, S. R. (1961). *A Life After Death*. Doubleday.

Schwarz, B. (1975). Telepathic humoresque. In Stanley Dean (Ed.), *Psychiatry and Mysticism* (pp. 79-94). Nelson-Hall.

Schwarz, B. (1977). The Men in Black Syndrome I. *Flying Saucer Review,* 23, 9-15.

Smith, S. (1975). *The Power of the Mind*. Chilton.

Uphoff, W., & Uphoff, M. J. (1975). *New Psychic Frontiers*. Colin Smythe.

CHAPTER 4

Bender, H. (1974). Modern poltergeist research. In Beloff, J. (Ed.), *New Directions in Parapsychology* (pp. 122-143). Elek Science.

Flammarion, C. (1921-23). *Death and Its Mystery* (3 volumes). Century Co.

Gurney, E., Podmore, F., & Myers, F.W.H. (1886). *Phantasms of the Living* (2 volumes). Trübner & Co.

Sidgwick, H, Sidgwick, E., & Johnson, A. (1894). Report on the Census of Hallucinations. *Proceedings of the Society for Psychical Research* 10, 25-422.

Rhine, L. (1961). *Hidden Channels of the Mind*. William Sloane.

CHAPTER 5

Cahill, Mary. (1953). A Call from Beyond. *Fate*, 6 (9), 73-74.

Hitchcock, A. (1955). My five greatest mysteries. *Coronet* (September), 75-77.

Mahony, P. (1973). *Who's There?* Manor Books.

Pritchard, R. (1960). Voice on the phone. *Fate*, 13 (1), 100.

Rees, W. D. (1971). The hallucinations of widowhood. *British Medical Journal*, 4, 37-44.

Rogo, D. Scott. (1980). A poltergeist in Los Angeles. *Theta*, 8 (4), 2-5.

CHAPTER 6

Bayless, R. (1959). Correspondence. *Journal of the American Society for Psychical Research*, 53, 35-38.

Franklyn, J. (1954). "Explain Please!" *Tomorrow*, 2 (4), 79-84.

Hunt, H.E. (1931). A telephone Interruption. *Light* (June 19th), 291.

Raudive, K. (1971). *Breakthrough*. Taplinger.

Rogo, D.S. (1977). Paranormal tape-recorded voices: A paraphysical breakthrough. In J. White, & S. Krippner (Eds.), *Future Science* (pp. 451-464). Anchor/Doubleday.

Smith, S. (1977). *Voices of the Dead?* New American Library.

Walker, D. (1956). *Spooks Deluxe*. Watts.

Welch, W. (1975). *Talks with the Dead*. Pinnacle.

CHAPTER 7

Eisenwein, W. (1968). An untelephoned message. *Fate, 21* (8), 61-62.

Ferrara, R. (1973). Phone call from Tinian. *Fate, 26* (12), 58-59.

Fisk, G.W., & Mitchell, A.M.J. (1953). The application of differential scoring methods to PK tests. *Journal of the Society for Psychical Research, 37,* 45-60.

Haynes, R. (1976). *The Seeing Eye, the Seeing I.* St. Martin's Press.

McConnell, R.A. (1955). Remote night tests for PK." *Journal of the American Society for Psychical Research, 49,* 99-108.

Talbot, M., & Biggle [Jr.], L., (1976). Quantum physics and reality. *Analog, 96,* 47-57.

Torkildson, G. (1976). Connection to the beyond. *Fate 29* (10), 92-94.

Roberts, U. (n.d.). *The Great Tomorrow.* Hale.

Schmidt, H. (1976). PK experiment with repeated, time displaced feedback. In J.D. Morris, W.G. Roll, & R.L. Morris (Eds.), *Research in Parapsychology 1975* (pp. 107-109). Scarecrow Press.

Schwarz, Berthold. Personal communication.

Wheeler, J. (1968). Superspace and the nature of quantum geometrodynamics. In C. DeWitt, & J. A. Wheeler (Eds.), *Battelle Rencontres, 1967 Lectures in Mathematics and Physics* (pp. 615-724). W. A. Benjamin, Inc.

CHAPTER 8

Carrington, H. (1939). *Laboratory Investigations into Psychic Phenomena.* Rider & Co.

Ebon, M. (1971). *They Knew the Unknown.* New American Library. [See Chapter 2: "Thomas Edison: A Machine to Contact the Dead"]

Geldert, L.N. (1918). *Thy Son Liveth.* Little, Brown Co.

Green, E., & Green, A. (1977). *Beyond Biofeedback.* Delacorte Press.

Hyslop, J. H. (1913). The case of Mrs. Blake. *Proceedings of the American Society of Psychical Research, 7,* 570-788.

Melton, F.R. (1921). Telephonic communication with the next world. *Light* (August 20th), 534-537.

Melton, F.R. (1921). *A Psychic Telephone*. E. Brown & Co. [Re-printed by Tricorn Books with an introduction by Callum E. Cooper, 2025]

Prince, W. J. (1920). Additional Notes on Two Books. *Journal of the American Society for Psychical Research, 14*, 615-26.

Sheargold, R. (n.d.). *Personal communications*.

Grierson, F. (1921). *Psycho-phone Messages*. Austin Publishing Company.

Weinberger, Julius. (1977). Apparatus communication with discarnate persons. In J. White, & S. Krippner (Eds.), *Future Science* (pp. 465-486). Anchor/Doubleday.

Wilson, D. (1915). *The ethereal transmission of thought. Light* (March 13th), 123-124.

POSTSCRIPT

Alvarado, C. (2005). Obituary: Raymond Gordon Bayless, 1920-2004. *Journal of the Society for Psychical Research, 69*, 238-239.

Anderson (1981). [Review of the book *Phone Calls from the Dead* by D. Scott Rogo and Raymond Bayless]. *Journal of Religion and Psychical Research, 4* (1), 66-74.

Barušs, I., Padilla, E., Gulyaprak, R., Mandoki, M., Ens, N., Shelvock, M., McMasters, P., Vasudev, A., Toporow, C., & Hutchinson, L. (2024). *After-Death Communication with Cell Phones: Interim Results*. Invited presentation of abstract, Bial Foundation Symposium "Behind and Beyond the Brain," Casa do Médico, April 3-6, Porto, Portugal.

Bayless, R. (1980). Electronic communication. *Journal of the Academy of Religion and Psychical Research, 3* (1), 37-40.

Biondi, M. (1984). Le telefonate dall' Aldila': Una nuova fenomenologia paranormale? *Quaderni di Parapsicologia, 15*(1), 60-67.

Biondi, M. (1996). Periscopio. *Luce e Ombra, 96* 92), 199-206.

Cohen, D. (1988). *Phone Call from a Ghost*. A Minstrel Book.

Cooper, C.E. (2010). Phone calls from the dead. *Anomaly, 44*, 3-21.

Cooper, C.E. (2010). Spontaneous cases concerning telephone calls and text messages. *Australian Journal of Parapsychology, 10*, 178-193.

Cooper, C. E. (2011). Test messages from the dead. *Paranormal Review*, 53, 10-12.

Cooper, C.E. (2011). Further comments on alleged phone calls from the dead. *Anomaly*, 45, 146-154.

Cooper, C.E. (2012). An interview with Dr. Elizabeth McAdams. *Paranormal Review*, 62, 18-22.

Cooper, C.E. (2012). *Telephone Calls from the Dead*. Tricorn Books. [2nd printing released in 2024]

Cooper, C.E. (2014). An analysis of exceptional experiences involving telecommunication technology. *Journal of Parapsychology*, 78 (2), 209- 222.

Cooper, C. E. (2019). D. Scott Rogo. *Psi Encyclopedia*. Retrieved from: https://psi-encyclopedia.spr.ac.uk/articles/d-scott-rogo

Cooper, C.E. (in production). *Rogo: The Life and Tragic Death of an Outspoken Parapsychologist*. Tricorn Books.

Dahl, R. (1983). *Book of Ghost Stories*. Jonathan Cape.

Elsaesser, E., Roe, C. A., Cooper, C. E., & Lorimer, D. (2021). The phenomenology and impact of hallucinations concerning the deceased. *BJPsych Open*, 7(5), e148.

Evrard, R. (2017). Ghost in the machine: A clinical view of anomalous telecommunication experiences. *Journal of Exceptional Experiences and Psychology*, 5(2), 21-30.

Holly, J.C. (1954). Grandfather's clocks. *Fate*, 7 (9), 25-30.

Jones, (Dr.) (2009). *Dr. Jones personal communication, November 26th*.

Kadiragha, D., & Baruš, I. (2022). After-death communication with cell phones [conference abstracts: SSE/PA connections, 2021]. *Journal of Parapsychology*, 86, 47-48.

Kasprowicz, L. (2016). *Quand les morts nous contactent. Enquête sur le phénomène des coups de téléphone post-mortem et autres contacts supposés avec les morts*. Chez l'auteur

Kasprowicz, L. (2024). *Des coups de fil de l'au-delà?* Les éditions Trédaniel.

Rees, W.D. (1971). The hallucinations of widowhood. *British Medical Journal*, 4, 37-44.

Rogo (1981). Author responds to book review: *Phone Calls from the Dead*. *Journal of Religion and Psychical Research*, 4 (1), 75-80.

Rogo (1986). *Life After Death: The Case for Survival of Bodily Death.* Guild Publishing.

Rogo, D.S., & Bayless (1981). *Llamadas Telefonicas Del Más Allá.* Editorial Diana.

Ross, I. (1974). Death can stop your clock. *Fate*, 27 (11), 95-97.

McAdams, E.E., & Bayless, R. (1981). *The Case for Life After Death: Parapsychologists Look at the Evidence.* Nelson Hall.

About the Authors

D. **Scott Rogo** (1950-1990) was an accomplished musician having attended the University of Cincinnati and California State University, Northridge, graduating with a B.A. in music in 1972. He majored in the psychology of music, and played the oboe and English-horn professionally with the San Diego Symphony and various other ensembles for two years. He was a self-educated parapsychologist and was notorious for being fiercely knowledgeable of the subject. Much of his early knowledge acquisition was thanks to the mentorship of Raymond Bayless and their collaboration in EVP research from the age of sixteen. He was a member of the S.P.R. and American S.P.R. and, for a time, research officer for the Southern California S.P.R. He'd held positions with the Maimonides Medical Center's division of Parapsychology and Psychophysics, and on the faculty of John F. Kennedy University's M.A. program in parapsychology. He was consultant editor for *Fate* magazine for a number of years, and began publishing with the magazine in 1968 on the topic of vampires before turning to parapsychology. He was the author of hundreds of articles and 30 books, to the point of his death at the age of forty in 1990. His murder shocked the world of parapsychology, and went unsolved for 30 years. Between 2021-2022, the mystery of his death was finally brought to a close.

Raymond Bayless (1920-2004) abandoned at birth; Raymond's true date of birth is unknown. He made his living, as a popular landscape and still life painter. He had famously provided fictional paintings for H.P. Lovecraft, H.G. Well's *War of the Worlds*, with some of his works hanging in the US National Art and Space Museum and public buildings. Within parapsychology, he is known as the experimental discoverer of Electronic Voice Phenomenon (EVP), having published a report on his recordings in the *Journal of the American Society for Psychical Research* in 1959. His books and writings mainly focused on interest in the survival of death hypothesis, such as *The Enigma of the Poltergeist*, *The Other Side of Death*, and *Animal Ghosts*. He was a member of the British and American S.P.R. and served for a number of years as the librarian and research officer of the Southern California S.P.R. Following his death, his wife, Majorie, believed that Raymond had made several ghostly returns—as he had promised!

Callum E. Cooper, Ph.D., was born in 1988 in Nottinghamshire, UK. He is a Fellow and Chartered member of the British Psychological Society (est. 1901). He is also a council member of the S.P.R. (est. 1882), Chair of its Survival Research Committee, a professional member of the Parapsychological Association (est. 1957) and Visiting Library Fellow of the Parapsychology Foundation (est. 1951). He is based at the University of Northampton, UK, and is co-director for parapsychology education at the California Institute for Human Science where he holds a Professorship for *Parapsychology and Public Understanding of Human Science*. Cal has received various awards for parapsychology, media and skepticism. To date, he has over 100 published articles and research papers, over two dozen chapters and forewords, and authored/edited 6 books including: *Telephone Calls from the Dead* (2012), and *Paracoustics: Sound and the Paranormal* (2015). Within his various media roles, he features as a guest psychologist and voice of skepticism on the hit BBC Radio 4 show *Uncanny* with Danny Robins, where *strange telephone cases* have become very popular, including episodes such as "Harry Called" (Series 2, Case 10) and "Dad's Phone" (Series 4, Case 2) which can be reheard anytime on BBC sounds. Visit: www.callumecooper.com

Index

A

Abbott, David, 65, 133-138
Abbott, Phillip, 65
Adams, Patricia (pseudonym), 18-20, 23, 29, 36, 60 171
AIDS, 171
Alex Tanous Foundation, 179
Alexander, David, 169
Alvarado, Carlos, 172
Amanda (*Uncanny*, radio show), 182
American Magazine, 144
American Society for Psychical Research (A.S.P.R.), 89, 104, 127, 133, 143, 194
Analog (magazine), 106
Anomaly (journal), 100-101
"Anniversary" cases, 59, 61, 68
"Anti-survivalists," 47
Apparitions and Survival of Bodily Death (Bayless)
Approach-avoidance conflict, 113
Association for the Scientific Study of Anomalous Phenomena, 176
Audubon (magazine), 100-101
Australian Journal of Parapsychology, 177

B

B., Mr., 36
Baby monitor, 175
Bander, Peter, 87-88
Barnard, Simon, 180
Barušs, Imants, 184-185
Battersea Poltergeist, The (podcast), 181
Battista, John, 172
Bayless, Marjorie, 91, 170-173
B.B.C., 175, 181-182, 194-195
Beard's Roman Women! (Burgess), 66
Behind the Scenes with the Mediums (Abbott), 133
Belli, Melvin, 110-111
Beloff, John, 105, 154-156, 161-167
Bender, Hans, 1, 50-51, 81
Bessor, John, 1, 61, 64
Beyond Biofeedback (Green and Green), 139
BIAL Foundation, 184
Bigfoot, 7, 173
Biggle, Lloyd, Jr., 106
Biondi, Massimo, 170-171, 179
Blackpool Gazette (newspaper), 177-178

Blake, Elizabeth, 133
Blue Room, The (Chapman), 140
Book of Ghost Stories (Dahl), 183
Brace, Iris, 42-44
Breakthrough (Raudive), 86-88, 123
Brier, Bob, 149
British College of Psychic Science, 129
British Medical Journal, 184
Broughton, Richard, 173

C

Cahill, Mary, 60-62, 64, 67-68
Cahill, Peggy, 60
California Institute for Integral Studies, 170, 178
Carrington, Hereward, 129, 131, 142-143
Carry on Talking (Bander), 88
Cell phone /mobile, 174-175, 177, 184-185
Chapman, Clive, 140
Chari, T.K., 97
Clark, Everett, 41
Clark, Jerome, 1, 61, 10-1032
Clark, Penny, 102
Clawson, George, 133-138
Clement, Father, 117-118, 120
Coast to Coast A.M. (radio show), 179
Colin Smythe Ltd., 87-88
Collins, Harry, 176
Connie, 69-70
Cooper, Callum E., 169-185, 194
Crosa, Giuseppe, 146

D

D'Alessio, Marie, 26, 37, 40-42, 54, 114
D'Alessio, Mrs. Sam, 37, 41

D'Alessio, Peter, 38
Dahl, Roald, 183
Dale, Alan, 178
Death and Its Mystery (Flammarion), 57
Death Studies (journal), 184
Death, interest in, 1
Delanoy, Deborah, 173
Detective, 172
Dimwiddie, Walter, 145
Doyle, Arthur Conan, 140
Duke University, 50, 149
Duncan, Barbara, 118-120
Duncan, Mary, 120
Dunninger, Joseph, 27
Dunwich Horror, The (Lovecraft), 68
Durrer, Lt. L.A. 172
Dutch Psychical Society, 143
Dynamistograph, 149-150
Dyne, Mark, 126

E

EDB (extradimensional being theory), 46, 56
Edison, Thomas, 144-145
Edson, Walker, 88
Eileen J. Garrett, 176
Eisenwein, William, 100-101
Electromagnetic theory, 78
Electronic Voice Phenomenon (EVP), 178, 185, 193-194
Ellison, Harlan, 169
Epps, Lee, 9-11, 17, 23
Erwood, Will, 140
ESP, 7, 11, 104
Everett, Hugh, 106-107
Evidence of Purpose (Richmond), 139
Evidence, standards of, 157, 159

Index

Evrard, Renaud, 180
Extrasensory Perception (Rhine), 50

F

Farragut, 43
Fate (magazine), 1-2, 9, 11-12, 20, 59-61, 100-103, 117
Ferrara, Mrs., 103
Ferrara, Robert, 103
Fisk, G.W., 104
Flammarion, Camille, 57
Franklyn, Julian, 82-83
Future intention, 111-112

G

Gandy, Arne, 66-67
Gandy, Mrs., 66-68
Gardner, Harry, 132-133
Garrett, Eileen J., 154, 176
Gary, 115-116
Gelb, Lester, 15-17, 23-24, 28-30, 34, 71
Geldert, Bob, 127-128
Geldert, L.N., 127-128, 144
Great Tomorrow, The (Roberts), 108
Green, Alyce, 139
Green, Elmer, 139, 150
Grierson, Francis, 131, 133

H

Hack, Gwendolyn Kelly, 144
Halloween, 169, 182
Hallucinations, 57, 101, 162-163, 165
　telepathic, 57, 163
"Hallucinations of Widowhood, The" (Rees), 63
Handmaker Jewish Nursing Home for the Aged, 25
Hansen, Eliza, 119
Hansen, Lavinia, 118-119

Harary, Keith, 172
Harlow, S. Ralph, 13, 31-32
Harvey, Richard, 136
Haunted (podcast), 181
Haynes, Renée, 101-102, 161
Hedgecock, Glenn, 42-43
Heywood, Rosalind, 158
Hidden Channels of the Mind (Rhine), 48
Hitchcock, Alfred, 65-67, 183
Hour 25 (radio show), 169
Human Behavior (journal), 63
Hunt, H. Ernest, 79-80
Hyslop, James H., 127-128, 133, 136-138

I

Inaudible Becomes Audible, The (Jurgenson), 87
Inside No. 9 (TV show), 182
Institute for Parapsychology of the Foundation for Research on the Nature of Man, 149
"Intention" cases, 21, 100-101, 103-105, 110, 114, 116
Instrumental Trans-communication (ITC), 185
iPhone, 175

J

Jamison, Benton, 102
Johlson, Enid (pseudonym), 24-26, 43, 54, 56
John F. Kennedy University, 154, 171, 193
Jones [Dr.] (pseudonym), 176-177
Journal of Near-Death Studies (journal), 184
Journal of Religion and Psychical Research (journal), 169-170

Journal of the American Society for Psychical Research (journal), 89, 104, 143, 194
Judd, Pearl, 140
Jung, C.G., 40
"Jungian," 180
Jurgenson, Friedrich, 86-89, 93-94, 131, 146-147, 151, 164

K

Kasprowicz, Laurent, 179-180, 184
Kastenbaum, Robert, 63-64, 70
Keel, John, 46
King's College at Western University Canada, 184
Koestler Parapsychology Unit (University of Edinburgh), 176

L

Laboratory Investigations into Psychic Phenomena (Carrington), 129, 142
Lana, 26-27
Landau, Lucian, 1, 81
Learning to Use Extrasensory Perception (Tart), 50
Lewis, Margaret, 133
Life after Death, A (Harlow), 13, 31-32
Life After Death: The Case for Survival of Bodily Death (Rogo), 170
Life After Death, The Case for: Parapsychologists Look at the Evidence (McAdams and Bayless), 170
Light (newspaper/journal), 80, 122, 125, 129
Lodge, Sir Oliver, 139
Luce e Ombra (journal), 171

Lupino, Connie,
Lupino, Ida, 72-73, 84-85, 159
Lupino, Stanley, 72-73, 85

M

MacConnell, Bonnie, 24
MacConnell, C.E., 24-27, 31, 34, 42, 54, 56
Magician, 170
Mahony, Patrick, 2, 74-75, 151
Maimonides Medical Center, 14-15
Manchester (England) *Evening Chronicle* (newspaper), 127
Manometer, 142
Marge, 23
Matla, J.L., 141-145, 149-150
McAdams, Elizabeth, 170, 172, 175, 178-179
McConnell, R.A., 104, 163
Medved, John, 34-36, 42-44, 78-79, 159
Melton, F.R., 129-133, 142, 145-146, 149-150
Melton, George, 130-131
Meyer, Andrew (pseudonym), 84-85
Mimi, 69
Mind Over Matter (Rhine), 14, 104
Mind Science Foundation,
Mitchel, A.M.J.,
Mortality (journal), 184
Moss, Thelma, 1, 33-34
Multivoiced calls,
"My Five Greatest Mysteries" (Hitchcock),
My Grandfather's Clock (song), 175
Mystére de la Mort, La [The Mystery of Death] (Matla and van Zelst),

Index

N

National Enquirer (newspaper), 110
New Psychic Frontiers (Uphoff), 2, 42
Ng, Suey, 110-111
Noory, George, 179
Nora, 118, 120

O

Omega: The Journal of Death and Dying (journal), 63, 184
Ouija board, 144, 149, 181
Out-of-body experiences, 71
Owens, Don B., 9-11, 13, 16-17, 23, 36, 42
Owens, Ethel ("Sis"), 10

P

Palmer, John, 1, 154-159, 163-166
"Paranormal Tape-Recorded Voices: A Paraphysical Breakthrough" (Rogo), 88
Paraphysical theory, 78, 84
Parapsychological Association, 111
Parapsychologists, 8, 105, 154-155, 157, 165, 172, 175
Parapsychology Foundation, 176, 194
Parent-Child Telepathy (Schwarz), 26
Patterson, David, 136
Paxton, Evelyn, 64, 67
Peck, Charles, 174
Pendleton, Elsie, 69-73
Phänomen Transzendentalstimmen [The Phenomenon of Transcendental Voices] (Seidl), 146
Phantom phone calls, 52

"Phone calls from the dead"
  "anniversary" cases, 59, 61, 68
  length of time, 55
  mechanics of calls, 77-97
  types of, 1, 11-12, 15, 20, 23, 42-43, 52, 17, 100, 103, 110, 114
"Phone calls from the dead?" (Rogo), 20
Phone Call from a Ghost (Cohen), 183
Pinch, Trevor, 176
PK-from-the-living, 62
Poltergeist(s), 11, 15, 50, 156, 164, 182
Poltergeist 2: The Other Side (movie), 183
Power of the Mind, The (Smith), 2, 24, 54
Precognitive message, 110
Price, Harry, 182
Prince, W. Franklin, 127, 144, 158
Pritchard, Ruth, 59-60, 62, 68
Psi, 156, 171
Psychiatry and Mysticism (Dean), 26
Psychic News (newspaper), 80, 132
Psychic telephone, 129, 150
Psychic Telephone, A (Melton), 129-132, 149-150
Psychokinetic (PK) force, 49-50
Psychophone Messages (Grierson), 131
Psychophone, 146

Q

Quaderni di Parapsicologia (journal),
Quantum physics as guide to phantom phone calls, 105, 107

R

"Radio", 87, 93, 132, 147, 150, 169
Randall, John L., 178
Random number generator (R.N.G.), 111, 125, 165
Raudive, Konstantin, 86-88, 93-95, 131, 145-147, 151, 164
Rees, W. Dewi, 63-64, 70, 175, 184
"Retroactive" PK,
Rhine, J.B., 50, 104, 147, 149, 158
Rhine, Louisa, 48, 56, 104, 157
Richmond, Kenneth, 139
Richmond, Zoé, 139-140, 150
Roberts, Arthur, 108
Roberts, Ursula, 108-110
Robins, Danny, 180, 194
Roe, Chris, 173, 176
Rogo: The Life and Tragic Death of an Outspoken Parapsychologist (Cooper), 191
Rogo, Jack, 178
Rog-Til, 109
Rose, Barbara (pseudonym), 118
Rose, Ray (pseudonym), 118

S

Sanderson, Ivan, 46
Schmeidler, Gertrude, 1, 118, 143, 154, 159-160, 164, 166, 170, 179
Schmidt, Helmut, 111-112, 165
Schnabel, Annemarie, 51
Schneider, Alex, 146
Schrödinger, Erwin, 106
Schwarz, Berthold, 1, 26-28, 37-38, 40-41, 52-53, 65, 114
Scientific American (journal), 145
Seeing Eye, the Seeing I, The (Haynes), 101
Seidl, Franz, 146
Sheargold, Richard, 146-147
Shearsmith, Reece, 182
Sheffield Hallam University, 179
Shepard, Jesse (see Grierson), 131
Sherrin, Mrs., 28-31, 42, 56
Sherwood, Simon, 173, 176
Sidgwick, Henry, 56-57
Smith, Mrs. (pseudonym), 31-32, 54, 88
Smith, Susy, 24-25, 88, 97
Society for Psychical Research (S.P.R.), 89, 104-105, 127, 133, 139, 143, 170, 172, 194
Southern California Skeptics, 170
Speiden, Norman, 145
Spiritistic theory, 56
Spooks Deluxe (Walker), 2, 84
Stanford Research Institute, 14
Steiger, Brad, 46
Stigmata, 173
Stone, Davis, 12
Stone, Ruby, 12-13
Stress and trauma, reactions to, 28
Subatomic processes, 106
Survival theory, 45, 70, 73
"Survivalists," 46-49, 156, 161
Synchronicities, 41

T

Talbot, Michael, 106-107
Talks with the Dead (Welch), 26, 96
Taped-voice phenomenon, 88
"Telepathic Humoresque" (Schwarz), 26
Telephone Calls from the Dead (Cooper), 178-179, 182
Television, 169
Terras, John K., 100
Thanatology, 63
Theta-agents, 47, 58, 67, 70

Index

Thy Son Liveth (Geldert), 127, 128, 144
"Time displaced" PK, 111-112
Tollen, Viola, 13, 17, 23
Tomorrow (journal), 82
Torkildson, Gus, 117-118, 120
Trailbush and Hedgecock, 42
Transcendental Physics (Zöllner), 108
Trasco, John, 41
Tricorn Books, 178
Twilight Zone (TV programme), 65

U

UCLA Neuropsychiatric Institute, 99
UFOlogists, 112-113
UFOs, 7, 17, 26, 113, 173
Ullman, Montague, 1, 15
Uncanny (TV programme), 181-183, 194
University of Bath, 182
University of Edinburgh, 178
University of Lorraine, 180
University of Northampton, 173, 178-180, 194
University of Virginia (DoPS), 170
Uphoff, Karl, 37, 40-44
Uphoff, Walter, 1-2, 40-42

V

Vandermuelen, Henri E. G. B., 144
van Zelst, G.J., 141-144
Venus flytraps as psychic detectors, 147-149
Voices from Beyond (Bayless), 138
Voices of the Dead? (Smith), 88, 91, 97
von Szalay, Attila (Art), von Szalay, 86, 88-96, 130-131, 133, 138, 145-146, 150, 164

W

Wallace, Edgar, 140
Weinberger, Julius, 147-149
Welch, William, 96
Wendy (*Uncanny*, T.V. program), 183
Wheeler, John, 106
Who's There? (Mahony), 2, 74-75
Wilhelm, Geri, 27-28
Will (*Uncanny*, T.V. program)
Wilson, David, 121-127, 145, 149-150
Wimshurst machine, 142
Wright, J. Gilbert, 132-133, 144, 150

Z

Zaalbert, Vandermuelen, 141
Zöllner, Johann, 107
Zoom (video calls), 185
Zwann, N., 132-133

www.ingramcontent.com/pod-product-compliance
Lightning Source LLC
Chambersburg PA
CBHW032225080426
42735CB00008B/714